THE APOLLO OF GOD

The Oracle and Festivals of Deliverance in Human History

R. ROBERT LARSEN

Order this book online at www.trafford.com
or email orders@trafford.com

Most Trafford titles are also available at major online book retailers.

Printed in the United States of America.

ISBN: 978-1-4269-1995-4 (sc)
ISBN: 978-1-4269-1996-1 (hc)

Library of Congress Control Number: 2010902133

Trafford rev. 02/19/2013

Trafford.
PUBLISHING® www.trafford.com

North America & international
toll-free: 1 888 232 4444 (USA & Canada)
phone: 250 383 6864 ♦ fax: 812 355 4082

TABLE OF CONTENTS

PROLOGUE

What if I told you the existence of God was a provable fact, that it was not an article of faith anymore? I'm talking about hard evidence you could prove in a court of law. This work is not a religious one. I don't support religion.

This experience can be compared with me telling you there exists a rifle that can shoot around corners. After the hysterical laughter began to die down, you would probably want to know what I'd been smoking.

But then I would take pen and paper and begin to diagram and describe my contention. At some point the chuckling would stop as you began to realize that my contention was becoming plausible. What you would see would be a traditional rifle stock modified to use modern, innovative camera and battery technology. All this would be fixed to a movable automatic pistol, also modified, and mounted on the front of the rifle stock. You'd probably want to kick the tires.

Take warning, however. Before we begin, I should tell you the road will be arduous in places. You must not be discouraged, however. You must commit to completing this trek to gain any benefit. *The Apollo of God* is an alternate history. Every now and then you will probably want to adjust your perspective. I know I did. *The Apollo of God* is unlike anything you've ever read.

The medium used to prove the existence of deity is the genuine oracle. The oracle is history written in advance. The genuine oracle can prove its own veracity both internally and externally. It can also be measured to show the contents were long known before they became realized in fact. When all the component parts of the oracle are assembled in one place, it must prove they are all connected and belong to each other. Finally it must prove its veracity is beyond the human pale. When we reach this point, the reader will have created the prism of God. This valuable gift will enable the reader to view religion and the biblical records and see them in a truer light. He or she will be better armed to see what is worth believing and what is not.

The pure word of God is the genuine oracle and nothing else. This will no doubt upset some fundamentalists who will want to add all kinds of addenda. But the truth about deity is an even smaller corpus, and its tenets are direct and simple. Give the religionists and philosophers the longest holiday anyone could get.

In addition, *The Apollo of God* will of necessity correct some long-standing notions held by our historians. Many grandiose explanations will come down to earth. This is generally true across the wide spectrum in our conventional wisdom these days. Archaeology and the scholarship that attends it are becoming much better and more inclusive. Its expansion in the world is bringing more knowledge and understanding of our history. The oracle adds another dimension to this inquiry. For instance, the seminal historian Edward Gibbon postulated the Roman empire fell after a long decline in 476 CE. The genuine oracle will demonstrate this is not the case. It fell much earlier and more quickly than has been thought. The period of decline was remarkably short.

Before we begin our journey, let me say a brief word about bibliography. Ultimately I decided not to include an extensive bibliography at the end of this work. The historical and other works I've used came from the public library system in the Greater Vancouver and Victoria area. Without their holdings and courteous assistance, this book would have been impossible. If you have a good public library system in your town, then you have a good bibliography also.

Some works do stand out, however. I used the Cambridge Ancient Medieval and Modern History as a final authority and made it the center of my reference. I also used authors like Ostrogorsky, Will Durant, and, of course, Edward Gibbon's excellent seminal work, among others. I used the classical authors extensively since they lived closer to the events they spoke of.

All verbatim biblical quotes are from the New Revised Standard Version Bible (1989) from Oxford University Press. All other quotations are in the public domain.

There are a couple of television documentaries I highly recommend to the history student. One is Jared Diamond's *Guns, Germs, and Steel*, from National Geographic Video (based on a book of the same title), and the other is *The Journey of Man* with Dr. Spencer Wells, from PBS Home Video.

1

THE MATERIAL THEOCRACY

The Bible is a history book, nothing more and certainly nothing less. Yet our Christian world has elevated this "collection of little books" into a religious monument based on stories and allegory that cannot be substantiated. Most people base life decisions on this type of literature simply because it's contained in the Judeo-Christian Bible. Nobody seems able to discern what is real and what isn't. Many Christians like to support their view that the Bible is the irrevocable word of God by quoting the apostle's words to Timothy. They like to conveniently forget the words of others, like the apostle John, who wrote, "Do not believe every inspired expression beloved but test them to see if it begins with God."

All historical information must be examined with caution. When possible, we must seek out proof that what is written is actually true. Where proof is lacking, then common sense can be helpful, so long as we realize it may not be conclusive. Much evidence has been lost to us. One can only wonder what was contained in the great library in Alexandria before it was destroyed. This puts a considerable premium on the information that has come down to us. Yet we must not lose sight of our ability to be objective; we must not become fools in love. Herodotus was very objective when chronicling the peoples beyond the Greek world. We can then be easily deceived into thinking his treatment of history in his own backyard was the same. This book will show it was not. Ethnic bias has always been very strong.[1]

---

1. For example, the Jewish historians portrayed the Philistines as an uncouth, unsophisticated nation in order to elevate themselves. In fact we will discover the opposite is true for good reasons. As the "Naked Archaeologist" put it, "The early Israelites were equivalent to the hillbillies showing up in Beverly Hills and eating off the billiard table."

There are also those who like to view history through the eyes of artisans and their creations. Artisans, we are told, are seekers of truth and beauty. They wouldn't lie to us! Perhaps not, but it's no guarantee they will give us an accurate perspective of what actually was. Some people understand allegory whereas others do not. Ancient coins were a much better method of communication with the populace than most art. People could be informed at more regular intervals. Those who attempt to tell history through art are simply those in love with art and not necessarily with history.

The Apollo of God is an alternative history that will look at the history of the world through the eyes of the oracle. However, there are some caveats to be noted first.

We must answer the question, "What is an oracle?" How do we test it to determine if it is genuine? There are at least twelve rules that I've discovered to be operative in this investigation. The first one is that, although all oracles are prophecy and prediction, not all prophecy and prediction are oracles. This book will examine why that is so.

The Bible is unique in that it contains two types of history: retrospective history that looks to the past, and an extensive "oracle history" that looks to the distant and near future. No other history book in existence accomplishes an onerous task like that. The history in the Bible's little books is expressed in three dominant voices. The retrospective voice is split into two main camps: the religious and the realists, who also at times try their hands at prediction, which is called prophecy. The quality of prose is often poetic. The third voice is the oracular voice. Though written by human hands, it looks long into the future and is spoken by a deity. From time to time, that voice will reference things from the distant past and project them into the future.

The reader of biblical history must first be able to determine what voice is speaking and when. The separation between them must become distinct and clear. Since *The Apollo of God* is not a religious work, we must identify

---

We must be careful not to be misled by their literary and ethnic sentiment or devices, nor to be offended by them. They are certainly common to others as well. They understood the audience they were writing for, and there was much they knew and didn't know. It's like a dozen frigates in the same navy. Each one was built at the same time as the others and performs the same way. Yet the sailors on frigate number four think theirs is the best ship in the world. It isn't, of course, but that is what they tend to think. The naval center of command encourages this kind of behavior in order to produce an espirit de corps. It is built on a typically human premise that in the end proves to be wrong. The true story must rise above that kind of propaganda, and it will certainly offend the fanatics.

the religious voice and then redact it. It is largely bombastic language that has no usefulness in our pursuit. Sad to say, of the three, it is the most dominant. For instance, the book of Genesis is not so much a statement of historical fact as it is a gateway into Judaism.

Once the overbearing religious voice is gone, we can replace it with the work of scientists, archaeologists, and scholars who have bequeathed to us a considerable amount of realistic information that better deserves our attention.[2] Pleasantly enough, the reader will discover we actually don't need a lot of detailed history to aid our understanding. Thus re-equipped, we can begin to reconstruct the history of the ancient Near East and the influence it has exerted over the centuries to the present.

---

2. For instance, the story of an antediluvian age and the so-called global flood that ended that era, as recorded in Genesis, is logistically impossible. However, that and the old Babylonian Epic of Gilgamesh may be based upon an actual event on a much smaller scale.

In the late twentieth century, a group of oceanographers probed the depths of the Black Sea. They discovered something quite unique. The Black Sea is largely salinated water, the same as the Sea of Marmora to the south, connected to the Mediterranean through the Dardanelle Straits. Yet at the bottom is a smaller body of unsalinated, toxic, clear lake water trapped by the salinated sea above it. Over the centuries, the two bodies of water have remained separate. The water at the bottom, which for our purposes we will call the ancient Black Lake, is at a much lower elevation than the Sea of Marmora. At the depth where the two waters meet, there is an ancient shoreline with early evidence of human settlement. The explorers also discovered a thirteenth-century Byzantine merchant ship in the clear, toxic deep, fully intact. This unique find may indicate the origin of the so-called Gilgamesh-Noaic flood story. It is reasonable to postulate the narrow land bridge along the Anatolian fault line between the Marmora and the much lower lake broke, possibly sometime in the dead of winter when the lake was frozen over, covering all the settlements in its reach. Gilgamesh or Noah and family may have been aware of this danger and countered it by building their homes on large log platforms in order to carry a few domestic animals and enough supplies to get to the new shoreline. These log platforms in time morphed into an ark and two of every kind of animal when the religious leaders decided to create an allegory to punish everyone but themselves. How's that for global genocide?

Those who survived in the Genesis account obviously lived on the eastern shoreline and moved in Anatolia to the great plain of Shinar, where they mixed with the Aramean peoples there.

In my considered opinion, this new information creates a much more plausible explanation for the Genesis flood story than what is actually contained in the book of Genesis.

Oracle history is truly global in its perspective of the world, past and present. It will serve to correct any bias, eastern or western. For centuries we have accepted the view of Edward Gibbon regarding the fall of the Roman empire. Although Gibbon's study is a remarkably good history, the oracle disagrees with the date of 476 CE for the fall of Rome, placing its collapse much earlier. The oracle also disagrees with the modern perspective that Rome only collapsed in the West. Upon re-examination, I had to change my view.

This work will not only deal with the subject of oracles but will attempt to apply some new insights and corrections to the conventional wisdom. This may sound pretentious to some, but this book will shine new light into areas long neglected or simply ignored by historians. In my research, I discovered a hidden history underneath the layers of religious bombast. The truth was there, but I had to excavate the conventional terrain to find it.

Merriam-Webster's Collegiate Dictionary defines the word *predict* as "to declare or indicate in advance; to foretell on the basis of observation, experience, or scientific reason." Currently, weather reports are a good example of predictive science at work. Forecasters can predict the time when the sun rises and sets or the ebb and flow of tides. The ancients likewise had a working knowledge of these things.

Prophecy is also prediction but of a different kind. The same dictionary defines *prophecy* as "an inspired utterance of a prophet: the inspired declaration of divine will and purpose." The world of the prophet is a murkier domain that relies little on science. The operative word here is inspiration. Prophetic work is usually poetic in nature or composition. It is also, in many cases, a secondary work inspired from an original and seminal source. Of the three terms used here, prophecy has the broadest meaning and application. It is also the most widely used. One can be an atheist and a functioning prophet.

The inclusion of a deity in a prophetic work is not conclusive evidence that said deity actually exists. It could be used as simply a metaphor. The prophet's inspiration could be cunning imagination or even mental illness. Any claims made by prophets or poets rest almost exclusively on faith. Although prophecy can be prediction, not all prediction is necessarily prophecy.

An oracle is a more exalted form of prediction and prophecy. Although all oracles are prophecy and predictions, not all prophecy and prediction are oracles. An oracle cannot exist apart from a deity, whereas prophecy and prediction can. The whole purpose of an oracle is to reveal deity to others. It is usually because deity cannot or will not appear visibly for one reason or another. Perhaps the experience would kill the prophet outright. Alternatively, the deity may want to appear more powerful than it actually is.

A genuine oracle is the utterance or Logos of a deity to a medium or prophet, who acts as a secretary by strictly recording, without alteration, what he sees or hears. The prophet's role is significantly subordinated to the divine voice, though the prophet shares a measure of the glory to come. The deity, the recorded prediction, and the divine message received, along with the prophet, are all part of the whole we call an oracle. A material shrine is commonly created in the aftermath, whereby the prophet or prophetess continues the function of the oracle by publishing, promoting, and preserving a memorial to the deity and its Logos. By this means, future generations can discover and learn about the divine appearance in their midst.

The passage of time and the revelation of events in the world of humankind serve to test the veracity of the oracle and the quality of its prediction. The sole purpose of an oracle is to identify the existence of a deity. As the prediction gradually aligns itself with unfolding human affairs, the oracle furnishes proof positive that it is genuine. The oracle then becomes a famous institution.

Since history can be written in oracular style, there must occur reliable markers along the way to clearly establish that the oracle is beyond the human pale. The quality and veracity of prediction also serve to test the power of the divine voice and its intentions. Inconsistency will reveal a deity of lesser power and influence. A deity that fails will speak through a multitude of oracles with different names. A genuine deity will create one oracle and remain true to it down through the ages. Oracles, like everything else, can be produced fraudulently.

An example of what an oracle is not can be found in the controversial clash that took place between the United States military and a Lakota-Cheyenne coalition at the end of June 1876. The battle took place at the Little Bighorn River in the state of Montana. Interestingly, an archaeological survey done on the battlefield in the 1980s brought some new facts to light. The native side maintains the great Lakota shaman Sitting Bull painted an oracle of the coming confrontation on a large animal skin at the conclusion of a sun dance. In usual surreal style, Sitting Bull painted blue men and horses falling upside down into an Indian camp.

The Black Hills Territory had been ceded to the natives in the Treaty of 1868, along with an adjoining stretch of land that led north to the Canadian border. However, the treaty was not intended to create a haven for lawbreakers, native or non-native. The Lakota had agreed to live peaceably and not use the Black Hills as a sanctuary or base for illegal activity. The government retained the mineral rights, and its agents were allowed unobstructed access to carry out official tasks. The option of expropriation was also included, but the chiefs balked at that. However, through their legal counsel, Red Cloud and his colleagues countered by demanding a seven million dollar price if the government expropriated. The government recoiled but ultimately agreed.

Sad to say, the chiefs were unable to contain the old lifestyle, and their young bucks violated the treaty stipulations and intent. To solve the problems created by the gold rush, the American president forced government gold reserves onto the open market and the price of gold collapsed. Two investors named Fisk and Gould had caused an artificial rise in the price of gold that led to the Black Hills gold rush. President Grant ended that in 1872. The miners and General Custer's troops departed in 1873. Unfortunately, the natives threatened to kill the general if he ever returned, and Grant had had enough. He signed the expropriation order and ordered the natives out of the Black Hills and onto reservations by end of January 1876.

February 1876 came and went, and the Lakota were now trespassing on government land. The natives refused to see it that way. War was inevitable.

Prior to the famous battle, Sitting Bull called for a coalition among his contemporaries, and the Cheyenne as well as others responded. Sitting Bull hosted a great sun dance sometime around April or May 1876. The climax of the sacred rite was his painting of a prediction in surreal imagery on a large animal skin.

Was this famous and controversial battle along the Little Bighorn River a manipulation? Or was it truly a gift of the gods to the Lakota-Cheyenne coalition and their supporters?

The only inexplicable part of the whole reconnaissance effort was the deliberate deception of Custer's chief scout, Bloody Knife, who took Major Reno on a wild goose chase that yielded nothing. The loss of trust between George Custer and his longtime friend proved very damaging to their part of the expedition. Custer, now a lieutenant colonel, no longer trusted him. When his Crow scouts told him it was the largest camp they'd ever seen, he refused to believe them, whereas Captain Bentine, his most experienced combat officer, allowed they may be right.

Trailing south with the Seventh, George Custer discovered near the Rosebud River a very recent battle site. General Crook's column was not in the area. Thinking like a general, Custer decided to take Crook's place and salvage the campaign, which was an astute military decision. In fact, as the mission continued, one is impressed by Custer's military acumen. He really was a general.

In my considered opinion, George Armstrong Custer did not originally intend to attack the Indian camp. He was there to fulfill a reconnaissance mission and nothing more. General Terry, his superior officer, had offered the Second Cavalry in support, but Custer had refused. He had no intention of inviting a native ambush. So long as he kept his personnel to the Seventh, he believed the Lakota and Cheyenne would just keep an eye on him for the time it took to complete his task.

However, once the scouts told him where the camp was and described the terrain, Custer thought he saw an opportunity. He was told the camp sat in front of a plain with bluffs on the further side of the Little Bighorn River. A unit the size of the Seventh could make an attack. Using the landscape, the element of surprise, and the superior range of the single-shot Springfield rifle, he could form an L-shaped skirmish line above and east of the camp and drive the Indians out on the plain, where the Springfield would do its deadliest work. But the attack failed because Custer lacked the necessary manpower. He lost the element of surprise he initially achieved, and made the mistake of splitting his force into five smaller groups. The native coalition's Henry and Winchester repeaters made short work of the soldiers.[3]

Although there is no extant evidence to say an oracle occurred, I believe in this case it did. Was it a genuine oracle? We cannot say it was because too much was known and the events were too close to each other. By February 1876, Sitting Bull knew a fight was coming. The appearance of the Crow army scouts would have signaled the army was near, and they had no intention of going. A battle was inevitable. "On that day it will be a good day to die," Sitting Bull is reported to have said. The prediction was a self-fulfilling one, and the coalition had committed themselves to it. Certainly the painting was a prediction and perhaps a prophecy. However, it was too close to the battle and too much was known ahead of time to identify it as a genuine oracle. The battle that ensued was the logical development of good and bad decisions, and there is nothing inexplicable that suggests divine intervention of any kind. It was simply a tragic defeat for both sides.

In the mid-twentieth century, some people tried to make something of the famous seer Jeanne Dixon's so-called prophecy about John F. Kennedy's assassination near the end of 1963. Miss Dixon was a well-connected person in American society who had access to influential people. Some were probably clients. Information and testimony which has come to light since then clearly indicate enough was known beforehand to conclude an assassination was entirely possible. Robert Kennedy, the president's younger

---

3.   See the segment on Battlefield Detectives—The History Channel.

brother, had committed the sin of rashness in his role as attorney general. He stepped on too many toes too quickly. His inexperience and impractical application of altruism led just as quickly to his brother's death. In the aftermath, he suffered the certain knowledge that his enemies were savoring the prospect of his own demise. An astute insider and those close to them could easily predict or prophesy the Kennedys' impending doom. Again, the prediction was too close to the event. Too much was known by too many beforehand.

On the other side, we have an example of what could be a genuine oracle among the ancient Aztecs of Old Mexico. It is a single-event oracle. It predicted the return of Quetzalcoatl, who was expelled by the Aztecs circa the tenth century CE. Quetzalcoatl was worshipped by the inhabitants of central Mexico prior to the Aztec invasions. His name means "plumed serpent," and he was the white god of the wind, the dawn, and the light. Quetzalcoatl embodied wisdom, knowledge, and civilization. Sometimes portrayed as a bearded white man, he invented agricultural processes, oversaw industries, originated the calendar, and was patron of the arts. His priests were educators and taught many of the children. He was the god of fertility and life. The planet Venus was his symbol.

Early in the tenth century, the Aztecs conquered central Mexico and sent Quetzalcoatl into exile on a ship to the east. The chief god of the Aztecs was the very bloodthirsty Huitzilopochtli, who granted the Aztecs an empire in exchange for a continuous supply of nourishment from human blood. Accepting this bargain, the Aztecs built a vast empire around their capital city of Tenochtitlan.[4] Today it stands as Mexico City. For six hundred years the Aztecs expanded their kingdom, and in so doing began a systematic extermination of many non-Aztecs through their ongoing pursuit of war and human sacrifice.

Prior to leaving Mexico to sail into the east, Quetzalcoatl vowed he would return in the year "reed one," March 1519 by the European calendar, to claim what was rightfully his and exact revenge on the Aztecs. The year "reed one" occurs every fifty-two years in the Aztec calendar. In November 1519, the Spanish conquistador Hernan Cortes appeared in Mexico with his troops and native allies. When he arrived in Tenochtitlan, the Aztec king Montezuma simply welcomed him as the returned Quetzalcoatl and turned the kingdom over to his rule. When Cortes attempted to introduce the god Jesus Christ to the Aztecs, the transfer of power became uneasy, resulting in war. However, by August 13, 1521, Hernan Cortes had become master of the Aztec empire. Indeed the bearded white man had returned.

---

4.   City of Tenoch.

This story of the oracle of Quetzalcoatl appears to have some of the indicators of a genuine oracle, albeit a single-event oracle. For nearly six hundred years, Spain had no idea of the existence of the Aztecs, nor did they know of the existence of the Americas. The Aztecs knew nothing of Europe prior to 1492. The epic voyage of Christopher Columbus is a legal milestone that proves the above is true and clearly beyond the human pale. In addition to the history left to us, we have new evidence emerging to say the white man was actually the first settler of North America, not the native Indians. Of course, aboriginals will not believe this concept, but the evidence is quite strong. Skeletal remains have been discovered in North America dating back to 12,500 BC and have been forensically reconstructed. To everyone's amazement, the remains were all Caucasian. The native community was somewhat upset at this discovery and a controversy ensued. However, this new evidence, when linked to the oracle of Quetzalcoatl, is a significant indication that will not simply go away. One day, Native Americans may have to accept they were not the first to inhabit the continent.

Once a genuine oracle has been fulfilled, it becomes recorded history. It is not laced with bombast requiring redaction. Rather, it can be relied on to give us an accurate account of what took place. Even those "oracles" that are written after the fact can be useful history if nothing else. As we will discover, parts of the books of Ezekiel and Jeremiah in the biblical record are bogus. Yet some of the information therein can be useful. Even a bogus oracle must make a serious attempt at getting the history right.

Finally a word about the sixteenth-century French seer, Nostradamus. He grabbed the attention of Catherine de Medici when it appeared he accurately predicted the death of her husband, King Henry II of France, in one of his unique quatrains. Many readers were attracted to his style of language and the dark quality of his verse. She responded by giving Nostradamus a pension, enabling him to devote his full time to his poetic work.

The fact is Nostradamus was not a prophet so much as an historian who wrote about the past in a unique style. As a devotee of astrology, he believed that history repeats itself. That belief is at the heart of sixteenth-century astrology in western Europe. He was ambiguously specific in his stylistic history but nonspecific about how or when that historical event would repeat itself in the future. Nostradamus's "predictions" are to be found in the past and not specifically in the future. Was it even Nostradamus's goal to become a futurist, or is that the ambition of his modern-day interpreters?

Is it a coincidence that Nostradamus predicted a great inferno in the year 66? He, of course, was looking back to the great fire in Rome when Nero was emperor. Today's historians have adjusted the date to 64 CE, but in the sixteenth century they accepted 66 CE. Some seventy years after Nostradamus, London lost a significant portion of the city to fire in 1666 CE. How this event affected the future and France's place in the world is unclear. It is somewhat out of sync.

Nostradamian interpreters have abandoned France since the end of World War II in 1945 and have shifted their focus to the United States. As we will see, this kind of breakdown in focus is not characteristic of a genuine oracle. Clearly the interpreters have it wrong.

Did Nostradamus have their aspirations in mind when he began his work? Or did he simply want to write history in a unique style to entertain his readers? When the biblical or Greek prophets spoke of other nations, they were talking about peoples who had been in existence for a long time and who would have a major impact on them in the future. These great powers were well developed in their own right and influential at the time the prophets spoke of them. When Nostradamus wrote his quatrains in the sixteenth century, North America was undiscovered. Nostradamus knew nothing about America then. The seer only looked to the past to forecast the future.

When it came to "the big one" that was to occur on July 24, 1999, later changed to August 11 according to the Nostradamian interpreters, that cataclysmic, earth-altering event never materialized. The dog days continued without interruption. In spite of that, the interpreters have rallied and are now forecasting the event will occur on December 21, 2012. Will Santa cancel Christmas? Don't bet on it.

As we develop the genuine oracle and draw it out of its traditional setting, we will see a real distinction between what belongs to humans like Nostradamus and the quantum leap required to associate an oracle with divine origins.

THE ORACLE BEGINS

The ancient world was filled with gods of every description. Most displayed some recognizable human characteristics and performed tasks useful to earth's population. Before long the contest for supremacy got underway as the various deities and the priests who attended them worked their ground and issued marching orders for the heady ride to the top of the heap. A supreme deity had to distinguish itself in some way, however. What better commodity for a supreme deity than knowledge of the future? What ruler and population wouldn't pay handsomely for that kind of information? It was an occasion that only a genuine deity could rise to.

The greatest prize for which the priesthoods competed was state patronage. If the ruling monarch was on your side, who would dare oppose you? All other deities would be subordinated to the will of the supreme god, whose power was absolute and wielded by the high priest. But rulers tended to be a cynical lot. Reliable advice was hard to come by, and most of their courts were self-serving in the end. Gods and priests were not above suspicion either. After all, information could be manipulated for evil ends.

In the ancient world, the gods were not seen as benefactors of humankind where monarchs and their families were concerned. Unlike the population at large, the ruling elite already had wealth and power. To them, the gods were only concerned with punishing the wicked. Like their deities, rulers knew the evils of wealth and power in the material world. The great unwashed, on the other hand, knew the evils of want. It was relatively safe ground to ask for wisdom, as Solomon did, to rule equitably among the people. Foreknowledge of impending danger to one's kingdom was also a reasonable request. Consequently, state patronage would be granted to the deity who could provide such information for the glory of the kingdom, the king, and the deity who so cared for them. It was a workable quid quo pro, provided it was contained within respectful boundaries.

However, change is inevitable in the human experience, and what suited the monarch of one time period became a burden to others. Deities, like kings, could rise and fall. State patronage was where the real power was invested. It became the goal of priesthoods to ensure the continuation of state patronage from king to king and dynasty to dynasty. This required a perfect performance from the reigning deity, however. The high priest and his organization had to ensure this was the case whenever and wherever possible. The oracle, which the deity was, had to develop a track record in each era that made it worthy to have around. The state expected good value for its money. Otherwise the priests and their temples would have to trade in the open markets to support the gods they worshipped.

With expectations raised to a high level, it is not surprising that oracles began to be manipulated from within to create the illusion of divine guidance. Information could be formed into predictions with favorable outcomes. History could be written in oracular style to give the impression that a god was directing events. Ambiguity was a servant that provided a wide range of flexibility for interpretation. Human psychology became a primitive science among the well-established priesthoods and oracle centers. Widespread intelligence-gathering became a constant occupation of priest and prophet alike. The ability of humans to predict outcomes was becoming a new science, and its limitations were being broken down. Prophecy was an honorable art form and greatly respected by many.

The story of Joseph near the end of the book of Genesis is an example of how an oracle or prediction could be used as a manipulative device to encourage a particular religious outlook. Pharaoh, it is said, dreamed he saw seven fat cows grazing in the reed grass that were consumed by seven gaunt cows. This scenario was then repeated with seven fat heads of grain consumed by seven thin heads. Troubled by this vision, Pharoah sent for his magicians. But in the end, only a descendant of Abraham through Jacob could give an interpretation.

In form, this story is remarkably similar to the one in Daniel concerning the dream of the Babylonian king Nebuchadnezzar.[5] The Judaic religious message is also the same: "The Almighty helps those who help us." This has been a very successful propaganda device for the Jews in every age, and it continues today.

This story, like many others, is a fanciful allegory woven around a skeleton of historical veracity. No doubt some or perhaps all of the characters mentioned were genuine historical personages. However, the real story is disguised by the insertion of religious nonsense.

What the historical and biblical student should take from this type of methodology is that the early Aramean-Israeli tribal system came about at a time when Egypt and its dynastic rulers were developing a system for the storage of grain and also increasing their herds of cattle and other animals. Extant records tell us the ancient Nile's annual inundation produced one bountiful year in five. In the other four years, the water level was either too high or too low, causing crop shortfalls and droughts.

There is no mention of seven successive bountiful years in Egyptian records. Like the adjustments in the calendar, it was the sacred duty of his majesty to more perfectly align the land of Egypt with the will of heaven. No king, or later pharaoh, would miss an opportunity to advertise his divinity to the priests and people at large. Yet the records are silent. The rabbinical Jews over the centuries would have us believe this monumental shift in Egypt's history came about from one Jewish jailbird named Joseph because the elite minds in the king's service couldn't determine these things for themselves.

The Deutero-Classical prophets have their monumental beginning with Moses. The first-century Roman historian Tacitus (ca. 55-117 CE) gives us an alternative history of the early Hebrews in book one of *The Histories*. The early Jews, he claims, originated in Crete near Mount Ida. He then quickly develops Ida etymologically into Iudea and has them boarding ship and sailing to Egypt like many other Mediterraneans. While resident

---

5.   Daniel 2.

in the Nile Kingdom, King Bocchoris consulted the oracle of Amun, who advised the king to rid his domain of all pestilent Asiatics. This led to the exodus of the Cretan Jews, led by one called Moyses.

The Pentateuch books of Genesis and Exodus give us a decidedly fuller account of the exodus. However, Tactitus's reference to the oracle of Amun as the instigator of a widespread persecution of the Asiatic populace in Egypt is an interesting one.

The description in Exodus 14 tells us this pharoah was among the seventeenth or eighteenth dynasty rulers. Verse 28 tells us his entire army consisted of chariot warriors. It was the so-called Hyksos rulers of the seventeenth dynasty who introduced chariots in a big way to their army. The standard Hyksos war chariot was drawn by two mules and mounted by one driver and two lancers. However, these Hyksos pharoahs and their armies were not Egyptian but Asiatic. The delta kingdom was overrun by Asiatics. This demographic was the enabling condition to bring Asiatic rulers into Egypt.

But upriver to the south, at Thebes, a strong aristocracy of ethnic Egyptians was unhappy with the proliferation of foreigners in the delta. They did not know Joseph like the Asiatic pharoahs would have. They wanted Egypt for Egyptians. They worshipped Amun.

The eighteenth dynasty is a better fit when we compare its characteristics to Exodus 14. These pharoahs placed Egypt on a permanent war footing. They developed the war chariot further by breeding horses especially for their chariots, and reduced the personnel in each chariot to a driver and an archer/lancer, who were the officers of the infantry during large campaigns. In times of relative peace, they were the pharoah's royal archers and rapid response army for quick dispatch. Their reputation and expertise grew such that their arrival in any number was enough to provoke fear and consternation. Later dynasties reduced the war chariot to one royal archer/driver per chariot, who steered his chariot into battle by placing one foot on the chariot tongue and maneuvered his direction that way. Consequently, the exodus pharoah is likely to be somewhere in the eighteenth dynasty. The nineteenth and twentieth dynasties are too late.

Here is where we begin the task of separating fact from fiction. Ten so-called plagues supposedly occurred in Egypt prior to the exodus. They fall into three groups: one through six, seven through nine, and finally ten, which includes for our purposes the Red Sea crossing.

Plagues one through six were, in fact, the nasty side effects of the Nile's annual inundation. First the river turned to blood and stank. This is a tricky combination of real and symbolic language. The annual inundation brought huge quantities of a reddish silt which the long river deposited on each bank as its journey slowed before it reached the Mediterranean. The silt looked like blood and in a symbolic sense could be viewed as the lifeblood of Egypt's agriculture, often referred to as the "miracle of the Nile." As its banks overflowed during the first half of its journey, before its speed decreased, the water would take with it all manner of debris, including animal and human excrement as well as dead carcasses in various stages of rot.

The floodwaters also brought the second plague: thousands of frogs. Along with the reddish silt, the debris and frogs were thrown up on the Nile's banks. Naturally, once the inundation abated, the soil would stink. The debris attracted the next two plagues: gnats and flies.

Since pharoah's officials wanted their twenty percent at harvest, there was no time to waste. The 20% wasn't calculated according to what the farmer actually produced, but what the land was capable of. Pharoah's officials knew this from the records. It followed that scratches would become infected, causing sores and other maladies.

Curiously, we hear nothing about the crocodiles that must have been washed down as well. Nor do we hear anything about the hippopotamuses. Each was a significant plague by itself. Why do they not appear on the list? The native Egyptian pharoahs would not have exterminated them because they were deified. Any license to hunt them would belong to the pharoah. The only explanation is that the animals were exterminated by a foreign power that had no tolerance for beasts that caused the kind of damage these two did on an annual basis. It was said these two creatures killed so many humans that the casualties they inflicted were only exceeded by warfare. An extermination policy could help the local population. This situation could have come about under the Hyksos rulers of the seventeenth dynasty, whose religious ideas were decidedly opposed to those of the Theban rulers upriver. However there is nothing to suggest such an extermination policy existed. The Thebans were in a position to alter that.

The other possibilities are the Persians, who were becoming monotheistic at the royal court, the Greeks, and finally the Romans. Early in the Greek conquest, we hear of Perdiccas's campaign to Egypt and the loss of many of his soldiers to crocodiles when they crossed the Nile in 300 BC. This indicates crocodiles were still a considerable problem there.

The most likely candidates are the Romans. The "sweat of Sobek" would have been relieved of its patron menace by the thirst for animal flesh and blood for her annual games in the arenas. From 30 BC, when Octavian took Egypt from Ptolemaic hands, to the end of the first century CE, when the Hebrew Bible was put down in its final form, the city of Alexandria would have witnessed a sharp decline in the crocodile and hippo populations, to the point where some wondered if the two beasts ever existed at all. Perhaps they were simply extinct, bygone specimens belonging to a distant age. It is my guess the Nile plague list that appears in Exodus probably came about in the Roman period near the end of the first century CE, when the Hebrew Bible was finalized by the rabbinic Jews.

The Egyptian priests and magicians would have followed their prescribed rituals each year to mitigate the six plagues, but to no avail.

The notion that almighty God transformed Pharoah into a hard-hearted robot ten successive times is utter nonsense. No reasonable mind can believe that. Yet today, people with good educations actually do believe it. They generally are people with superstitious values.

This example will give readers something of an insight into how the Jewish mind-set works, in particular their use of Scripture to create an allegorical history instead of a real one based on all fact. The decision to opt for an allegorical history was to promote the religion of Judaism. In so doing, they also left us some dots of real history. The Judeo-Christian Bible is an elaborate tapestry of stories and religious themes woven around a skeletal frame of real events and characters.

Plagues seven, eight, and nine, for reasons we will explore later, did actually happen. To fully understand why I say this, a foundational understanding must be established.

Plague ten and the Red Sea crossing did not occur. Almighty God does not do business like that. These two fictional events are once again the product of the Jewish mind-set, looking back from the first and second century CE through the Ptolemaic era, when the Greek Septuagint appeared, and finally to when the Aramaic Bible was first written by the Jews in Babylonian exile (586-538 BC). The Egyptian rulers and their people were allegorical surrogates for the Babylonians, Greeks, and Romans, who caused the Jews suffering over the centuries. The notion that the pharoah, after ten plagues, would chase the Aramaic-Egypto-Israelites into the Red Sea is calling him and his army stupid. The notion that almighty God cancelled the pharoah's free will and forced him into self-destruction is, as stated, ridiculous. However, understanding that the Bible was written to promote a Judaic point of view, it all starts to make some sense. These religious, allegorical references come together to promote the idea that God punishes the wicked and rewards the faithful. Of course today, we know this is often not true. Perhaps it's more disconcerting to understand that many of the stories that promote the above idea are also not true.

Let me here say *The Apollo of God* is not a polemical work. I don't hate the Bible. It's a valuable history book and deserves genuine respect. However, to get the benefit it offers, we cannot literally accept what's written there.

We must use our sensibilities and reasonable minds to avoid the pitfalls of religious fanaticism that can only lead to disappointment.

The Aramean descendants of Jacob[6] journeyed by intervals into the Sinai desert. For some six thousand people,[7] water was critical. They would have traveled about fifteen to eighteen kilometers a day and carried enough water for three days. After one month, they came to a place called Elim on the east side of the Gulf of Suez.

After a rest in Elim, they trooped to Mount Horeb, arriving one month later just as the summer was beginning. The Jews remained there for close to one year. There would have had to have been an oasis at Horeb that gave the people enough water to drink. An oasis would also mean a community was already living there before they arrived.[8] The Sinai was probably less of a desert then than it is now. What the Aramean-Israelites would have found there was a community of priests and prophets dedicated to the deity Yahweh. The name Yahweh simply means "the one who proves to be."

They had developed a simple law code outlining their knowledge of and relationship to Yahweh and each other. First and foremost, Yahweh was a monotheistic deity. Among the Yahwist community at Horeb, their divinity had no rivals. He could not be represented as an idol of any description. He was above every god known and was higher than any zenith or pinnacle known to humankind. The name Yahweh was not to be made a brunt of jokes or used in a worthless way. In their relations with each other, the community at Horeb followed seven precepts for living peaceably together. The institution of slavery was apparently frowned on, but anyone who employed a slave was to grant him one day of rest in seven. This rule applied to slave owners as well. The number seven was sacred to this community. The act of coveting what did not belong to you was viewed as the origin of murder, adultery, thievery, and false witness by the Yahwists. This indicates these priests and prophets lived a somewhat Spartan existence and struggled with austerity like everyone else. Finally, animals were to be handled with intelligent consideration, indicating the people were including their herds in the divine equation. Here in Horeb, Mosaic law was written down and developed from the above principles which we now know as the Ten Commandments.[9]

---

6. Deuteronomy 26:5.
7. Deuteronomy 7:7-8. The promise to Abraham of making his seed like the "stars of heaven" in Genesis 15:5 allowed the Bible writers to extrapolate the numbers.
8. Modern day Hashem el Tarif.
9. In the gospel of John, not once did Jesus or the Jews ever refer to the Mosaic law, in part or whole, as God's law: a very telling non-reference. The

This new nation was to be a religious experiment among the Aramean-Israelites. The descendants of Jacob, formed into twelve tribes, were the initial promised seed of Abraham, and they made up the exclusive amphictyon of Israel. However, it was allowed by Moses and Aaron, his brother, that the Egyptians with them and the descendants of Esau, known as Edomites, could be admitted to the amphictyon from the third generation onward as legal Israelites.[10]

The community of priests and prophets also had decided ideas of what heaven was about. The temple shrine of Yahweh was constructed at Horeb to reflect their notions. The inner sanctum was the Holy of Holies and could only be approached by a well designed high priest once a year. In the inner chamber, human religious society was segregated by degrees. And so the mountain of Yahweh at Horeb was translated by the Aramean-Israelites to continue their lifelong journey of discovering who Yahweh was.

However, not all of the Israelites were interested in the new amphictyon[11] of Yahweh. Roughly half their number created another amphictyon centered on calf worship. Their ancient polytheism was centered on a new image. The symbolism of the calf is something of a puzzlement and may be a syncretism of some kind. From its inception, Mount Horrible, as some probably called it, was the site where Israel openly split over religious differences. The Aramean-Israelites had been a polytheistic society, like most in the ancient world, and not all of them were receptive to abandoning their pagan ideas for an unknown deity. Out of the approximately six thousand Israelites who left Egypt, half were devoted to the same sentiments as Abraham, their Aramean progenitor. To them it was Yahweh who had "proved to be," not some deity represented by a calf idol. To the other half, the polytheistic Israelites, Yahweh had proved nothing. They believed the Yahwists had no proper idea what God even looked like!

Monotheism was embraced by Abraham, who actually had no idea who God was. The son of Terah from Aramean Chaldea, Abraham did not subscribe to pagan polytheism. He may have been an atheist for a time. Abraham was an extortionist who accumulated considerable wealth by blackmail. He used the "My sister is actually my wife" deception to sting

---

apostle Paul tells us in Romans 2:14-15 that it is possible for non-Jews and Christians to develop good law and obey it. The notion that Mosaic law and the Ten Commandments are God's law was cultivated after centuries of generational reinforcement. The law of God in Ezekiel was the law regulating the priesthood, temple worship, and the festivals.

10. Deuteronomy 23:7.

11. Greek word meaning "oracle community," usually divided by tribes.

men wealthy enough to buy their way out of public embarrassment.[12] Sarai couldn't get pregnant, which guaranteed no complications and furthered the con game. This may be why Terah had to leave Ur in Chaldea. It was certainly the reason Abraham was exiled from Egypt. There, Abraham and Sarai had become so odious that their son Isaac was later advised not to settle in Egypt.[13]

In Gerar of Philistia, Abraham once again succeeded with his "My sister is actually my wife" sleight of hand on a local ruler named Abimelech.[14] Abimelech was forced also to pay out a huge indemnity. Abimelech on another occasion would not do business with him until Terah swore an oath not to deal fraudulently with him. Abraham was not a righteous man.[15] Indeed, Abimelech and the ruler of Egypt were more righteous than the Israelite forebear.

Although Abraham did not know who God was, he had definite ideas about what God was not. He was convinced the ultimate deity was not represented by any idol he had ever seen.[16] In time Abraham developed faith in a God who would eventually reveal himself; a God who would "prove to be." This deity who relied on individual and collective faith found its way among the community of priests and prophets at the oasis near Mount Horeb. This deity they called Yahweh was the one who "proved to be." This was the new amphictyon created at Mount Horeb during the first year of Israel's residence there.

Sometime in the early winter months, the camp separated into two religious nations. Half remained polytheistic while the other half embraced the Yahwist shrine and its legal code.[17] The account of this split in Exodus and Deuteronomy gives us a confused outcome. Those who were not Levites but were caught inside the holy precinct were probably killed, but

12. Genesis 12:13-20; 20:1-16; 26:6-11.
13. Genesis 26:2.
14. Genesis 20 is decidedly out of sequence and should directly follow chapter 12. It was placed in its current location in the Hebrew canon for etymological reasons, not based on content. The chapter only makes sense when it becomes chapter 12:21-38 instead of 20:1-18.
15. Deuteronomy 9:4-6.
16. He may have reasoned that a world of peace could only come about under one supreme deity who was also a peaceful entity. He saw all around him a world dominated by multiple gods who vied with each other for supremacy and the chaos such conflict produced. Endless religious wars sapped the strength of the human population so that human blood became the nectar of the gods.
17. Exodus 32:28, 34-35; Deuteronomy 9:8-21.

polytheistic Israel remained largely intact. Aaron, who made the calf, was unharmed. At length it appears Moses prevented retribution by either side. But the religious wounds had been opened, and the separation would be troublesome indeed.

The process by which the biblical history is degraded in modern eyes begins with the use and abuse of numbers. Other ancient records, of course, are also guilty of the same sin. The Bible does not stand apart in this respect.

As we will see later on, the nineteenth dynasty in Egypt is contemporaneous with Saul, David, and Solomon. This is additional evidence that the Exodus pharoahs would have had to have been the eighteenth dynasty. This raises serious doubts about the biblical chronology in Genesis 15:13. The shorter distance in years is more in keeping with the smaller size of the group of Egypto-Arameans under Moses.

An assembly the size of the Persian host under Xerxes that invaded Greece was such a rare occurrence that it became an historic moment.[18] The logistics of moving such a large number of people was enormous and took months of planning and diplomatic skill. Yet the Bible writers toss the same level of numbers off the tips of their pens in such a cavalier manner that one would think such armies were commonplace.

There are, of course, reasons for this abuse, and we will deal with them as our analysis progresses. For now the reader should be aware of the numbers game and its relationship to the information it is a part of. Are the numbers suspect, or is it the information that bears closer scrutiny? In time, the student of the biblical history will begin to master the use of numbers provided therein.

The Ten Commandments is one of the most honest documents originated by humankind and the only one accepted by the Almighty. It became a part of the covenant relationship at that time. The Ten Commandments acknowledge the route to degradation taken by humans that ultimately strips them of their worthiness before their fellows and the monotheistic god taught by the priests at Mount Horeb. The path to degradation begins by rejecting the Almighty for other deities. Then comes the process of representing those competitors as graven images of various kinds. The third commandment applies when humankind begins to refer to God in derogatory terms. Even today, people blame God for all kinds of things and give him credit for things that God has never done. Humans have consistently tried to form a partnership with the supreme Deity by degrading God to their own level, rightly or wrongly. In many instances the

---

18.   Herodotus, Bk. 7.

absolute authority of God is denied its place. This was largely the experience of the ancient world.

Next comes the removal of parental authority in one's life: the lack of respect and care for those who cared for us. We actually disrespect our own flesh from whence we came.

It's at this point we encounter the awkwardness of a human document. The commandment of keeping the Sabbath holy is listed as fourth when it should be fifth. Perhaps this is a corruption. What we can say is it lacks the precision of a genuine oracle. Also, the tenth commandment is an awkward, purely local expression of the law concerning work animals only. Any law on animals would have been much broader in its application if it were of divine origin. The authority of a father and mother would be more important than a day off. Consequently the law of Sabbath should occupy the fifth place.

The law of Sabbath takes aim at slavery in the ancient world. Many slaves were simply worked to death. All flesh and blood creatures require adequate rest from their labors in order to live a reasonable life. But those who had removed the institutions of godly authority in their lives had no regard for their fellows. They had no respite from their enemies. Once an enemy, always an enemy. You won, they lost, too bad.

The next four commandments can be easily collected under one law that says, "Thou shalt not covet what belongs to another." This would make it sixth and include the whole spectrum of coveting instead of limiting this practice to four. Coveting what belongs to others is usually the root cause of wars. The experience of war has a profound, degrading effect. Sometimes thousands, even millions, of noncombatants are killed or maimed for life. The destruction of property and expense of supporting armies can cause ruin for years in the future. The wounds of hatred for others can continue for centuries without healing.

The seventh and last commandment regards work animals. This is the last stand of a degraded human. When our love of animals comes to an end, there is not much left to salvage. We have been thoroughly degraded. At least this was the view of the ancient priests of Horeb.[19] As a human document, the Ten Commandments did not contemplate the degradation of the planet itself, which a genuine oracle would do. It is an excellent law code, but of human origin and not divine, for the reasons already given. Its only claim to divinity is its inclusion in the covenant along with other provisions. The actual law of God given to Israel through Moses was the law concerning the temple, the priesthood, and the rituals that served the

---

19. Unlike today, many domesticated animals in the ancient world were considered more valuable than humans for obvious reasons.

seven festivals every year. That law served as a model by which humans could approach the Almighty and symbolized future events.

The festival cycle was to prove a distinctive grid that displayed the importance of the Sabbath, the provision of rest, to humankind. The festival grid was laid out over a period of fifty years. Every seventh year was a Sabbath year. This cycle was repeated seven times for a total of forty-nine years. The fiftieth year was a Jubilee year and also a Sabbath. All property, includingslaves, were returned.

The festival grid had a larger application within which the oracle and miracles of almighty God were set. Anything outside this framework was an event not performed by the Almighty. The fact that this was hidden from humankind for so long not only protected the work of God but shows this process is not from humankind. It originates from the Most High and cannot be concluded otherwise. It is the pattern of his work.

This pattern or divine grid is the reason for singling out the seventh, eighth, and ninth plagues as actually taking place in Egypt. They fit the divine grid perfectly. The tenth plague and the Red Sea crossing do not for the reasons already given. The seventh plague of fire and hail was the first instance of almighty God's intervention in human affairs. Other miracles ascribed to the period prior to the seventh plague are Jewish allegorical inventions used to teach the precepts of Judaism. This use of allegory to teach religion was widespread, then and now, and should not be viewed with any kind of excessive emotion. It is simply a fact and we should leave it there. It is only important that we finally recognize it and put it to good use.

As stated, the book of Genesis is not factual history but an allegorical gateway into Judaism. We should not be troubled as we say goodbye to the great flood story. It was not a global catastrophe but probably a disaster that was more local. The PBS television documentary "The Journey of Man" makes a very persuasive case the the human race originated from one couple, but locates that couple among a group of hominids in Africa. We don't know exactly what happened at the beginning but we shouldn't speculate on something we can't know at present. We'll be dealing with the Garden of Eden at a later time, when it becomes more appropriate.

The story of Abraham sacrificing Isaac on Mount Moriah[20] and the vision of Jacob's stairway to heaven[21] are also allegorical creations. The characters probably really existed, and that is the skeletal history contained in the Bible. However, the allegorical, religious tapestry that is woven into

---

20. Genesis 22:1-19.
21. Genesis 28:10-15.

the stories belongs in the realm of religious fantasy. Even early Christians were deceived by it.

In particular, the story of Abraham and Isaac has been seen by Christians down through the centuries as a messianic message. It is nothing of the kind. In fact, the Jews of Jesus's day rejected his claims to be the messiah because of this story. The message of Judaism was that almighty God accepts animal surrogacy but rejects human sacrifice. The prophet Jeremiah berates Israel for engaging in human sacrifice. Such a thing, he tells them, "never came up in Yahweh's heart."

Christians, on the other hand, believe that almighty God does accept human sacrifice under very special and specific circumstances. Jesus Christ was not murdered by those who killed him; he was sacrificed. He and the church that grew up after him were vessels chosen by God and anointed with holy spirit so that the Almighty could receive them at their appointed time. These special conditions were not determined by any human but only by the Most High himself. Any unauthorized human sacrifice was murder. That is why the Ten Commandments are in error when they use the word *kill* and not *murder*. Almighty God does permit killing under specific conditions. Murder is killing without God's permission. Only a human law would prohibit God from killing. This is another reason why the Ten Commandments represent not God's law but man's.

The shrine of Yahweh was an elaborate tent meant to symbolize heaven and its approach. The first compartment was the Holy of Holies and contained the ark of the covenant. The high priest would enter once a year; no one else was allowed to enter on pain of death. The Holy of Holies represented heaven and the presence of God was symbolized by the *shekinah* light suspended above the ark. Heaven was separated by a curtain from the holy which represented the state of grace conferred upon the priests who performed rituals there. The entrance to the tabernacle always faced the east. On the north wall of the holy was a table for ritual bread, and on the south side was a seven-stemmed candelabrum to give light. On the west side, in front of the curtain in the middle, was an altar.

Outside the temple was an outer courtyard segregating the priests from the nation at large. There was a larger bronze altar in front of the temple entrance where sacrificial smoke was made for the people outside the courtyard. The legal code specified sacrifices which the nation and priests could make to Yahweh for various reasons.[22] The priests wore special

---

22.   Leviticus, chapters 1-9.

garments for their service and became the nation's first religious lawyers. The new tabernacle was also an oracular shrine.[23]

After almost a year, the camp of Israel left the community of priests and prophets at Horeb and made the usual three-day journey northward into the desert. From that time forward, Horeb became a site of sacred pilgrimage for the devoutly religious of Israel. The next stop for the transient nation was Hazeroth. Here the function of the tabernacle as an oracular shrine was to take on some important changes.

Most oracles of the ancient world responded to petitioners with a simple yes or no answer. The oracle of Amun in Egypt would respond to questions in this manner. If the answer was yes, the priests would take one step forward; if no, then one step back. In most other shrines, sacred lots were cast to give a yes or no answer. Sometimes a more complicated formula was followed. The Shrine of Fastuna among the Romans in the early period had a system of wooden tiles with messages written on them. A child would randomly withdraw one or more tiles, and the ancient messages would be interpreted to insert the petitioner.

The oracular shrine of Yahweh began in the same way. The ephod breastpiece of the high priest contained two sacred lots called Urim and Thummin.[24] We have an example of how these sacred lots were used.[25] Although Saul could get no other kind of answer from priest or prophet, he could, in the end, resort to Urim and Thummin. It appears to have worked by process of gradual elimination until the answer he was looking for appeared. Based on these lots and their outcome, Saul was quite willing to kill his son and heir Jonathan. But the people would not allow it on that occasion.

However, at Hazeroth, the oracular shrine of Yahweh was to be elevated beyond this primitive beginning. Dreams and visions used by prophet and priest to determine future outcomes were to become a thing of the past. At that time, Moses was the prophet of Yahweh, and any oracle would be communicated only through a representative of the temple. At Hazeroth, the official community of judges/prophets was created.[26] The community began[27] with seventy-two members who received the spirit of prophecy, seventy inside the temple precinct and two men outside in the camp, named Eldad and Medad. On hearing of the two men outside the tabernacle courtyard, Moses opened the door for the expansion of the prophetic

23.   Exodus 28:30.
24.   Exodus 28:30.
25.   1 Samuel 14:36-45.
26.   Numbers 11:16-17; 24-12:9.
27.   See Exodus 7:1.

community by expressing his wish for all Israel to become prophets. The independence of the shrine was now protected by two power blocks. The first line of defense inside the temple precinct was the priests.[28] The second line of defense was the community of prophets made up of men and women drawn from all other non-Levitical tribes.

The two groups who served the interests of Yahweh's sanctuary were variously known as messengers of the Lord or "angels of the Lord." Many Bible readers think any reference to an angel denotes some otherworldly creature. This can be true at times, but for the most part the name refers to men and women who serve the Yahwist temple.[29] The account in the book of Judges interchangeably uses the terms *prophet*, *angel of the Lord*, and *the Lord* to denote the person sent to Gideon from the Yahwist sanctuary.

The priests and prophets inaugurated at Mount Horeb believed they spoke with Yahweh's authority. Where there was no audible response from the deity inside the oracular shrine, which was very often the case,[30] the priests and prophets could fall back on their written histories and the legal code.[31] If those failed, there were always the sacred lots Urim and Thummim. Consequently, when we read the expressions "the Lord says" or "Yahweh says," it is the voice of the priests or prophets speaking with their understated authority from the Yahwist temple. For the most part such statements were based on information already known and spoken by men or women who were held in high regard by most of the Israelites. Except in very rare instances, it is erroneous to think God spoke audibly from the Holy of Holies.

Because the tabernacle was routinely silent, but stood as a representation of the national deity, it was essentially impossible to convince the high priest and his colleagues that a fraudulent prophet was genuine. Time was always on the side of the shrine. Only the passage of time, with some legal milestones along the way, could establish a genuine prophet of God. Yet speaking in Yahweh's name could be abused and was at times. This power was usually abused outside the temple to impact on the population at large.

---

28. Exodus 32:27
29. Judges 6:7-14; Revelation 2:1; Judges 13:6; 1 Samuel 29:9; 2 Samuel 14:17.
30. 1 Samuel 3:1.
31. The prophets also relied heavily on their knowledge of the locals and their understanding of events. They were constantly engaged in information-gathering. According to John's gospel, the Samaritan woman at Jacob's well was impressed when Joshua ben Joseph informed her she had previously had five husbands. She responded, "I see that you are a prophet" (John 4:19). The locals were well aware the prophetic community knew these things. Information was power.

Charlatans did pose a genuine threat to the Yahwist institutions and were usually dealt with quickly.

The community of priests and prophets worked closely together, yet each was also a check on the other. As messengers or angels of the Lord, the community of prophets performed various functions on behalf of the shrine. The account of Balak, the king of Moab, in the book of Numbers gives us our first indication that prophets bore arms in Israel's defense. Since he couldn't afford to prevent the invasion of Canaan by the wandering Israelites, King Balak decided to hire a prophet named Balaam ben Beor, who appears to have had a well-known reputation. When Balak's envoys proposed that Balaam curse the new invaders, the Aramean prophet took the high ground and rejected their request. After all, no one can hire God to speak what they want to hear. The standard prophets' contract specifies complete artistic freedom at all times.

However, the fee of Balak obviously was a considerable inducement, and Balaam saddled up. Hearing of this, the Israelites decided to turn it to their advantage. Taking up weapons, a small group of prophets was able to intercept Balaam at some point on the king's highway. Sensing danger nearby, the donkey left the road without saying a word to anyone. The armed prophets cornered Balaam and threatened him. The prophet could keep the money and perform his task, but he had to see to it that every oracle came out in Israel's favor. Assuring Balaam his life hung in the balance, they probably escorted him to Bamoth-baal.

Interestingly, the apostle Peter quotes this story in his second letter and actually believes the talking donkey part of the text. As we all can appreciate, donkeys don't articulate in Aramaic, but they can sense nearby danger and the presence of humans and animals well before homo sapiens can. Peter Johnson fell victim to the Jewish bombast that permeates the Hebrew Bible,[32] as some people still do today.[33] Yet by redacting such religious nonsense, an interesting and very human story emerges of an essentially ordinary people guided by grand principles couched in the Mosaic legal code. The Bible is an historical corpus invaluable to the modern historian, but like all ancient documents, it must be approached with a mixture of respect and skepticism.

---

32. 2 Peter 2:16.

33. The part about the talking donkey is a device to suggest Balaam engaged in beastiality. The donkey speaks to Balaam as an abused wife or prostitute would do. Usually people hated by the Israelites/Jews were given an ignominious death of some kind, but in Balaam's case the Bible writers decided on a sexual slander.

Of all the books of the Pentateuch, the most important is Deuteronomy. It contains the essential history of the Aramean-Israelites, the legal code, the song of Moses, and the blessing and curse. In Israel, Mount Gerizim came to be known as the mountain of blessing and Mount Ebal as the mountain of the curse. After setting out both,[34] Deuteronomy makes a prophecy. The foolish, stubborn, and rebellious Aramean-Israelites will fall victim to the curse. This was a new element upon which many of Israel's seers were to base their prophecies: the blessing and malediction.

After the death of Moses, the oracle shrine of Yahweh fell silent until such time as a representative chosen by the deity suited the holy and appointed service. Till then, the community of priests and prophets used what they had to perform their designated function within the nation. Their faith and understanding would mold their service for better or worse.

The Mosaic legal code provided that Israel's firstborn children, particularly males, belonged to Yahweh and could be recruited to serve as Nazirites. Parents could offer their children into this service voluntarily if they wished. This was one of the functions of the priests, who could also use distinguished prophets in that capacity. The young child Samuel was recruited in such a fashion. His father Elkanah had two wives, and out of respect for his first wife, Peninnah, he had no children with his second wife, Hannah. This put great stress on Hannah, not only because she wanted her own children, but because the appearance of barrenness brought odium on Israelite women then. A married woman without children was presumed to be an adultress or cursed according to Mosaic law. It could also mean her husband hated her. For Hannah the latter, we are told, was not the case. However, Hannah was not happy with her situation.

Each year, Elkanah and his two wives traveled to Shiloh, where the tent of Yahweh had been located for some time. There Hannah would make her offerings and pray for a child. If it was a son, she promised she would dedicate him to the shrine of Yahweh. On one occasion when the tears of her pain were flowing freely, the priest Eli rebuked her for being drunk. Such behavior was obviously something the priests would see at times. However, Hannah used his rebuke as an opportunity to tell Eli what was troubling her. Eli listened with interest. After consoling her, Eli kept in mind what she requested.

Sometime afterward, an angel of the Lord paid Elkanah a visit and instructed him to provide Hannah with a firstborn son, who would be dedicated for Nazirite service.[35] Since this was a request from Yahweh's

---

34. 27:11-30:20.
35. Numbers 6:2-21.

shrine, Elkanah was favorably disposed to comply.[36] Elkanah and the wife he loved the most did have a firstborn son they named Samuel. After weaning the young boy, Hannah took the child to Shiloh and there gave him to permanent sanctuary service. At this religiously pleasing point, the exilic Bible writers inserted a lovely psalm, perhaps an excerpt from the popular Book of Jashar, to give the story of Samuel a poetic and glorious send-off.

In the same manner, an angel of the Lord was sent to Jerubbaal ben Joash, also called Gideon, to commission him as military leader against the punitive invasions of the Midianites.[37] Not only did they steal what they wanted, but they destroyed what was left. At this time the Israelites were building mountaintop refuges and walls around their towns and caves, where they could hide themselves away. A secretive defensive network known only to the Israelites began to develop. When the danger from the invaders passed, they could return to their homes and crops. In the case of the Midianites, the Israelites were returning to fields and stock pens not only ravaged but also destroyed. It became necessary to mount a military campaign against them. The Israelites had the choice of death by the sword or starvation.

Like many people then and today, Gideon was perplexed by Yahweh's inability to prevent Israel's dire straits. The prophet brushed aside these concerns and simply told him he had the job. Gideon decided he wanted to see a sign. Among their duties, the prophets had to be magicians on occasion. Gideon explained he would lay a wool fleece on his threshing floor. If in the morning the fleece was covered with morning dew but the threshing floor dry, then Gideon would know the Lord would help him defeat the forces of Midian.

During the night while everyone slept, the prophet and any assistants he may have recruited removed the fleece and covered the threshing floor. Before Jerubbaal woke, they removed the covering and placed the wet fleece on the dry surface. But then Gideon wanted to see the reverse. At this request, the prophet knew Gideon would be leading the troops. The second request was easier than the first. All he had to do was keep the fleece dry overnight. Yet Gideon accepted this plausible sleight of hand as a sign from the Lord.

The rule here is if humans can create it, they probably did. These types of illusions were not uncommon to religious shrines in the ancient world.

---

36. If the child was a daughter, there would be no inheritance problems. A son would be problematic, however. This may have been why Elkanah was reluctant to give Hannah children. Perhaps there was land a son would have inherited during Jubilee.
37. Judges 6:7-18.

Some had artfully created statues or idols that moved, spoke, or even bled. Pagan oracle sanctuaries were more talkative than the one at Shiloh, and the Israelites were still a primitive polytheistic society.[38] It took centuries for the Yahwist faction to gain the upper hand. Until then, pagan practices found their way into Israelite religion. It isn't until the Second Temple period after the exile that religious Israel became a truly monotheistic society with the post-exilic advent of a new creation called the Jew.

Although the nation required their military leaders to be decisive and bold of action, they were careful to select men who were suitably humble, with little or no political ambition. Once the emergency had come to an end they wanted their heroes to return home to their fields and farmer lives and leave governance to priest and prophet. Gideon was such a man. Jephthah was an outlaw and carried the odium of being a prostitute's son, and he was willing to settle for amnesty. After the successful conclusion of the Ammonite war, he returned home and was given the dignity of a judgeship.

---

38.   Deuteronomy 32:16-18; 1 Samuel 8:18.

The Festival Cycle

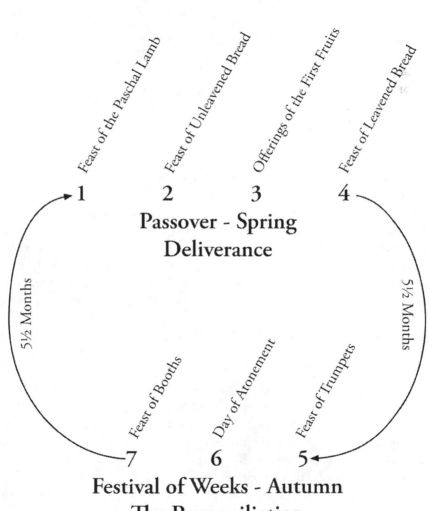

Feast of the Paschal Lamb

Feast of Unleavened Bread

Offerings of the First Fruits

Feast of Leavened Bread

1   2   3   4

Passover - Spring
Deliverance

5½ Months

5½ Months

Feast of Booths

Day of Atonement

Feast of Trumpets

7   6   5

Festival of Weeks - Autumn
The Reconciliation

2

THE RISE OF KINGS
AND THE GOLDEN AGE

Only one of Gideons' sons, Abimelech, made an overt attempt to become king before Saul. The difference between Abimelech and Saul was the latter was the choice of a prophetic community, whereas the former was financed by the lords and merchants of Shechem Israel's first important capital city. Abimelech received money to raise an army and was officially installed as king of Israel at Shechem. Saul, in fact, was not Israel's first king. However, the principal men of the capital used the first kingship to profit by robbery and corruption. Naturally, the new king was angered at these developments, and relations with the merchants of Shechem significantly deteriorated.

To solve their problem with the king, the merchants financed a rival named Gaal ben Ebed, provoking a civil war. The two rival forces clashed in the countryside and ben Ebed was forced to fall back on the capital. The troops of Abimelech laid siege to the stronghold in the city and succeeded in taking it, killing all his political opponents within. However, the kingship of Abimelech abruptly ended after three years of rule. He was killed during the seige of Thebez. There is no further mention of a king in Israel until we get to the selection of Saul ben Kish. Saul's short reign would produce an important transition for the political and religious life of Israel.

One of the major influences impacting life and politics in southern Palestine was the rich caravan trade crossing the North Arabian desert. From the oasis towns of Tema and Dedan, the lucrative trade in spices and luxury goods would wind its way to Egypt and the Mediterranean. Both towns were directly east of Thebes across the Red Sea. From Tema, north of Dedan, this route snaked through the Arabah, south of the Dead Sea, into the Negeb and then along the valley of Salt, south of Judah, to its terminus in Philistia. The transport of these goods was controlled wholly by the Arabs. This caravan trade was the honey in the expression "land of milk and honey."

Needless to say, the Arabs resented any interference in their monopoly. Their wealth could exercise a major influence in the political and economic life of the Near East and did so well into Roman times.[39] Edom, Judah, and the tribe of Simeon to the south of the Valley of Salt could benefit directly from the caravan trade passing through and along the borders of their territory. The prosperous economic life of Philistia made these merchants natural allies of the wealthy Arab traders. So long as the other three groups did not interfere with the caravans' passage, they could all live at peace and enjoy the peripheral benefits. Arab money took up permanent residence in local government.[40]

The governance of Israel by priest and prophet did not disturb peaceful relations with Philistia and the Arab traders. Samuel was opposed to a king in Israel because a permanent monarchy would lock the Hebrews in a death struggle with Philistia. At that time, the Israelites were vassals to the wealthy and powerful Philistines. To inaugurate a royal system would be an open declaration of war. From the Arab perspective, it may not have mattered who their customers were, so long as their routes remained open and unencumbered.

Watching all this from Thebes and Memphis, Egypt had a long-term interest in the Near East. The caravan trade affected them as well. Although controlled by the Arabs, it was coveted by everyone else who appreciated the wealth it generated. It could be as troublesome as it was enjoyable. Too many fingers in the honey pot was a recipe for political headaches.

Even as far north as Babylon and west into the Mediterranean, the great powers of the ancient world invariably cast an interested eye on the trade in spices and luxury goods flowing into Egypt and the Near East. As a general policy, they tended to placate the Arabs at the expense of the locals. If their initial peaceful overtures were not appreciated by local governance, the great powers would invariably follow up with ruthless subjugation.

The Arab trade was controlled by the Assyrians, who were destroyed by the Medo-Babylonian coalition. From the time of Nebuchadnezzar II (Cyrus the Great), the Arabs enjoyed another respite until Cambyses. After that, the Arabs had to accept the Greek and Roman hegemonies.

---

39. Indeed, the age of exploration launched after the fall of Constantinople was a direct reaction to the eastern trade routes through Byzantium falling into Turkic hands. The Americas became known to the world.

40. 1 Samuel 8:2-3.

Today the Arabs have control of the oil market and OPEC. They even have an office with direct contact to American power brokers. Only fools and religious zealots would openly oppose the powerful capitals of Beer-Sheba and Gurbaal, the seats of Arab control in the region.[41]

It is not surprising that the extreme outcomes of interference with the caravan trade inspired religious zealots to see the hand of God in the lives of themselves and the people at large. Religious rationales would have to find reasons why a wicked king presided over prosperity and a righteous one suffered defeat and poverty. The hand of Yahweh would somehow have to be maneuvered to account for any and all contradictions that might arise. Thus was born religious bombast in the Hebrew Scriptures. Today, Bible students have the task and duty to remove the layers of religious bombast in an attempt to allow the real and down-to-earth human history of the ancient Near East to surface.[42]

According to the Muratori canon, which came forward at the end of the second century CE, Christians simply adopted the Septuagint canon already preserved by the rabbinic Jews who escaped the destruction of Jerusalem in 70 CE. Christendom did not recognize the extensive Jewish religious bombast layered into the Hebrew text. They accepted it as-is without making any changes. As a result, they were unable to recognize the influence of zealotry in the Christian Greek scriptures.

Over the centuries to the present day, dedicated Bible readers gradually began to adopt the same religious perspective as the zealots and eventually manifested religious bombast in their own behavior, becoming unreasoning fanatics. Today we see the comedic spectacle of a monumental contradiction: modern-day Christians exerting enormous effort to become Judaizers. This is a huge step backward, never intended by the early apostolic church. Consequently, the thrust of Christianity as a road to truth and redemption has been lost to humankind, abandoning the moral high ground to science.

Before the advent of Saul as Israel's first king, the Hebrews were always a military contingent in someone else's army. As the songs of Deborah and Barak allude, whenever any part of the caravan trade was interrupted,

---

41. Herodotus's designation of Sennacherib as "King of the Arabians and Assyrians" is viewed by modern historians as a mistake (Herodotus Bk. II-141), but is it? When one realizes the power wielded by the Arab traders, this is hardly an error on the historian's part but an insight into the way things were. See Herodotus bk III.

42. It is safe to say the Bible is, for the most part, that part of the apocrypha the redactors missed.

nations went to war.[43] In those days, Israel offered a force of ten thousand to the unmentioned host army. The deliberate exclusion of any mention of a host army is another reason why the numbers of the enemy are always greater than those of the Israelites in the biblical record. Likewise, Jewish history in the future will document the Holocaust of World War II (1939-1945 CE) as a contest between Nazi Germany and six million Jews who died in concentration camps. The millions of non-Jews who died to stop Adolf Hitler and his latter-day praetorians will gradually be excluded from their pages. It is a quirk of Jewish history.

Prior to Saul's election and before Samuel, Israel's great judge, the Israelites attempted to break the Philistine yoke on their own. Here for the first time the community of prophets weighed in to the fighting with a large force of thirty thousand. These prophets were honored as Israel's chosen men when David ben Jesse came to power.[44] However, the war with Philistia did not go well with Israel, and they were badly defeated near Aphek. If that wasn't bad enough, the ark of the covenant was captured by the Philistines and paraded in their cities until the priests were able to obtain it back, probably after paying out a large sum of money.

The defeat of Israel's sacred troops and the loss of the ark were major blows to religious sympathies and the Yahwist sanctuary at Shiloh. For almost twenty years, the sacred chest was abandoned in someone else's field. Shiloh had lost the people's respect.

At this point, Israel was on the fulcrum of a dilemma, from the viewpoint of the Yahwist camp. The nation was poised to fall headlong into pagan polytheism if the Yahwist faith collapsed. Israel's religious future hung in the balance.

This was the problem facing Samuel during his first years as Israel's great judge. Perhaps the Yahwist faith needed a stronger leader to reorganize the threatened monotheistic state from within. Against this background, Saul ben Kish became Israel's second king and the first to be anointed by Yahweh's community. In fact, Saul was chosen by Urim and Thummim, the sacred lots of the priesthood, in front of Israel's tribal leaders, after Samuel had specifically chosen ben Kish ahead of time. This shows the sacred lots could be manipulated by the priests.

At Mizpah, Saul was hailed as king with a suitable display of humility, and Samuel presented him with the *Book of the Rights and Duties of the King*. Saul's army was made up of three thousand prophets, including Saul

---

43. Judges 5:6-13.
44. 2 Samuel 6:1-5; 1 Chronicles 11:20-21.

himself and his son Jonathan.[45] To Jonathan, Saul committed one thousand prophets, and Saul kept two thousand, who would become officers over the chosen of Israel, numbering thirty thousand. The number three was the organizational division in the military at that time.

When Nahash the Ammonite besieged Jabesh-Gilead east of the Jordan, the new kingship sprang into action. Organizing the thirty thousand prophets under his standing army of three thousand, plus seven thousand Judeans, who hired themselves out as mercenaries to other armies, Saul clashed with the forces of Nahash in a night ambuscade while they camped outside Jabesh-Gilead.

However, a dispute over Saul's kingship arose in the territories east of the Jordan. Consequently, Samuel organized a great coronation of Saul at Gilgal. On that day, a thunderstorm caused rain, and the people took it as a sign that Baal was pleased with the choice.[46]

It appears the Philistines did not feel threatened by Israel's choice while they observed from their garrison at Michmash. Perhaps they did not take part in the defeat of Nahash at Jabesh-Gilead farther to the north. However, when Jonathan took the Philistine garrison, the armies of Philistia were mustered to put down the Israelite revolt. Saul then sent out a call to arms to assemble at Gilgal, but the Hebrews went into hiding,[47] as had been the custom since the invasion of Midian. Many fled to refuge east of the Jordan river.

At Gilgal, Saul's standing army began to desert since Samuel didn't arrive on time. The Philistine military might was descending on Michmash, and Jonathan was forced to quit the captured garrison he led with his reduced force. Saul was truly up the Jordan without an army. His own command had shrunk to some six hundred loyal troops. They managed to keep Israel's supply of weapons out of Philistine hands, but they were too few in numbers.

From Michmash, the army of Philistia spread out in different directions to find the rebel king and his supporters. Saul and Jonathan had become fugitives in their own country. The only military action they could pursue was hit and run night raids. Eventually Saul was forced into hiding until the Philistine campaign forces withdrew leaving a smaller occupying force to hunt the Israelites down.

Saul now had to rebuild his forces. The community of prophets had abandoned him, and Samuel continued to support him reluctantly. The

---

45.   1 Samuel 10:10-13, 26.
46.   1 Samuel 12:18. The Iliad of Homer portrays Zeus as a thunder god.
47.   1 Samuel 13:6.

incident at Gilgal revealed Saul to be a wavering Yahwist who may have sacrificed to Baal instead. However that may be, Samuel decreed the end of Saul's rulership at that time. It appears Samuel and Saul repaired their crumbling relationship, and Saul undertook a campaign against Amalek south into the Negeb.[48] This expedition used the Israelites' recorded history and Mosaic authority in the wake of "the Lord says" to perpetrate a genocide on the nation of Amalek. Men, women, children, animals, and property were to be destroyed. This genocidal revenge was to be unconditional. Saul and his warriors did carry out the national genocide, but they kept the best of the animals and made King Agag their captive. It was Sauls' intention to offer them as a holocaust to Yahweh at Gilgal in order to complete the genocide.

But Samuel was displeased with Saul's plan. He only wanted news the final solution had been carried out. The prophet wanted no evidence of it in Israel. If that wasn't bad enough, the Israelite king was going to present that evidence on the altar of Yahweh. Samuel took a sword and "hewed Agag to pieces," completing the genocide.

The great judge also used the occasion to rid himself of Saul for good. Samuel had grown dissatisfied with the king's performance. The community of prophets had abandoned Saul, and the nation was not roused to arms under his leadership. Saul represented the prophetic community's first major failure. The religion of Yahweh had been undermined even further under this king. These were dark days indeed.

Saul's failure was also Samuel's failure. The two were tied in a co-regency role. Saul was the dependent member. After agonizing over his poor choice, Samuel stimulated all his experience and faculties and chose another candidate from the community of prophets: David ben Jesse, a Judean.

The rejection by Samuel left Saul out in the cold. Hunted by the Philistines and spurned by the religious community of Yahwists, the Israelite king became desperate. To continue he would have to appeal to the polytheist nation inside his borders.

The young ben Jesse was an ardent Yahwist and a member in good standing of the prophetic community. He was a musician who loved poetry and song. If he had not become king, David may have become one of Israel's great prophets. Samuel's choice had seriously widened the division between the Yahwists and polytheists in Israel. Each would have their own king.

Although completely loyal to the Yahwist cause, David loved and respected Saul. He was the Lord's anointed and became his father-in-law.

---

48. Probably Amalek threatened the community of prophets at Horeb at this time. It should be realized Yahweh had sanctioned no genocide.

The young ben Jesse had begun his military career as a slinger in the king's army. Slingers were skirmishers in ancient times, used as an advance unit to provoke their opponents into premature attack or to lure them into an unfavorable position. It was dangerous work, and slingers were the only ones who could flee back to the ranks with dignity.

At Socoh near the Philistine border, David and his fellow slingers caught a warrior named Goliath in a badly exposed position. He had foolishly left the protection of his ranks and strayed too close to the Israelites. Seeing this, Saul ordered his young slingers to confront the reckless Goliath. Swarming on the Philistine, they got the better of him and killed the big guy with his own sword. Goliath's weapon became David's first battle trophies, and he dedicated them to Yahweh. Saul would have enjoyed watching the challenger being taken down by a group of boys and impressed with ben Jesse's part in it. The young man liked the taste of blood and was eager for combat. In time, David's fame grew and Saul gave him his daughter Michal for a wife, making David a member of the royal family. David ben Jesse now had a legitimate claim to the Israelite throne.

The transition of kingship from Saul to Davide represents a transition in the Yahwist community from a primitive religious system to a more progressive one. The shrine of Yahweh was in tatters. The ark of the covenant no longer occupied the Holy of Holies at Shiloh. Yahweh had become one of Israel's peculiar cults; another version of Baal. Even the prophetic community was using primitive methods derived from pagan norms. Popular at that time was frenzied dancing used to induce prophetic trances.[49] Saul and David were not strangers to this practice. In later years, prophetic frenzy appeared in the pagan shrines of Asia Minor and European Greece.

The sacred lots of Urim and Thummim were still being used to manipulate events. The Amalek genocide was a horrible indictment of the Yahwist congregation. The manner in which Samuel jeopardized Saul's position in the co-regent role and then manipulated it to slaughter a whole nation was evil incarnate.

The Israelite nation was more divided than ever. The polytheist population and its practices were gaining the upper hand, and the Yahwist society was not a positive influence on them. Shiloh had been repudiated in their midst. What was needed could not be achieved under Saul, and so before his death, Samuel anointed David ben Jesse to replace Saul.

It was a good choice. Under David, Israel would enter a religious renaissance that would progress for years to come.

---

49. 1 Samuel 19:20-24; 2 Samuel 6:1-5.

The two years of Saul's solo reign seriously demonstrated his dependence on Samuel. Saul was similar to Gideon in many respects, a bold man of action yet humble and "small in his own eyes." After the emergency of Nahash the Ammonite had been concluded, ben Kish should have simply returned home to continue his usual life. That old system would have worked well with Saul. However, as a permanent monarch, Saul fell victim to a bad choice. An effective king was made of other stuff. The prophetic community failed to recognize this essential requirement and thrust Saul into a royal system he was not suited for.

Watching from the sidelines, David saw this deterioration in the monarchy and realized Saul was being unfairly victimized. David loved Saul, and the king loved ben Jesse as his own son. Saul sought David's life on more than one occasion, yet the young Judean could talk to Saul's heart and move him to affection they once shared. It wasn't that Saul was an evil man; he had been caught in an evil system, and he struggled as best he could. The nation had demanded a king and then abandoned him at the worst moment, making Saul and Jonathan fugitives in their own land among their own people.

David understood this and refused to victimize his father-in-law as the rest had done. He would not lay a violent hand on Israel's king, nor would he tolerate any disrespect for Saul. In David's eyes, ben Kish and Jonathan were mighty warriors of magnificent stature.[50] But the forces against them from within and without were too strong, and they were finally overwhelmed on Mount Gilboa.

> Saul and Jonathan, beloved and lovely! In life and in death they were not divided; they were swifter than eagles; they were stronger than lions.
> O daughters of Israel, weep over Saul, who clothed you with crimson, in luxury, who put ornaments of gold on your apparel.
> How the mighty have fallen in the midst of the battle!

Saul was succeeded by his son Ishbaal at Mahanaim while David was made king of Judah at Hebron. A state of civil war now existed between Judah and Israel. Near the pool of Gibeon both forces clashed, and

---

50. This was where David's heart met with approval from the Almighty. David understood clearly that Yahweh was dealing directly and only with Israel's king. This mutual understanding is what led to the Davidic covenant and why ben Jesse's dynasty lasted so long. It was one of the ancient miracles (1 Samuel 24; 26:8-11).

Abner's troops were badly defeated by Joab, the commander of David's army. Eventually, Abner defected to the Judeans, leaving Ishbaal without a commander. After a rule of two years, Ishbaal was murdered and David became king of Israel by acclamation.

Before rising to the kingship of Judah at Hebron, David had been a fugitive in Philistia for sixteen months. He was employed by a wealthy ruler named Achish of Gath, who used David and his six hundred warriors as mercenaries. He based his military operations in the Negeb from the town of Ziklag. Although Achish trusted David, the five lords of the Philistines did not. They would not permit Achish to use him or his troops in their battles.

When news reached the Philistine rulers that David had become king of all Israel, they mounted a military campaign against him. Unlike Saul, David was supported by the community of prophets and his own troops, giving him the army he needed to defeat the Philistines at Baal-perazim. The five lords mounted a second campaign into Israel near the garrison at Michmash, and this time David surprised them by attacking in their rear, creating panic and causing the foe to retreat. David then took the citadel of Jebus, renaming it Jerusalem.

The ark of the covenant was brought up to the new capital while David and his fellow prophets engaged in frenzied dancing in the ark's train.[51] Once the sacred chest had been lodged in its own tent, David decided to build a permanent temple to Yahweh in Jerusalem. He put the proposal to the prophet Nathan, who informed him the temple would be built by his son and successor. The response, given in 2 Samuel 7:4-16, is known as the Davidic Covenant, an important document in Israel's history.

Before Jacob ben Isaac died in Egypt, he cast a prediction over his sons. In time it became a prophecy and had an influence on the distribution of Canaan among the Israelites. Ultimately this prediction/prophecy rose to become a genuine oracle. It is one of the rare exceptions to the general rule. The two most extensive partitions of Israel's prophecy concern Judah (Genesis 49:8-12) and Joseph (Genesis 49:22-26). The unfolding of Israel's history reveals the molding effect these patriarchal pronouncements had on the political life of the nation. Concerning Judah, the prophecy stated: "The scepter shall not depart from Judah, nor the rulers' staff from between his feet until he comes to Shiloh; and the obedience of the peoples is his"

In the case of Joseph, the great patriarch had given him extensive praise, but no specific role was assigned to his younger son. In recognition of Jacob's prophecy, the nation had a specific marching order during the years in the

---

51. 2 Samuel 6:1-5, 20-22.

wilderness. The camp was arranged in a symmetrical form that placed the tribe of Judah in the leadership role. The tent of Yahweh always opened toward the east, and the tribe of Judah was always positioned directly in front of the temple entrance. Joseph, represented by the tribes of Ephraim and Manasseh, was directly opposite Judah in the west.

Over time a rivalry developed among these three tribes. During the period of the book of Judges, there was much looser governance among the tribes, but Ephraim and Manasseh exercised a larger role in governance than most, while Judah remained in the forefront. The Davidic Covenant was a further development in Jacob's prophecy and served to sharpen the distinction between Judah and Joseph. The kingship would be a Judean regency. Ephraim and Manasseh would be excluded from royal power. David's marriage to Michal, Saul's daughter, brought Benjamite women in as wives for the Judean dynasty, but all other tribes would be subjects. This was the theocratic model the prophecy of Jacob and the Davidic Covenant imposed on the nation of Israel.

Once the issue of royal power had been addressed from Jerusalem and preparations for the grand temple of Yahweh had begun, David turned his attention to securing Israel's borders from within. Philistia had suffered two decisive defeats at Israel's hands, and her garrisons were no longer within her control. Israel was now for the Israelites. Strengthening his hold from within, ben Jesse began systematically to subdue Israel's old enemy. To protect their retail exports, the Philistine merchants bowed to the inevitable, becoming a vassal kingdom and paying tribute to their new suzerain. A destructive war would have been bad for business. They would bide their time and wait for the right opportunity to resist.

Using the new source of revenue from Philistia, the Israelite king cut the king's highway at Medeba, launching a strike south and taking Moab into tribute as well. Philistia and Tema held their breath. Was Edom next? Instead, the Israelite army moved their next military action to the far north, leaving a collective sigh of relief behind.

King Hadadzer of Zobah had thrown the Aramean world into turmoil by laying siege to Hamath on the Orontes River. He was joined by the Arameans at Damascus in this effort. King Tou sent to the Assyrians for help, and David journeyed up the king's highway to assist the Assyrians in their relief of Hamath. Hadadzer and his allies were defeated at Hamath and their armies reduced to a police force. David was granted the territory belonging to Damascus, in which he established garrisons.

David had made allies in the north and had secured a listening post there. When ben Jesse's forces returned, he moved on to Edom in the south, putting in place more garrisons there. However, the troubles in the Aramean world were not over. In Rabbah, the capital of Ammon, King Nahash died, leaving his son Hanun on the throne. Hadadzer of Zobah had continued to work behind the scenes and succeeded in organizing another coalition force made up of King Maacah of Mesopotamia and Hanun of Ammon.[52] Maacah had a huge mercenary force of over thirty thousand chariots. One can only wonder how much Arab and Philistine money greased that big wheel? King Maacah and his force linked up with the Ammonite king and his army at Medeba. Hadadzer of Zobah remained in Zobah as a reserve.

Joab realized the enemy force was too large to defeat and sent word to David. From Jerusalem, ben Jesse organized the community of prophets, bringing the thirty thousand chosen men to the Jordan at the north end of the Dead Sea. He probably sent word to Assyria and King Tou of Hamath and possibly to the pharoah in Egypt. These were probably heady days for the Arab traders.

However, before battle was joined at Medeba, the forces of Maacah and Ammon withdrew northward. They were joined by Shophach, the commander of Hadadzer's army. David joined forces with Joab, and they came up behind the Aramean coalition of Kings Maacah, Hadadzer, and Hanun, cutting their line of retreat. Obviously a large Assyrian force was moving south on the king's highway.

A massive battle at Helam took place, inflicting serious casualties on all parties. Hadadzer, Maacah, and Hanun went down in defeat. The following year, Joab returned to Ammon, subjugating them in their turn. All their wealth was confiscated, and the Ammonite crown of Milcom was placed on David's head.[53] Shortly after this contact with the northern Arameans, Palestine was ravaged by a widespread plague that caused some seventy thousand deaths.

The battle of Aramean forces near Helam was probably the biggest battle ever fought east of the Jordan during the history of the Israelite nation. Some one hundred thousand lives were lost. The majority died by pestilent infection inside Israel and the surrounding areas. How widespread the plague was in the Aramean world is not known.

King David was devastated by the horrific number of deaths inside his kingdom. How was it that Yahweh had given Israel its independence from the pagans through a series of military successes, yet had punished innocent people with plague? The reign of David also had suffered a three-year famine. The priests and prophets had reconciled the plague with a census that David

---

52. 1 Chronicles 19:7; 1 Samuel 13:5. Perhaps David was able to defeat the Philistines because their numbers had been reduced by plague.

53. 1 Chronicles 20:2. 18:7-8, 11.

had ordered over all of Israel. However, the census was not to include the Levites, which was also done.[54] This was how some seventy thousand deaths were explained away. It becomes clear to them from the text at 2 Samuel 24:13 that the famine of three years was also a punishment from Yahweh. The priest and/or prophets were able to convince David it was because of an injustice done to the Gibeonites, who were not Israelites. They demanded a human sacrifice from Saul's family. David gave them two of Saul's sons and five of his grandchildren. All seven were impaled.[55]

The history of David ben Jesse was recorded by three prophets of the Yahwist community. Samuel wrote about the early years; Nathan recorded the middle years and early kingship; and the seer Gad covered the last years of David's reign and the beginning of Solomon's reign.[56] It is the writer Gad who first introduces the concept of Satan to Scripture—Yahweh's great adversary. The seer Gad appears to be something of a religious fanatic who likes wielding the power of a prophet and adviser to the king. When he orders ben Jesse to buy the threshing floor of Araunan, the Jebusite at the capital, the king does. Though prohibited by the priests and the community of prophets to build the new temple of Yahweh, David undertakes massive preparations. The wording of the Davidic Covenant would allow that: "He shall build a house for my name, and I will establish the throne of his kingdom forever. I will be a Father to him, and he shall be a son to me."

Although the ark of the covenant had been brought to Jerusalem by David and the thirty thousand chosen men, the tent of Yahweh originally transported through the Sinai wilderness by Moses had been moved from Shiloh to Gibeon. This new location became another of Yahweh's "high places" frequented by Israel's king. However, the numerous high places of Yahweh were to acquire a new perspective from the priests and prophets when the new permanent shrine was completed. To this end, David assembled all the royal officials and dignitaries in Israel and raised Solomon to be co-regent with himself. The temple of Yahweh at the capital would be built by Jedidiah ben David, he announced. From that time forward, the Davidic Covenant would have the force of law.

Before David died, Adonijah made a bid for the throne. Since Solomon had officially been made co-regent, the result would be civil war. Adonijah had acquired the support of the army commander Joab and the priest Abiathar, two powerful allies. To prevent a death struggle inside his kingdom, David

---

54. Numbers 1:47-49.
55. Here we see a pagan practice which was to become a horrible feature in successive Israelite reigns.
56. Samuel's work is found in 1 Samuel 1-24. Nathan writes between 1 Samuel 25 and 2 Samuel 22, and Gad continues from 2 Samuel 23 onward.

had the priest Zadok and Nathan the prophet take Solomon to the throne room, where Solomon was officially anointed and proclaimed Israel's king. The palace coup planned by Adonijah collapsed. Although Solomon spared Adonijah's life, he was ultimately forced to execute him when Adonijah tried to marry Abishag the Shunammite.

Locating the shrine of Yahweh at Jerusalem would effectively draw the tribe of Levi into the Judean hegemony. Mosaic law had prohibited allocating a tribal land portion to the Levitical priesthood, confining them to those lands connected to the sanctuary and its function. In addition to their exclusion from royal power, the tribe of Ephraim would lose the shrine at Shiloh. The monarchy would be supported by four power bases: the tribes of Judah, Benjamin, and Levi, and the community of prophets. These were the main pillars of the new Israelite theocracy resting on the foundational Mosaic covenant. This structure would serve to elevate the roof of heaven above their heads. Above this roof sat the throne of Yahweh. Around this structure, the remaining ten tribes of Israel, those not part of the community of prophets, would gather to stand in awe and serve at heaven's gate. This, in fact, was the real temple at Jerusalem. From its inner sanctum the religious life of the nation would aspire beyond the old, primitive norms. Paganism would be rooted out of the new theocracy. Instead, the vision of an exclusively Yahwist state would finally be realized and would stand as a testimony to the nations abroad.

Solomon's reign was spent consolidating the material theocracy of Yahweh inside the Israelite state and rooting the Judean hegemony on the throne. The crown of Milcom would rest on the Davidic dynasty, just as the prophecy of Jacob and the Davidic covenant specified. The words of his son Rehoboam to the Israelites at Shechem indicate Solomon met some opposition to this royal concept from within. The new king departed from his father's foreign policy and made an alliance with Egypt instead of Assyria. Jedidiah ben David married the pharoah's daughter, becoming a client king of greater Egypt, to the glory of the Nile Kingdom.[57]

In ancient times, the extensive bitumen pits in the Valley of Siddim supplied the kings of Shinar and involved the Arameans in eastern Palestine and the Negeb. The destruction of Sodom and Gomorrah and their neighbors had effectively ended their interest in the Near East. This natural disaster and the spread of the North Arabian desert made Egypt's influence

---

57. Among the Israelite kings, Solomon was the builder king just like the Ramesside pharoahs who were his contemporaries. Solomon put in place Israel's infrastructure before the gold supply in Egypt and the Near East ran out.

predominant in Canaan. David ben Jesse's contact with the Arameans in the north had brought their politics and disputes into Israel's backyard. The battle at Helam and the devastating plague that followed was a horrible price to pay for Aramean adventurism. Israel was better off under the aegis of the pharaoh and the Nile Kingdom.

As a dowry for his daughter, the pharaoh, probably at Solomon's request, marched his army to Gezer, the Canaanite stronghold that still remained in northern Philistia, and destroyed it. The Canaanite genocide was then complete and the Yahwists mention it no more.

Naturally, the pharoah's daughter introduced Egyptian style into the Aramean-Israelite court. In the fourth year of his reign, Solomon began construction of the temple complex, and completing it late in his eleventh year of rule. Solomon's wife had her own house built on an elevation above Jerusalem. She probably had a spectacular view of Israel's geography, east and west. Solomon then built his famous palace, the Millo, which took an additional thirteen years. He also constructed six main fortresses in his kingdom. In the north, there was one at Hazar and one at Megiddo near the Carmel mountains. There were two inside Philistia, at Baalath near the coastal Mediterranean and at Gezer close by. The remaining two were at Beth-horon, some fifteen kilometers east of Gezer, and at Jerusalem, the capital. Spread out over this defensive system was an elite corps of fourteen hundred war chariots and horse teams imported from Egypt and supported by twelve thousand cavalry. The Israelite military was a combination of Egyptian and Aramean styles.

One of the more popular references about Solomon, particularly among men, is the notion that the son of David had three hundred wives and seven hundred concubines. Another is that ben David was the wisdom king, the greatest of all the Orientals.[58] Naturally the Hebrew propagandists would like us all to believe that. Solomon was not the wisest man in the world, nor was he the greatest of all the Orientals. His neighbor to the south, the Egyptian pharaoh, was.

No ruler in Egypt had more wives than Ramesses II, before or after. Recently a huge underground burial chamber of the size of a royal palace was discovered by archaeologists in Egypt. It was built for the children of Ramesses II, who lived to a grand old age. He outlived the first twelve of

---

58.   In the same way, Jewish braggadocio has Abraham extorting wealth from the pharoah. This, of course, was not the case. But Jewish megalomania will not settle for a lowly official. Father Abraham must rip off the king of Egypt. Why not go directly to the top?

his successors. His thirteenth son by the queen, named Merenptah, took the throne upon Ramesses II's death.

By giving Solomon a thousand wives, the Hebrew propagandists were loaning the reputation of Ramesses II to their king.[59] It is also possible the number was derived from a list of dependants who received the royal stipend, most of whom would have been widows whose husbands died in the king's service. In my considered opinion, I would generously concede thirty wives and a harem of seventy concubines, or a number thereabouts.[60] The logistics of a thousand are insensible.

When Solomon had finished building his palace and temple, he gave King Hiram of Tyre twenty cities in the north as a reward for his generosity and help in supplying Solomon with expensive timber and gold. Hiram was insulted at the gesture; those cities were worthless real estate as far as he was concerned. It could have been that, twenty years into Solomon's reign, the gold supply was now exhausted in the Near East, as it had become in Egypt under Ramesses III.

Solomon certainly was a wealthy ruler, considering he was a vassal and client king. Each year he received six hundred and sixty-six talents of gold and a huge amount of silver in tribute. He bought and sold Egyptian war chariots and their horse teams with the northern Arameans. At Eziongeber on the northern tip of the Gulf of Aqaba, where the king's highway terminates, Solomon launched a fleet for a journey to Ophir to bring back four hundred and twenty talents of gold. Not a wise investment, considering it averaged a return of 1.05 talents for every year he ruled.

The Arab traders paid tribute to ben David to secure their passage to Philistia.[61] It was probably a peaceful and protected transit, but in this situation it was not a wise policy from the splendor king. Paying tribute to the Israelite state made goods sold for export into the Mediterranean more expensive. In prosperous times, the cost could be and was passed on, but when times became difficult, paying tribute became an irritation for the Arabs and the Philistine merchants. In effect, Solomon created a hostile mind-set against his kingdom among these businessmen. It was not exactly

---

59. The notion that Solomon was the wisest of all the Orientals is also negated by the famous law case involving an infant and two female claimants. Solomon, if the story is actually true, was about to commit an act of murder to achieve justice. This contradicts the whole notion of justice. This example in effect says, "a wrong can produce a right," or, as the Jesuits taught, "the end justifies the means." See 1 Kings 9:11-13; also I Kings 10:15.

60. 2 Chronicles 11:21.

61. 1 Kings 10:15; 2 Chronicles 17:11.

an astute decision reflecting the wisdom of the ages. In years to come, this issue would prove to be troublesome.

After inaugurating the grand new Yahwist temple at Jerusalem, the kings of Israel no longer needed to travel to and sacrifice at Gibeon. From the viewpoint of the Levitical priesthood, the high places of Yahweh spread out over the kingdom were no longer needed. Three times a year, the population of Israel would journey to Jerusalem for the great festivals instead. Consequently, the high places of Yahweh were placed off-limits for worship.

The last twenty years of Solomon's rule addressed the problems and discontent brought about by the changes in the Israelite theocracy. Many Israelites began to complain of its heavy burden.

The verse 2 Chronicles 8:3 indicates somewhat vaguely that Solomon, sometime around the twentieth year of his reign, took part in a military expedition to Hamath in Zobah, just as his father had done. On this occasion, however, it appears Hamath had already been taken by siege, requiring the rescue coalition to invest the city on their arrival. When David ben Jesse and the Aramean army he supported had relieved the city in years previous, defeating Hadadezer, one of his associates named Rezon ben Eliada had been reduced to an outlaw operating around Damascus. He and his heirs eventually became a dynasty of rulers of that city and permanent enemies of Israel.

On his return from Hamath, David had subdued Edom and had his military kill every male they could find in Esau's domain. However, this genocide failed to catch the young prince Hadad in its net. Hadad and his royal entourage escaped to Egypt, where Queen Ptahpenes granted him asylum.[62] He also was a permanent enemy of Israel for very good reason.

One can only wonder about ben Jesse's time as suzerain in Aram after the first defeat of Hadadezer, when he had invested the city of King Tou. Did he also practice genocide there? The genocide in Edom was obviously sanctioned by the Israelites in the Yahwist religious community. It was never mentioned as a cause for the famine or the plague that occurred during the reign of "Yahwehs' friend." Yet killing the Edomites was clearly a violation of the Mosaic dictum found in Deuteronomy 2:5 and 23:7-8. The Israelites were to treat the Edomites as their brothers and not their enemies. The genocide that the Egyptians practiced on the Arameans during the days of Moses had clearly found its way into the Israelite religious psyche. It is often the case among those who suffer at the hands of an oppressor that they become guilty of the same opprobrium.

---

62. Queen Tawosret.

Here we have psychological evidence emerging in the genocidal behavior of the Aramean-Israelites that gives credence to the Egyptian persecution against the Asiatics. There seems to be enough evidence to indicate the god Amun was a genuine deity. Perhaps Tacitus's description of the oracle of Amun during the reign of King Boccharis has some veracity after all. By impressing a persecution mentality on the Asiatics prior to the exodus, the deity Amun created the same mind-set among those unsuspecting humans, who eventually practiced genocide on one another. This kept their populations small and divided. The Asiatics became their own worst enemies outside the borders of Egypt. The god Amun was indeed looking after his own.

In an attempt to cure the damage done to the Israelite mind-set by this cruel deity Amun, one of their latter-day rabbis counseled them to "love your enemies also." Joshua ben Joseph used the Greek word *agape* in this context meaning the Israelites should have a principaled love for their enemies in order not to become like them. One can hate another to the point that one begins to mimic the oppressive behavior of the other. The point made in the New Testament is that one can love one's enemy even when resisting his oppressive machinations.

When Absalom's attempt to usurp ben Jesse's throne at Jerusalem failed, in the aftermath of the battle in the forest of Ephraim, a Benjamite named Sheba ben Bichri tried to shift the rebellion to a new sentiment. "We have no portion in David, no share in the son of Jesse! Everyone to your tents, O Israel!" The division between David and his son Absalom changed to a civil war between Judah and the rest of Israel. The days of Ishbaal had returned. The rebel leader raised the cry among all the other tribes and made his headquarters at Abel of Beth-maachah. The army commander Joab immediately invested the city. From the conversation between Joab and one of the women of the city—perhaps a prophetess?—it is clear that Beth-maachah was a high place and oracle center prior to the institution of the kingship. That same woman betrayed ben Bichri, whom Joab called an Ephraimite, by having him killed and then throwing his head over the wall. The siege was lifted and the Judean hegemony was restored. However, toward the end of Solomon's reign, this old sore would rise to the surface once again.

By one means or another, some of Solomon's wives prevailed on him in his old age to allow them to build altars to Milcom, Chemosh, and Astarte, the Sidonian goddess. Perhaps the crown of Milcom, placed on David's head, had become more than a war trophy. However, Solomon had not only alienated outer Israel but had offended the community of prophets, who had consistently supported the Judean monarchy.

Jeroboam ben Nebat, another Ephraimite and one of the king's taskmasters, was singled out by the prophet Ahijah from Shiloh after leaving the capital. In the open country, Ahijah took off his new outer garment and dramatically tore it into twelve pieces. Ten pieces he allowed to Jeroboam as a "sign" that the Ephraimite would be Israel's new king. Judah and one other tribe would continue in the Judean hegemony. Ahijah was well aware that the tribes of Joseph's sons Ephraim and Manassah had been eliminated from royal power, and that Shiloh had been removed as the site of Yahweh's temple. Although the high places had been prohibited, they continued to function as usual. The rebel ben Bichri had articulated the discontent that was real enough.

The community of prophets decided to use this discontent to punish Solomon and his former wives by creating a second state as a check on the Judeans. One state would watchdog the other. However, Solomon received word of this new rebellion and ordered Jeroboam arrested. Hearing of this, ben Nebat fled to Shishak, seeking asylum in Egypt.

The wealth and prosperity of Solomon's rule gave impetus for a cultural development that would reflect the intellectual progress of the Near East. Living next to the empire of Egypt would also foster a hubris of its own derived from a competitive spirit among the Aramean population. Once the great building works of Solomon had been accomplished, his court turned its attention to other interests in the arts. It appears from the extant Hebrew Bible that literature, both religious and non-religious, begin to proliferate at this time. It is likely the story of Adam and Eve first developed during this golden age.

The story of Adam and Eve is a moral allegory based on a real event. The study of human genetics in recent years tells us that genetic markers contained in the blood of all human males could trace the human race historically to a single male and a single female ancestor. It is also postulated by scientists and archaeologists that this first human couple lived somewhere in Africa.[63] Muslims believe that the dwelling place of this first human couple was in western Arabia. The Aramean-Israelites developed the notion that the garden of Eden was always Israel.

Israel could see for themselves their shrine at Shiloh and in the Sinai desert would not communicate or favor anyone guilty of disobedience. For his disobedience, Moses was not allowed to enter Canaan. Clearly the Adam and Eve story would have developed after this accumulated experience with

---

63.   See the excellent PBS documentary "The Journey Of Man," hosted by Spencer Welles. Personally I suspect human history began in India.

the shrine of Yahweh. Indeed, the story of Saul's disobedience would have still been quite clear in the minds of the Israelites.

The concept of everlasting life was believed without reservation by the Egyptians, and after centuries of observing what appeared to be an everlasting Judean monarchy emerging in their midst, it wasn't a stretch for the Israelites to adopt the concept for themselves. Zedekiah was a later Adam who disobeyed God by refusing to accept the angel Jeremiah's warning and was duly expelled from Eden.

The description given in Genesis 3:24 indicates this premise. To the east of Eden lay the North Arabian desert, a powerful geographic symbol that contrasted sharply with the park-like paradise of God ruled by the successors of David ben Jesse. The other symbols, including the tree of the knowledge of good and bad, the tree of life, the tempter serpent, and the naked human body were understood by the ancients. It was then reasonable to use these symbols to syncretize what likely happened at the beginning of human existence. Because all had to die, God removed the prospect of everlasting life from the first couple. It couldn't be otherwise. And so the allegorical moralists of the Near East adapted these symbols to serve the ends of the Yahwist religion in the Talmudic tradition.

The story of Adam and Eve may be based on the first human pair but has more to do with the kings of Israel than with human origins. Solomon and his queen were the "first couple" of the kingdom who enjoyed Edenic wealth and prosperity given them by the grace of God. The prophet Samuel presided over the breakup between Yahweh and the Israelite nation.[64] The Almighty would no longer listen to their complaints. He would deal with them through their king. Consequently, in a very real sense the Israelite kings and their wives were alone before Yahweh as the first human couple were.[65] The knowledge of good was, of course, the law of Yahweh and insight into the Almighty's will. The people of Israel owed their obedience to the king as their service to God. The king was to strictly enforce the Yahwist religion in its purest form according to religious and civil law. This strict obedience would translate to the nation as a whole. The knowledge of bad was to abandon the will of Yahweh and pursue a defiant course into pagan belief and practice.[66]

---

64. 1 Samuel 8:7; 17.

65. Eve was an allegorical Israel who led her kings into sin.

66. The first oracle cited in Genesis 3:13 had an allegorical application to Israel and its king. With the passing of time, it has become in every sense part of the genuine oracle that applies to a future king and the contest that will come about. Interestingly, the book of Revelation makes reference to Satan as an ancient serpent but does not link him to Genesis 3:13. However, it is

Solomon, like Adam, succumbed to pagan religion at the behest of some of his wives and gave tacit permission for the nation to do the same. This was the sin of disobedience that caused the fall of the first human couple in Eden. Clearly, the Jews who preserved this story while in exile in Neo-Babylonia viewed Israel as the true garden of Eden in the holy land of God. It was the park of prosperity and untold wealth lost to humankind because of the sin of disobedience.

---

likely intended to describe him as Israel's greatest enemy during the era of the kings.

3

THE DUAL MONARCHY

The remaining years of Solomon's rule were relatively peaceful. Jeroboam was in communication with the separatists in Israel. Upon the king's death, ben David was succeeded by his son Rehoboam. In Shechem, the leaders of outer Israel came together to inaugurate a change in the rulership. Rehoboam decided to hold his coronation there instead of Jerusalem. The symbolism was not lost on the new king. Shechem was the capital city of Israel's first king, Abimelech ben Gideon. The lords of Shechem had made Abimelech king without the sanction of the Levite priests, and Israel was prepared to do it again. Jeroboam ben Nebat had returned to Ephraim from his exile in Egypt to be the neo-Abimelech. Would the new Judean king be able to avert the coming revolution?

Many historians have consistently misunderstood the confrontation that took place at Shechem between Rehoboam and the Israelite leaders. "Your father made our yoke heavy," they told him. "Now therefore, lighten the hard service of your Father and his heavy yoke that he placed on us, and we will serve you." True, Solomon spent the first twenty years of his reign building Israel's monuments, but the last twenty years was "lighter" in that respect. The heavy lifting was long over. The conscripted labor consisted of conquered subjects and alien residents. The pharoah's daughter would have helped her husband organize effective use of these conscripts. Solomon never conscripted any of the Israelites.[67] In fact, the Israelites lived in a privileged society. Many of them had the best jobs and best estates.

What then was the heavy yoke? Most of the money and materials for Solomon's construction projects had been assembled by David. Was the heavy burden taxes? Most of Solomon's wealth came from foreign tribute

---

67.   1 Kings 9:20-22; 2 Chronicles 8:9.

and private enterprise. He had twelve officials who provided him with one month's food supply each in the year. He was allowed to tax the Israelites one-tenth of their wealth, and the sanctuary tax was one half shekel per male over twenty years of age.[68] In Egypt, the pharoah owned the land and taxed its produce at twenty percent. Most considered that fair. Egypt was filled with temples from one end to the other. It never caused a nationwide revolt. Temples in the ancient world were often the bank of last resort. The temple of Yahweh contained a huge amount of gold reserve.

Building preparations made ahead of time, large foreign revenues, cheap tax rates, large reserves, foreign conscription—what was the heavy yoke?

The heavy yoke was the Davidic covenant. The monarchy was closed to all except the Judeans. The house of David would produce the royal dynasty. This requirement was based on the prophecies of Jacob and Nathan. Both had the full support of the priesthood, now located at Jerusalem, and the community of prophets. David's marriage had included the tribe of Benjamin in the power structure. Ephraim and Manasseh had been shut out of the royal court and the power that went with it. Jerusalem had become the seat of Yahweh's sanctuary and worship at all other high places was prohibited. This was the burden of Israel that Rehoboam would have to address at Shechem.

The king deliberated for three days with his counselors, whose advice split along two age groups. The elders recommended the king give the Israelites what they asked for, whereas the younger men advised him not to yield anything. After three days, Rehoboam appeared before the elders of Israel and told them, "My little finger will prove thicker than my Father's loins. Now, whereas my Father laid on you a heavy yoke, I will add to that yoke. My Father disciplined you with whips, but I will discipline you with scorpions."

This response may sound harsh and cruel, yet Rehoboam and his young advisers were simply telling Israel the new monarchy and the Yahwist sanctuary embodied in the Davidic covenant were here to stay. The sons of David would not lift the prohibition on Yahweh's' high places, and Yahwist Israel would make the journey to Jerusalem for the great festivals. Any disobedience to these injunctions Solomon punished with whips. Rehoboam promised to punish rebellion with harsher service. He would

---

68. The military lists in Scripture and the numbers given were recorded for the purpose of collecting the sanctuary tax. It wasn't the actual size of the military used by the king; it only provides the basis for the money collected.

punish them as if with scorpions.[69] They would suffer severe pain. The Davidic covenant would be a permanent feature of Israelite life under Rehoboam, like it or not.

The leaders of Israel were disappointed in the king's pronouncement, but Jeroboam ben Nebat was encouraged to believe he would become Israel's new king. He and the leaders of Israel raised the cry of Sheba ben Bichri: "What share do we have in David? We have no inheritance in the son of Jesse! Each of you to your tents, O Israel! Look now to your own house O David!"

The nation was now in a state of civil war. The first act of violence against the Judean king was the killing of Hadoram, who was Rehoboam's taskmaster in the north. The Judean king fled with his entourage to Jerusalem while Jeroboam ben Nebat was crowned king at Shechem.

What part the Arab traders and Philistine merchants may have had in Israel's breakup is not known, but it worked to their advantage. Isolating Judah in a small kingdom in the south while Israel went its way in the north was a step in the right direction. A destructive and costly civil war would have been even better. However, the community of prophets intervened. One named Shemaiah advised Rehoboam not to engage the rebels in war. He convinced the king that the hand of Yahweh was in the events. Instead ben Jedidiah placed Judah and the territory of Benjamin on a defensive footing by building fortresses along the western border with Philistia, up in the Judean foothills. Another string of forts north to south were built in the mountains from Jerusalem to Ziph. The new Yahwist Theocracy was a fortress kingdom in a hostile land.

Yet the prophetic community was reasonably certain the rebel nation would gradually return to Jerusalem as its capital. The internal consolidation and strength Judah acquired under Rehoboam and his co-regent Abijah would ultimately persuade them the Judean banner was their best defense against a hostile world.

In the north at Shechem, the new Israelite king, Jeroboam ben Nebat, was becoming aware of the same possibility. Consequently, he decided to split Israel along religious lines as well as secular. He was familiar with the separation in religious sentiments that had occurred at Mount Horeb in the Sinai peninsula when Moses was their leader. Perhaps Jeroboam had made a pilgrimage to Horeb while he was exiled in Egypt. Half of Moses camp became dedicated Yahwists while the other half remained

---

69. The scorpion was a particular kind of whip with knots in the strands. From (akraub) Maaleh—Acrabbim = a pass in south Judea; aqrâb = scourge; Skŏrpiŏs = to pierce from a concealed place.

polytheists. Jeroboam may have learned many of these things from Hebrews who remained in or returned to Egypt during the wilderness years. Moses' brother Aaron had given polytheist Israel its golden calf idol. Although the idol had been destroyed, pagan sentiments continued among many of Jacobs' children. After all these centuries, polytheism was still alive, engaging the pagan deities of Canaan such as the Baal and Astarte. Therefore, Jeroboam intended to champion pagan orthodoxy instead of the new Yahwist burden. Israel would be a nation that reached back to Jacob through Joseph and Reuben instead of Judah. Aaron would to be the patriarchal high priest who gave them the calf deity.

Jeroboam built two calf idols at Baal in the south and Dan in the north in order to diminish the pilgrimage flow to Jerusalem thrice a year. Ephraim now had its own king at Shechem and its age-old religion.

Israel's new/old religion had its own festival commemorating the split with the Yahwist camp, celebrated during the month of Heshran on the fifteenth day. A new priesthood was inaugurated to offer sacrifices to all the calf idols in the country. Ahijah, the prophet from Shiloh, was disappointed in his choice of Jeroboam, much as Samuel had been in Saul. When ben Nebat's wife sought his help with her son's illness, Ahijah reacted very much like Samuel but with a more direct and brutal pronouncement.

> I will cut off from Jeroboam every male, both bond and free in Israel, and will consume the house of Jeroboam, just as one burns up dung until it is all gone. Anyone belonging to Jeroboam who dies in the city, the dog shall eat; and anyone who dies in the open country, the birds of the air shall eat; for Yahweh has spoken.

Ahijah told her that Abijah, her sick son, would die, and would be the only son of Jeroboam to receive a decent burial. He indicated her husband's successor would be murdered by someone appointed by the prophetic community. Assassins would be readied. This was to become a pattern in Israel in the future. The prophetic community would become "scorpions" in Israel, stinging them with prophecies in Yahweh's name and calling forth the blade of the assassin.

In Rehoboam's fifth year of rule, the pharoah Shishak invaded Judah with twelve hundred chariots and sixty thousand cavalry. The Egyptians stripped the Kingdom of Judah's wealth and Abijah was taken hostage. The king replaced his son with Asa, his grandson, as co-regent with himself. All the gold showpieces in Jerusalem were replaced with highly burnished bronze. Civil war with the new state of Israel was now out of the question.

The wealth of Jerusalem and Judah was probably the prize dangled in front of Shishak when Jeroboam sent envoys to Egypt. Without the support of the Yahwist prophets, who had now adopted a wait-and-see policy punctuated by surgical removal, and with the loss of its considerable wealth, Rehoboam and his grandson Asa turned inward to govern the much smaller but more dedicated Yahwist theocracy.

Until recently, it was thought the pharoah Shishak was the first Libyan dynast Shoshenk. This conclusion was based on a very loose etymological association. There are only two Egyptian records that document expeditions into Israel. One is the so-called "Israel stela" of Merenptah, who documents his father's military campaigns. One was into Palestine. The other is written on an archway in Karnak and tells of Shoshenk's expedition into Israel some three to four hundred years after Ramesses II.[70] Ptahpenes is probably Queen pTahwosret who ruled prior to the twentieth dynasty. The experienced Egyptologist will notice the P is dropped from the Queen's name. The proper spelling is Pthapenes. The P is silent. Ptah is the artificer and builder god of the Egyptians prominent among the early Ramesside pharoahs. However Ptah is not exclusive to them. Shishak is a Hebrew transliteration of Sisa or Sysa. Shoshenk is actually Sosenq. David Rohl has postulated Shishak or Sysa is inscriptionally identified with Ramesses II and III. This association is carved in stone at Karnak. Rohl has revealed some impressive evidence to say Shishak is not Sosenq. His archaeological discoveries include a chronological list of royal architects that places Sosenq close to the fall of Samaria in 722 BC. I agree with Rohl that Shishak is not Sosenq. In my humble opinion Sosenq, is King So of the Bible.[71]

There can be no question that archaeological evidence to date clearly identifies Shishak and Ramesses together. However, there were a number of Ramesside pharoahs. Solomon and his fictional thousand wives probably came after Ramesses II, since the Bible propagandists patterned Solomon in the pharoah's mold. The Israel stela could be talking about the campaign the pharoah made against Gezer, the Canaanite stronghold, which he destroyed as a wedding present to Solomon and his daughter.[72] Perhaps Solomon accompanied the pharoah on an expedition to Hamath in Zobah as ben Jesse did with the Arameans.[73] As Shishak's ally, he would have had

---

70.   1 Kings 11:19-20.
71.   2 Kings 17:4.
72.   1 Kings 9:16.
73.   2 Chronicles 8:3.

no choice. Perhaps this is what is meant by the Egyptian bombast that "Israel is prostrate; his seed is no more." The latter line may refer to Saul. The biblical Shishak could also be and probably is Ramesses III. Egypt's seemingly inexhaustible supply of gold disappeared during his reign. He was the last of the great pharoahs. The confiscation of Israel's gold would not only have prevented civil war in Egypt's buffer zone but also satisfied his need for gold. However, this association of the early Ramesside pharoahs with the early Israelite kings leaves a considerable gap between the new kingdom's dynasts and the nineteenth dynasty of some two hundred years. Is this possible?

The rule of Ikhnaton, the so-called heretic king, attempted to supplant the old Egyptian religion based on Amun, which was a religion of the night among the living dead. Ikhnaton's new religion worshipped the power of the sun—the aten—a monotheistic concept that dominated the day and centered on life. It was the antithesis of the old, morbid religion. The four priestly tribes in Egypt were horrified at the revolution of Amenophis IV/ Ikhnaton. They decided Ikhnaton needed a new city away from Thebes to inaugurate the new faith. The pharoah agreed and chose a site halfway between Thebes and Memphis. He named the new city Akhetaten; we know it today as Tel el-Amarna. Gradually the priests isolated Ikhnaton until he died. He was succeeded by the now-famous Tutankhamen, who restored the old religion. When he died after a nine-year rule, the kingdom was ruled by a vizier, Ay. Was there a long gap in pharoanic rule after Ay?

The name Ramesses embodies a syncretism of Ra + amen + sisa. Ramesis or Ramesses. These pharoahs ruled far away from Thebes in the Delta at Tanis. Incorporating the sun god Ra and the traditional god Amun into a single deity would have taken some time. Any syncretism would have met some considerable opposition. Ikhnaton's revolution had an enormous negative impact on the priests of Amun, who may have banished the pharoahs altogether in upper Egypt. There is a gap of some one hundred and fifty to two hundred years in the Apis bull chronology, which is contemporaneous with pharoanic chronology. Of course, absence of evidence does not necessarily mean evidence is absent. It may still be undiscovered. We wait to see.

Today, the conventional wisdom is under fire and Egyptologists are not giving a good account of themselves. Other disciplines are entering the field, resulting in a turf-war mentality from the guardians of the conventional wisdom. Egyptologists are currently at odds with geologists, who have concluded that the sphinx on the Giza plateau and the temple that sits in front of it may be the oldest monuments on the planet. The erosion from the top down on the Sphinx was done by the desert winds, say the

Egyptologists; not so, say the geologists. The type of erosion evidenced was created by water in a savannah-like environment dating back to 7,500-10,500 BC. "Show us potsherds or other evidence," is the rallying cry of the Egyptologists, unwilling to yield. Of course, in a savannah or tropical climate, potsherds and other evidence would have disintegrated quickly.

What about the evidence that is available? Currently, there are more questions than answers, and more artifacts are being discovered by archaeologists on a regular basis. Who knows what the future will reveal?

On Rehoboam's death, Asa's father Abijam returned from exile in Egypt to wear the crown. As soon as he took the reins of government, he launched a military expedition into Israel. Jeroboam's forces confronted him in the hill country of Ephraim, where Abijah took a defensive position on the slopes of Mount Zemeraim. The Judeans were outnumbered by two to one.

Jeroboam's commanders made a fundamental error by splitting their force, sending half their troops to attack Judah in the rear. Once they were out of sight, Abijah attacked the Israelites in front, routing them. He then followed the path of the ambuscade and attacked those troops, inflicting a devastating defeat on Jeroboam's army. The Israelite troops suffered a sixty percent casualty rate. As a result, some of Ephraim's territory was lost to Judah, and the doors to Shechem lay open.

However, before Abijam could follow up on his victory, the Judean king died after a three-year reign. His son and co-regent Asa assumed the royal duties, and Asa deliberately decided not to capitalize on Israel's crushing defeat. Instead, like his grandfather, he turned his efforts to strengthening Judah and Benjamin from within.

Many Israelites were immigrating into his kingdom, and Asa was busy rooting out pagan and prohibited practices in his jurisdiction. The king was a dedicated Yahwist determined to enforce pure religion on his subjects. He was fully supported by the priests and prophets.

The first line of defense was his standing army of chariots and cavalry. In times of war, they became the king's officers over his conscripts. The backbone of the conscript army was the community of prophets, who were ardent nationalists. If they prophesied in favor of a war or military action, the king had no difficulty in conscripting their service. The prophets would infect his army with an invaluable espirit de corps. If they abandoned the king in an emergency, it was an uphill struggle in an atmosphere of doom and gloom. Better to have the prophets onside. Yahweh always took care of his prophets. Asa believed it was true and responded to their counsel.[74]

---

74.   2 Chronicles 15.

After some ten years of Asa's rule, Philistia hired the army of Zerah the Ethiopian to break the Judean grip. Marching northward along the coast, he laid siege to Mareshah in the Judean foothills.[75] We do not know the exact size of Zerah's army, but using the formula in Leviticus 26:8, we can postulate Asa's army contained between ten and fifty thousand troops. The number of three hundred chariots in Zerah's army is the only clue we have to work with. That number of chariots indicates a cavalry force of between fifteen hundred and two thousand. The Libyan infantry would have been some ten thousand in strength.

Mustering his troops at Adullam, Asa marched them to the valley of Zephathan to confront the invasion. It appears the Judeans had superior numbers because the mercenary army withdrew. Asa followed up the Ethiopian desertion with a punitive campaign inside Philistia around the city of Gerar. The king returned with an enormous amount of booty. In his fifteenth year, Asa renewed the covenant with Yahweh by opening the east gates of the temple, which was the custom.[76] It also became a law among the Judeans that those not seeking Yahweh in the kingdom would suffer the death penalty. It seems Asa launched a religious persecution.

Many historians consider the death of Solomon as the end of a golden age and the beginning of decline for Israel. Solomon's demise may have ended an era, but the golden age continued for some time. For Israel, it was truly a golden age denied to them at Mount Horeb. They could be openly polytheistic in a state governed by a more tolerant king. The calf deity could be developed fully inside their kingdom, and they could have as many altars as they wished. New opportunities were created for many people who had been shut out of the Yahwist theocracy. Israel could determine its own economy and its polytheistic influences.

In the south, Judah also went from strength to strength. The Yahwist theocracy was probably never stronger than it was under Asa and his son Jehoshaphat. The Israelite kingdom acted as a protective buffer to the north, east, and south. The tribe of Simeon below the valley of Salt would have presented Jerusalem with an interesting dynamic, however.

The Arab caravans traveled along the common border between Judah and Simeon. Beer-sheba was a transport stop shared by Israelite and Arab. Eventually the Arabs built their own city directly east at Gurbaal, making it the seat of their power and influence. Although hardly mentioned in scripture, Gurbaal was connected to Tema and became one of the major capitals in Palestine. It was an Arab listening post in the region, and Judah

---

75.   2 Chronicles 21:16; Micah 1:15.
76.   2 Samuel 19:9, 15, 31. Held on Pentecost.

ignored Gurbaal's might and wealth at its peril. So long as the Yahwist theocracy remained strong from within, it could manage its relationship with the Arab traders and Philistine merchants. Both kingdoms at Jerusalem and Shechem could be corrupted or persuaded by Arab and Philistine money.

However, Hanani's son Jehu went to Baasha at Tirzah and pronounced the prophetic death sentence on the king's future dynasty. Afterward, one of Baasha's chariot commanders, Zimri, was anointed in secret to carry out the slaughter of Baasha's house when he died. Baasha knew this would take place from his own experience. Consequently, he warned his son and successor Elah that an assassin was in their midst. The prophets were seeking the death of his entire family.

After Baasha died, Elah managed to rule for two years before he was murdered by Zimri. Elah was a guest at the house of a palace official, Arza, when he was killed. The king was drunk at the time. Zimri ruled for only seven days, but he massacred Baasha's family and servants.

Two dynasties had been ruthlessly destroyed by prophetic injunction in Israel. The prophets were determined the Davidic covenant would not have a successful rival in Israel. This much had become clear to all aspirants to the throne at Tirzah. The news that Zimri had murdered the king raised Omri to the kingship by acclaim of the army, which was besieging Gibbethon in Philistia. Omri lifted the siege and moved on Tirzah. On his arrival, he took the city by assault and Zimri committed suicide. Interestingly, although Zimri never had a chance to change anything in Israel, he is still condemned by the Bible writer for Jeroboam's sins.

The balance of Asa's reign was peaceful enough, making Hemani's prophecy against Asa a bogus one. In fact, it was in Israel that a war of succession was taking place. Hanani should have stayed in Israel instead of intruding in Judean politics. In fact, the wars were in his own country. The city of Gibbethon had rebeled twice and Damascus was now at war with Israel. When Omri became king at Tirzah, he had to face a civil war with a rival nameed Tibni ben Ginath. After a contest of some three years, Omri gained the support of Israel against Tibni. He was recognized as king from Asa's thirty-first regnal year.

Omri moved Israel's capital to the hill of Shemer, naming it Samaria. This became the permanent capital of Israel, and ancient documents referred to the nation as Omri-land. Before he died, Omri was careful to warn his son Ahab that the community of prophets would seek his life in the same way they had disposed of Nadab and Elah. Someone would be anointed in secret to be Ahab's assassin. Omri and Ahab may have planned for this eventuality well ahead of time because we hear of no rival or prophetic pronouncement against Omri. We can safely conclude the anointed assassin and successor was apprehended and executed. Perhaps the prophet or prophets involved suffered punishment as well. Ahab ben Omri ruled Israel for twenty-two years.

Jehoshaphat continued the internal policies of Asa and his great grandfather Rehoboam. He kept the military strong and added garrison fortresses in the conquered territory of Ephraim. Each fortress now had forces assigned to it. Under his rule, Judah remained a Yahwist state. In order to help his subjects "seek the Lord," he had five of his officials organize a teaching circuit traveled by eleven priests who educated the people in Mosaic law. This may have been where the Talmudic tradition began. At Jerusalem, a court was inaugurated to hear and decide disputes. It also was used as a platform to continue the teaching process for all who attended. Jehoshaphat was a great teacher or rabbi in his kingdom. He appreciated his father's injunction to seek Yahweh. Those who knew the law had an obligation to teach it as well as live by its precepts.

Jehoshaphat married one of Ahab's daughters, forming an alliance with Israel. His son and successor Jehoram also married a daughter of Ahab named Athaliah, who bore him Ahaziah. Two of Ahab's sons were also named Jehoram and Ahaziah. Relations between the royal families were closely tied together at this time. Jehu ben Hanani criticized Jehoshaphat for this integration but was ignored. This prophet and his father do not seem to have been well received by the Judean kings. It would appear Jehu's father Hanani was not a very good prophet. Jehu probably raised his own stature when he criticized Jehoshaphat for his close association with ben Omri when he returned from his bloody Aramean adventure in his eighteenth year. After the horrific body count, Jehoshaphat may have accepted Jehu's words as just punishment. The history of ben Asa was reported by Jehu ben Hanani in his annals, which were included in the book of the kings of Israel.[77] In the twenty-third year of his reign, he engaged in a joint venture with his grandson Ahaziah for a fleet at Ezion-geber which did much worse than Solomon's naval expedition. The fleet was destroyed before it made any money.

The most serious threat to Judah was a massive invasion of raiders from Moab and Amon, who entered Edom first. They clashed with Edomite forces at Mount Seir and killed as many as possible to protect their rear after looting the country. From there they journeyed north along the west bank of the Dead Sea until they got to the Ascent of Ziz, east of Hebron. Hearing news of this danger, Jehoshaphat moved his forces to Tekoa. However, before he could engage the invaders, they began to die en masse. As often

---

77.   2 Chronicles 20:34.

happened in the ancient world, large, undisciplined, and unruly hordes ultimately became their own worst enemy. Bad sanitation and poor diet exposed them to infection and plague. Sometimes they were infected from contact with the enemy. This seems to be what happened on this occasion. In some cases, infected troops turn their swords on each other to escape the agony of a slow, ignominious death.

Ahab ben Omri went to war with the community of prophets. He did it for very practical reasons. Because his father had changed nothing in Israel, both sides knew the prophets would seek to kill Ahab and his household. Ahab decided to stay alive at their expense. And expensive it was. The king of Israel went outside his borders and married Jezebel, the daughter of King Ethbaal, who ruled at Sidon. Sidon was an export economy in the Mediterranean and a seagoing people. They worshipped Baal, the god of rain and thunder. Jezebel brought many prophets and priests of Baal and Asherah to Samaria.

The reason Ahab and Jezebel were viewed as more wicked than any of Israel's rulers was because they systematically hunted the prophets down and killed them. The war between the community of prophets and the Israelite monarchy had become dog eat dog, and Ahab had determined he would bite first and hardest.[78] It wasn't because of the Baal religion, because Israel had worshipped Baal for centuries. To many Israelites, Yahweh was simply another manifestation of the Sidonian rainmaker.[79]

To escape the persecution, many of the most distinguished prophets fled to Mount Horeb in the wilderness, which had become a pilgrimage site for the religious of Yahweh.[80] Perhaps it was a pilgrimage site for calf-worshippers also. Many would have escaped to Judah, but Jehoshaphat had married into the royal family of Israel and the Judean king's son and successor Jehoram had married Ahab's daughter Athaliah. Both were Baal worshippers. This did not bode well for the kingdom to the south.

As a symbol of their devotion, many decided to leave Palestine altogether. From their headquarters there, the grand prophets and their council directed the rank and file of the prophetic community still alive. The aged Elijah was one of their servants and a prophet of distinction. He was head of a cell of fifty prophets at Tishbe on the east side of the Jordan in Israel. While Ahab ruled the northern kingdom, Palestine suffered a serious drought. The grand council at Horeb decided to use this drought in

---

78. 1 Kings 18:4.
79. 1 Samuel 12:18; Judges 2:11.
80. Mount Horeb continued to be a holy site of some significance after Jerusalem was destroyed. In Ezra's day, it was still recognized as the mountain of Yahweh (2 Esdras 2:33-41).

their favor to recall ben Omri to his senses and end the persecution against them. They sent Elijah from Gilead to perform this task.

Arranging an audience with Ahab, the prophet told him, "As Yahweh the God of Israel lives, before whom I stand, there shall be neither dew nor rain these years, except by my word." After putting ben Omris in this mind set, Elijah left for Tishbe and let the king ponder his words. Elijah and his group of prophets, who were probably known as ravens, lived near the Wadi Cherith until the water supply became exhausted. They then packed their grips and move to Zarephath on the Mediterranean coast just below Sidon. Here they discovered from the maritime traders and sailors when the drought would probably end. They took up local employment and bided their time.

Prophetic communities in the ancient world were intelligence networks. As prophets moved about the country performing their various tasks, they assembled a working knowledge of the geography, local customs and beliefs, industry, the workings of other royal courts, and troop movements, among other useful information.[81] They connected to a network of other prophetic communities and traded in information. It was a primitive Internet without computers. Much of this information, if deemed to be useful, was recorded for future use.

Ancient kings and rulers quickly appreciated this vast network of information and stayed close to the prophetic communities, whether they believed in the deities at the oracular shrines or not. The information network was worth the effort. Manipulating this network made the prophets and their leaders very powerful. They were a secret kingdom among other kingdoms and usually welcomed by other prophetic communities and their royal courts. There was prestige, insight, and adventure.

The life of an active prophet was not dull. The ranks were open to men and women and gifted children. They learned to be cautious, eloquent, and crafty. Considering the amount of travel involved, they were probably physically strong and experienced in handling weapons. Most were working men and women, and only their most distinguished leaders drew from a common fund.

The war between Israel's prophets and the monarchy had reached the place where realpolitik was needed. Ahab was successful and Jezebel was supplanting the prophets. When the time came, Elijah proposed a contest between the prophets of Baal and Asherah and the prophets of Yahweh. Ahab could decide who would serve him best. Sidonian Baal had to rise to

---

81. 2 Kings 6:8-13.

the occasion and bring the drought to an end. But Elijah would show the king that the prophets of Yahweh were better.

To accomplish this, Elijah determined the site of Mount Carmel at the southeast side. From the northwest side, he could position trusted members of his cell of prophets, who would be able to keep Elijah informed of any weather developments in the distance. He could set in place a courier system with fifty prophets all the way to Sidon. When word came from the Phoenician coast that rain was imminent, he could begin the contest.

Sacrificial holocausts were common in the ancient world. To persuade onlookers that sacrificial smoke was fire from heaven required a special kind of preparation. The fire had to be spectacular in appearance, yet intense enough to consume flesh down to the bones quickly. In time, priests and prophets developed compounds or discovered substances similar to "Greek fire" used later by the Byzantines.[82] Greek fire was a highly volatile substance that exploded into fire even on water. For centuries, it was kept a state secret. The same was true of the substance used in sacrificial holocausts. What Elijah and his associates used is not known to us, but water had no effect on it. Like explosions in the movies today, the superstitious mind in the ancient world was taken in by spectacular sacrificial holocausts. It had to be fire from heaven. Normal fire didn't behave like that.

The time finally came when Elijah arranged another audience with ben Omri. By then, the drought was severe enough that the Israelite king was willing to entertain anything. Assembled on the southeast slope of Mount Carmel, the contest began. Elijah invited the prophets of Baal and Asherah to begin. They may have worked for a day or two or possibly weeks. When Elijah heard along his communication system that clouds were rising out of the sea, he took his turn at the altar. Once the sacrificial victim had been set in place, and the altar and carcass laced with whatever substance he used, Elijah said a prayer to Yahweh and then ignited the water-soaked sacrifice. He then went to an isolated spot on the mountain and waited for news about the coming rainstorm. When that news arrived, in good time he sent word to Ahab to leave for Samaria right away to avoid getting bogged down in the mud. The king departed. Elijah then maneuvered his servants and the prophets of Jezebel's court down into the Wadi Kishon, where he had them all killed. When the Sidonian queen heard of it, she sent word to Elijah that his life had now become worthless.

Clearly Yahweh did not answer Elijah. Only the king was granted the privilege. Yet people want to believe that Yahweh does answer their prayers.

---

82.   Isaiah 30:33. See also 2 Maccabees 1:21-22, 36.

The whole merit of the exercise on Mount Carmel was to propose a reconciliation between the king of Israel and the prophets of Yahweh. Ahab should consider the long and successful reign of Asa and the promising rule of his son Jehoshaphat. These kings, along with Rehoboam and David ben Jesse, listened and responded to the counsel of the Yahwist prophets. They all properly recognized the power wielded by these servants of God. As a result, their kingdoms prospered. Seeking the lives of both royal families in the case of Jeroboam and Baasha had only made matters worse. It was now time for ben Omri to seek Yahweh and the power the community of prophets could add to his rulership. It was time to reject Baal and his prophets.

Did they succeed in summoning Anat to perform her act of restitution? In spite of their entreaties, Mot still ruled. In fact, it was Yahweh who had ended the drought. Of course, by implication, it was hoped Ahab would assume on his own that Yahweh, not Mot, was the one who brought the drought also. Surely the king would realize the intelligence networking of Israel's own prophetic community had outsmarted the prophets of Baal in their own forum. However, Ahab and Jezebel were now seeking his life. The persecution would continue. Elijah fled south to Horeb to give the grand council there his report.

Leaving his servant at Beer-sheba, on the border between Judah and Simeon, Elijah journeyed a day's distance into the wilderness. At a place near the desert's edge, he stopped awhile among a local group of prophets. There he bulked up on food and drink before making the long trek to Horeb. On his arrival, he gave his sad account to the grand council of prophets and then retired for rest and nourishment. He engaged in a time of contemplation and reflection on his long career as one of Yahweh's prophets. Most of it was under Baasha and Omri in Israel. He had lived through the elimination of two possible dynasties, civil war, and transmigration inside both kingdoms. Jehoshaphat was a good king like his father, but his closeness to the Israelite royal family was worrisome and dangerous. Ahab and his father Omri were waging a successful war against his fellow prophets. The young Ahaziah and Jehoram would follow ben Omri's footsteps, if for no other reason than to preserve their own lives and their families. They really had no choice.

What of the young Jehoram of Judah? Ahab was his uncle. Would he follow his father's footsteps or would he abandon Yahweh as his cousins had? Were they all fighting the good fight, or was it all in vain? What of the Yahwist cause? Like Abraham, Elijah did not know who Yahweh was, but also like Abraham, he had decided ideas about who Yahweh was not. Their god was not in the wind, earthquake, or fire.

Long before Elijah's day, the ancient world was aware of the four main Aristotelian elements. Of the four, wind was the most mysterious. Its effects on earth, water, and fire were evident, but the wind appeared to be immune to the other three. Such power was godlike in its manifestations. Nature yielded to its exhalation. To many in the ancient polytheistic and superstitious world, the wind became identified with the spirit world and ultimately God. If you lived near a forest, mountain, sea, or desert, you felt the motions of gods and goddesses. But only a superior deity could destroy the earth's face with fire or split it apart with an earthquake.

Yet Elijah realized that Yahweh was not any of these. The Almighty was a royal, discerning personage. The prophet had read of the miraculous birth of Isaac to the aged Abraham and Sarah. In Egypt, Yahweh had performed two miracles that identified him as a discriminating, royal deity. It also determined that all of earth's firstborn creatures belonged to God for his disposal. Humans had nothing to say about it.

Finally, at Mount Horeb, where he now was, Yahweh had condescended to send a royal servant to speak with Moses, the greatest of all Yahweh's prophets. Were they not the voice of Moses in their day? The persecution of ben Omri had driven them back to the mount of God. Their grand prophet was like a latter-day Moses, and his grand council the seventy elders and prophets. Eldad and Medad now numbered some seven thousand who had not bowed to or kissed Sidonian Baal.

Elijah had come to Horeb to retire, but the grand council had one more assignment for him. He would anoint Elisha to succeed himself; then he would instruct Elisha to anoint Hazael to begin a holy war against Israel. People wanted to believe Yahweh answered their prayers. The sin of Jeroboam ben Nebat had to be effaced from among the people of God.

> Whoever escapes from the sword of Hazael, Jehu shall kill; and whoever escapes from the sword of Jehu, Elisha shall kill. Yet I will leave seven thousand in Israel, all the knees that have not bowed to Baal and every mouth that has not kissed him.[83]

When ben Omri had invited his son-in-law to take part in a military campaign against the Arameans, Jehoshaphat was not satisfied with the prophets who attended them. All the prophets admonished them to go ahead with their expedition. There was no dissenting voice.

---

83.   1 Kings 19:17-18

Finally, Ahab summoned a prophet named Micaiah ben Imlah to the Samarian court held in one of the gateways of the city. The messenger sent to ben Imlah instructed the prophet to give a favorable forecast. So Micaiah did. This irritated Ahab because this prophet normally gave the Israelite king difficult words. He criticized him and demanded the truth. So ben Imlah did tell him the horrible truth of what had been decreed against him by the grand council at Horeb.[84]

"Who will entice Ahab of Israel, so that he may fall at Ramoth-gilead?" asked the grand prophet.

After some discussion a volunteer came forward and announced. "I will entice the King."

"How will you do it?" inquired the grand council.

"I will become a lying spirit in the mouth of all his prophets." came the reply.

The decision of the grand council was then commanded by the grand prophet. "You are to entice him, and you will succeed at it; go ahead and do it."

The prophet Zedekiah ben Chenaanah standing nearby was stunned at ben Imlah's words. He was telling the Israelite king secret words the king was not meant to hear. Zedekiah walked over to Micaiah and slapped him in the face. "Which way did the spirit of the Lord pass from me to speak to you?" Zedekiah, it would appear, was the spirit offering his service to the grand council. But Micaiah despised Ahab and told him the truth as a warning to Jehoshaphat. The Israelite king, he calculated, would not believe it anyway. In this, ben Imlah was right.

The war with Aram began with a siege of Samaria with a small force of thirty-two chariots, indicating an army of fewer than five thousand cavalry and infantry. Ahab collected a superior force and Ben-Hadad withdrew.[85] The following year both kings clashed at Aphek, and Ben-Hadad was defeated and captured. He agreed to a treaty with ben Omri, granting him bazaars in Damascus for Israelite goods. For three years, Samaria and Damascus were at peace.

Meanwhile, Elijah returned from Horeb and learned ben Omri had Naboth of Jezreel judiciously murdered at the hands of his wife Jezebel. When Elijah, accompanied by Elisha, came to Naboth's vineyard next to the king's palace, he found Ahab admiring his new property. Elijah said

---

84. 2 Chronicles 18:18-24.

85. Haddad was the storm god of Phoenicia, symbolized by a meteorite. Zeus was also a storm god. A falling meteorite produces shock waves in the atmosphere that can sound like thunder.

to him, "Have you killed and also taken possession?" Finally after some fifteen years, Ahab heard the prophetic death sentence against him. "In the place where dogs licked up the blood of Naboth, they will also lick up your blood." The same would be true for Jezebel and his entire house. The king would not leave a dynasty behind him. By now the scorpions of Yahweh had surrounded him.

Ahab feared the worst. He tore his clothes as a sign of grief and exchanged his royal robes for sackcloth and his crown for ashes. Consequently, the prophecy was revised, allowing Ahab to live. The disaster would fall on Jehoram instead. However, the overall judgment would remain unchanged.

In 859 BC, Ahab ben Omri placed Jehoram on the throne because Ahaziah had been badly injured in a fall and was not expected to live. He died that year or shortly thereafter. Elijah had passed the mantle to Elisha, and at about that same time he departed for the mountain of God, allegorically pictured by a flaming chariot in the text. But Elisha agonized over the task now before him: holy war against his own country and people. As he saw Elijah disappear southward, he called after him, "Father, Father, the chariots of Israel and its horsemen!" But it was too late. Jehoram and Athaliah would succeed Jehoshaphat in Judah, and Jehoram ben Ahab was already in a co-regency. Jehoram ben Jehoshaphat would become co-regent in 855 BC. All of them were Baal worshippers. Because the prophecy against Ahab had been revised, Elisha had to wait until he died. Ramoth-gilead, where Jehu ben Nimshi was, would have to be delayed.

Elisha would not have to wait long. The northern Aramean world was in turmoil. The Assyrian war machine was on the move. Shalmaneser III (859-824 BC) had set his sights on Hamath of Zobah. King Irhuleni of Hamath had contacted Ben-Hadad of Damascus and ben Omri to join him in the war against the Assyrians that was sure to come. Ahab had asked Jehoshaphat to join him at Ramoth-gilead, Israel's eastern staging area, for the campaign into Zobah.[86] The Judean king agreed and mustered a force of two thousand chariots to lead an army of ten thousand. Assembling at Hamath, Irhuleni moved his force of sixty-three thousand north to the city of Qarqar.

In 853 BC, the coalition army engaged the forces of Shalmaneser in a bloody contest resulting in fierce casualties. The Assyrian "Monolith"

---

86. Ramoth-gilead was the eastern approach to Palestine. Ahab and Jehoshaphat waited to see where Shalmaneser would begin his invasion. Irhuleni and his troops meanwhile guarded the western approaches until it became clear where the Assyro-Babylonians would appear. There was no doubt a well-established relay between Ramoth-gilead and Megiddo.

inscription, housed in the British Museum, reports fourteen thousand. A statue inscription from Ashur puts that number at twenty-nine thousand. Ahab was killed in the battle, and Jehoshaphat made a narrow escape. It appears Ben-Hadad's illness may actually have been wounds from the battle.

Hearing news of Ahab's death, Elisha set in motion the holy war against Israel. In 852 BC, he journeyed to Damascus to anoint Hazael king of the Arameans in Assyria. Hazael killed Ben-Hadad and prepared for the war. Sometime about 848 BC, Elisha sent a young prophet to anoint Jehu ben Nimshi king of Israel.

The material theocracy of Israel was a representation of what the descendants of Abraham had created among themselves. In the early period, the holy mountain of God was in the Sinai peninsula. It was only much later that Jerusalem came to represent the mountain of God. Yahweh was a mountain deity. In the days of Moses, the wind on the holy mountain was the breath of Yahweh, and his power was expressed in fire and earthquake, but by Elisha's time many in the prophetic community had progressed beyond that level of manifestation. Yahweh became a royal court, expressed by his stand-ins the grand prophet and his council, who walked about on a sea of glass. They were daily attended by their angels, who traveled about the land in service to their Lord. It was a material theocracy, not a heavenly one.

Joshua ben Joseph, in the first century CE, reenacted the days of Moses and Elisha as a sign to Israel. The man had very good insight into his own history. He did not elevate it to a grandiose level. Herod was a latter-day Ahab and Pontius Pilate was the undisputed, absolute authority of God on earth. It was a material theocracy. Tiberius was the Most High in the Roman world. The material theocracy had progressed beyond Palestine and had embraced the Mediterranean world. Joshua viewed himself as a member of the community of prophets, and John ben Zechariah as his Elijah gave him legitimacy. It was a material theocracy and nothing more. Although nothing is mentioned about it, we can safely assume the community of prophets at Mount Horeb still existed in Joshua's day. His pilgrimage to Horeb was one of the first things he did after John baptized him.[87]

Early in the reign of Jehoram of Judah, he had all his brothers and anyone who could rival him executed. His wife Athaliah was Ahab's daughter, and both introduced Baal worship into Judah. Edom revolted and Libnah in Philistia also rebelled. In his first campaign, he was captured by the Edomites while his army fled. He was probably either ransomed to

---

87. 1 Kings 19:4-8; Matthew 4:1.

the Arab traders or used as a ploy to capture Jerusalem.[88] At any rate, the kingdom of Judah fell to the Philistines and Arabs in the first half of his reign. They confiscated the wealth of the kingdom and took his entire family hostage, with the exception of his youngest son Jehoahaz to succeed him.

When Jehoram died, he was buried with no honors. His son Jehoahaz or Ahaziah succeeded him. In his first and only year of rule, he went with Jehoram ben Ahab, his cousin, to war with Hazael of Aram. At a battle near Ramah, Jehoram was wounded, and both he and his cousin traveled to Samaria for rest and recuperation.

Unknown to them, Jehu ben Nimshi at Ramoth-gilead had been anointed to replace ben Ahab. The young prophet had instructed Jehu to exterminate Ahab's house, throw Jehoram's body in the vineyard of Naboth at Jezreel, and kill Jezebel also. When Jehu returned, his officers inquired about the young "madman." Jehu brushed him aside as a typical "babbler." But his officers wouldn't let their questions drop. They called him a liar and demanded to know. Ben Nimshi relented and told them what the young madman had babbled to him. They couldn't proclaim him king fast enough. Although they may have resented the real power wielded by the community of prophets, they were quick to use it when it dropped into their laps.

Anointed by the prophet and hailed by the army, Jehu mounted his chariot and marched his cavalry to Samaria. When he came near Jezreel, Jehu quickened his pace to close the gap between him and Jehoram. When the first rider did not return, the king and Ahaziah drove out to meet him. When they came close enough, Jehu killed both with his bow. Jehoram's body was dumped onto the ground of Jezreel. Ahaziah escaped to Megiddo, where he died from his wounds.

Now the slaughter in Israel began. Jehu killed Ahab's house, including Jezebel. When he came across forty-two relatives of Ahaziah on the way to Samaria, he killed them also. When Athaliah heard her son Ahaziah was dead, she wiped out the royal family in Judah as well and made Baal the chief god at Jerusalem. Only the temple precinct of Yahweh was closed to her. But Jehosheba, Ahaziah's sister, and her husband Jehoiada took Ahaziah's young son Joash to the temple to escape Athaliah's murderous purge. There, in the Jerusalem sanctuary, the infant prince spent the first six years of his life.

After Jehu's bloody purge of the royal family in Israel, he called for a national demonstration of allegiance to Baal. Ahab had honored the Canaanite deity in a small way, but Jehu would be magnanimous. He ordered the priests to organize a mass ritual observance at his temple in Samaria. All

---

88. See Ezekiel 27.

were required be in attendance, and there could be no recognizable Yahwists among those assembled.

Most of what we know about Baal of Canaan comes from tablets discovered in Northern Syria at Ras Shamra. This site of ancient Ugarit was the location of his temple dating back to the second millennium BC. In the Semitic languages, the name Baal means lord or owner. Its use has a very broad scope. Baal was a fertility god of the soil and cattle of the field. He was the cloud-rider or rainmaker who fought his enemies, died, and then was reborn. One of his chief enemies was Mot, who ruled the season of drought. After numerous sacrifices, his sister and consort Anat was called forth to battle with Mot, whom she killed. The remains of Mot were pulverized and sown on the parched land, making it live again. Baal was resurrected and spread his productive rain on the thirsty soil, summoning up its produce. Baal was therefore entitled to an offering of the first fruits, vegetable, animal, and human.[89] Egypt embraced this deity in the fourteenth century BC.

Another of Baal's enemies was the god El and his wife Asherah. El had a long period of development in the ancient world reflected in the biblical texts. Eloah is usually used to designate a pagan deity and idol, while Elohim indicates a deity or magistrate in the superlative sense. It was this later term Elohim that the Aramean-Hebrews latched on to to elevate their essentially unknown god above all other deities. It was during the period under Moses that Yah first appeared among the Israelites, a word that means "the lord most vehement." It is in the book of Exodus that Yahweh first appears, the lord who will prove to be in the most vehement sense. Here we have etymological evidence to suggest the three miracles in Egypt did take place as the record says.

In time, El-Yahweh was given Asherah as wife, becoming Baal's enemy. Like Baal, he was the rain god,[90] but he could also be Mot.[91] Yahweh was lord of the first fruits, with the exception that worshippers were prohibited from offering human sacrifice. Yet El-Yahweh could slaughter the firstborn of the enemy. He could confiscate the firstborn of believers for holy orders or special service.

One of the problems faced by the Israelite religious community was that Baal already had a fully developed persona, whereas El-Yahweh was still shrouded in considerable mystery. The human desire for tangible revelation

---

89. Jeremiah 19:5.
90. Leviticus 26:4, Deuteronomy 11:14.
91. 2 Chronicles 6:26, Haggai 1:11.

could easily syncretize the two, whether consciously or subconsciously. Baal often could fill the gap when answers about Yahweh were absent.[92]

The main difference between the two was couched in Mosaic law. Yahweh was an uncompromising moral absolutist and Baal was a moral relativist, enforcing law by expedience. In a dangerous world, moral absolutes are difficult and seemingly impossible to manage. Fear is a great obstacle. Evil despises moral excellence. However, moral relativism is highly deceptive. It is often not the safe haven it appears to be. Those who seek refuge in moral relativism can suffer in other ways. We live in a dangerous world, and the thrust of the Mosaic code was that neighbors should not harm one another. The law extended beyond actual harm and property damage: neighbors were not to pose a threat of harm or damage.

On the appointed day when the Baal worshippers had assembled at the temple in Samaria, Jehu had his most loyal soldiers positioned at the entranceways of the sanctuary and probably at all the gateways into and out of the city as well. Between the two would have been a military perimeter to prevent any possible escape. On the king's signal, the slaughter began. Only those who knew of any secret passageways had hope of escape.

When the purge ended, Baal's temple was converted to a public toilet. This event probably occurred sometime in Jehu's sixth year of rule, before he became the vassal of Assyria. It may have been the result of ben Nimshi's purge to bring Shalmaneser III and his forces down on Israel to protect the worship of Sidonian Baal in the region. By the time the killing stopped in Israel and Judah, the holy war had become a river of blood. The power of the grand council at Horeb could no longer be taken for granted. They were there to enforce the material theocracy by whatever means they determined.

---

92. Hosea 2:16.

4

THE NEW AGE PROPHETS

The purge of Baal worship in Israel gave the priests of Yahweh's temple at Jerusalem the impetus to depose Queen Athaliah. She had spent her six years on the Judean throne ruling the country on behalf of her suzerains, the Arabs and Philistines. Like her parents, she was a Baal devotee and had extensively promoted the religion in the region. Only the temple of Yahweh at Jerusalem had avoided the religious infiltration by the pagan rainmaker. The doors to the temple precinct had been decisively closed against Athaliah's rule. However, in Jehu's sixth year of rule, which coincided with Athaliah's sixth year, the priests of Yahweh used the successful purge of Baal in Israel to launch a takeover of the government and to purge Judah of the Baal religion as well. Arming themselves, they opened the gates to Jerusalem and siezed the throne for Jehoash, capturing Athaliah and executing her outside the palace.

In Judah, the new king was managed by the priests and his co-regent uncle, Jehoiada, until he reached a suitable age. The young boy's kingdom continued under the thumb of the Arabs and the Philistines, who were the de facto rulers. In concert with the priests, Jehoash and his uncle turned their efforts to repairs needed at the temple. Although the priests collected money, no repairs were actually done until Jehoash's seventeenth year.

In the meantime, Jehu had become the vassal of Assyria in about his eighth or ninth year of leadership. This event is depicted in the Black Obelisk at the British Museum. The obelisk shows ben Nimshi bowed before Shalmaneser III while his attendant pays the tribute. Shalmaneser had failed to take Damascus, but he had conquered the coastal territories, including Israel.

When Shalmaneser died, Hazael took advantage of the gap in power to invade Philistia and Jerusalem. Jehoash paid Hazael a ransom, after which he withdrew. Hazael was careful to bypass Samaria. Toward the end of his reign, after his uncle Jehoiada had died, Jehoash saw his kingdom become polytheistic when his officials forced him to concede to religious freedom in Judah. His officials no doubt had the full support of the Arab traders and Philistine merchants, who saw the fragmentation of Judah's internal affairs as a good thing for themselves. As a result of Jehoash's concession, in addition to the Yahwist high places worship and the altars of Baal, Asherah and other pagan deities began their reappearance in Judah.

In Israel, Jehu had been reprimanded for not removing calf worship. Although Baal had been expunged from prominence in Israel, some of the ritual practices of Baalism had been syncretized into calf worship.[93] With Assyria as their new suzerain, it was simply a matter of time before Baal was once again triumphant.

Consequently, the remaining years of Jehu's reign and the rule of his son Jehoahaz saw a growing, more intense activity among the prophets. The activity was organized, refined, and began to be written down. Because Judah and Israel were vassal kingdoms, their kings were limited in their actions, and the grand council at Horeb adopted a more lenient attitude toward both monarchs and their families. The prophets decide to leave ben Nimshi and his dynasty alone to the fourth generation. If prophetic sanction was not given to the fifth member of Jehu's dynasty, then that descendant would be murdered by a usurper.

In Judah, the return of the Baals and Asherahs in all their manifestations incited similar prophetic activity, spearheaded by Zechariah ben Barachiah. But the success of their efforts brought charges against ben Barachiah, who was judged and sentenced to die. Jehoash granted the death penalty, and Zechariah was stoned to death inside the temple precinct. In the first century CE, Joshua ben Joseph drew attention to Zechariah ben Barachiah prior to his own death.[94]

The Bible student will notice that Zechariah, though the son of Jehoiada, had a different last name.[95] Zechariah's biological father was deceased, and Jehoiada adopted him. King Jehoash did not bear Jehoiada's name either, although he was raised by his uncle and aunt. Perhaps Zechariah's father Barachiah died in the purge inflicted by Athaliah.

---

93. Hosea 13:2.
94. 2 Chronicles 24:19-22; Matthew 23:35.
95. The name "ben Barachiah" may have been omitted by the rabbinic Jews of the first and second century CE.

It is reasonably clear that Jesus did not have the writers of the prophetic work in mind when he drew attention to Zechariah. The situation ben Joseph faced before he gave his great prophecy paralleled the situation ben Barachiah suffered. Therefore, the student of Bible history can use the history of Jesus Christ as a guide to expand insight into the later reign of Jehoash ben Ahaziah. Jesus was referring to himself as a metatype of Zechariah.

The most reliable gospel is John's. He was the one disciple Jesus trusted completely. John ben Zebedee wrote his gospel to set the record straight. This is why his account is at variance with the other synoptic gospels. At the time when John wrote his history, many misconceptions and stories had grown up about Jesus's life and ministry, many of which were included in the synoptic gospels. Matthew's gospel was probably the first and became badly corrupted over time. However, the Sermon on the Mount, the ten parabolic oracles, and the prophecy in chapters twenty-four and -five are worth preserving. Mark's gospel is unnecessary, and Luke's is the most unreliable of all. The last three, except where noted, could form the first books of the christian apocryphal writings. There are more reasons to take this position which I will address later on in this work.

Assyrian power began to undergo internal turmoil during the reign of Jehoahaz of Israel and the last half of the reign of Judah's Jehoash. At the end of Shalmaneser III's reign, a civil war broke out with his eldest son. Shalmaneser was succeeded by his second son, Shamshi-Adad V (824-810 BC). When he died, his widow Sammu-ramat (Semiramis) became co-regent for the young Adad-nirari III (810-782 BC). The reign of the latter became a time of internal weakness for Assyria. After Adad-nirari, Assyria essentially disappears from the geopolitical map until Tiglath-pileser III appears in 745 BC.

King Hazael and his son Ben-hadad III took advantage of this breakdown of Assyrian power and attempted to become the hegemonic power in Palestine. The internal conflicts among the northern Arameans was mirrored in the destructive wars among the southern Arameans in Palestine. To protect its kingdom from Assyrian aggression in the north, Damascus had to ensure there were no enemies in the south. The Arameans readied for war and moved on Israel and Judah.

Sometime about 804 BC, Israel was subjugated by the Syrians.[96] They established a garrison at Aphek near the east side of the Sea of Chinnereth. The following year or thereabouts, the conquering army from Damascus invaded Judah and began devastating the kingdom. Jehoash's army was

---

96.   2 Kings 13:7.

badly defeated, and the king himself was seriously wounded. In 802 BC, all his troubles abruptly ended when he was assassinated in his bed.

In Israel, the new king Joash ben Jehoahaz determined to throw off the Syrian weight and sought the blessing of the ailing prophet Elisha. About that time, King Hazael of Damascus had been, or was about to be, succeeded by his son Ben-hadad III. Joash may have waited for this outcome before he began his campaign against Syria by overthrowing their garrison at Aphek. He probably placed his son Jeroboam in a co-regency with himself before beginning the war. Joash defeated Ben-hadad III in three successive campaigns, recovering his lost territories and eliminating the garrison at Aphek. He was supported in his efforts to restore his kingdom by the community of prophets. No doubt they used this occasion to strengthen their hand inside the realm to bring about religious reforms.

In Judah, Amaziah came to the throne a year after Joash with the same desire as the Israelite king: to rid himself of the suzerain. Amaziah signaled war by placing his son Azariah on the throne as a co-regent rule in the sixth year of his reign. After executing his father's assassins, he made ready for a war on Edom. Although a Mosaic injunction[97] prohibited any interference with the Edomites, Amaziah, like David ben Jesse's commander Joab, not only warred against his kindred but perpetrated genocide on them.[98] This is one of the most disturbing aspects of the material theocracy: the venomous and self-righteous attitude among the prophets, who despised all outsiders. Their merciless and murderous view of the Gentile nations is reflected in the writings of the prophets, such as the books of Obadiah, Nahum, and the Gentile portions of other works. Yet they excused themselves of genocide with regard to their own kindred, the descendants of Jacob's brother Esau. When Amaziah returned, he was criticized by the religious community for returning with some of Edom's idols as trophies of war. David ben Jesse accepted the crown of Milcom on his head, the abomination of the Ammonites. Yet the prophets plotted the assassination of Amaziah.

Flushed with his success in the genocide on his brethren, Amaziah turned his attention to Israel and proposed war against Joash. The Judean king had intended to hire Israelite soldiers for his campaign against the Edomites, but the prophets had counseled against it. Amaziah was admonished to forget the payment already made and proceed with his own troops. Heeding their advice he disbanded the mercenaries and sent them home. However, while he was away slaughtering his kindred, the Israelites had vented their frustration by sacking towns and villages on

---

97. Deuteronomy 2:2-6.
98. 2 Chronicles 25:11, 12.

Judah's northern border. The mercenary army burned, looted, and killed many of their Judean brethren before retiring.

Indignant at this affront, Amaziah demanded reparation from the Israelite king. Joash declined, telling the Judean to stay home. Joash laid the blame at Amaziah's feet for creating the mercenary beast to begin with. Mercenary armies were unpredictable at best and slew for pay, not national idealism. It would be better, Joash counseled, to refrain from adding any more victims to the tragedy. But Amaziah would not listen.

Realizing the Judean king would not take no for an answer, Joash marched his army into Judah and clashed with Amaziah at Beth-shemesh. Just as Joash had foreseen, the outcome was disastrous for Judah. Amaziah's army was defeated, and Amaziah was taken prisoner to Samaria. Joash tore down a large section of Jerusalem's walls, exposing the capital to easy sack and pillage. All the gold and silver was confiscated, leaving Amaziah's son and co-regent Azariah in difficult straits.

Amaziah was soon released by Joash's successor, Jeroboam II. When Amaziah returned to Judah, he left Azariah on the throne in Jerusalem and made Lachish his capital instead. During the remaining fifteen years of his rule, the second capital became an important center for Judah's polytheistic population.[99] Located in the western foothills, further to the south, the city was closer to Egypt's border, giving the pharoahs' forces quicker and easier access should the city need relief from siege. This new location was beneficial to Egypt as well, and the decision to make Lachish a fortress was probably made with their counsel and assistance. Lachish was also closer to Beer-sheba and Gur-baal, serving the interests of the Arab caravan route and the Philistine merchants. While Jerusalem remained the citadel of Yahweh and his priests, Lachish in the Shephelah became the military and civil capital of Judah.

The kingdom of David was in the process of becoming two domains. The polytheists and monotheists were once again separating into two religious nations. Jerusalem's developing similarity with the traditional Mount Horeb caused a shift in religious symbolism. From this time onward, Jerusalem became the symbolic mountain of Yahweh. The holy site of Mount Horeb in the Sinai peninsula faded, becoming more of a pilgrimage site and a tourist curiosity as time passed. The Levites and new age prophets had a permanent capital they could look to. Mount Horeb and its wilderness communities continued as as a safe haven and part of the prophets' domain, but Jerusalem had replaced Horeb in importance.

---

99. Micah 1:13.

Like his father, Amaziah fell victim to assassins while at Lachish, and his body was returned to Jerusalem for burial. He was the fourth Judean king to die violently at the hands of fanatics. The old material theocracy believed their actions were sanctioned by their ancestor Moses and his brother Aaron. They were Yahweh's prophets who called to them over the centuries, giving them authority to keep the nation religiously clean. To facilitate this divine mandate, the prophets put words in Yahweh's mouth and then carried them out.

The "new age of prophets" mentioned by ben Barachiah[100] was much less bloody-minded than the seers from Horeb. The message of his disciples was very simple. Those who obeyed Mosaic law would enjoy a peaceful relationship with Yahweh even if they suffered at human hands. Those who transgressed the law would not. The internecine bloodbath had made matters worse. Healing, tolerance, and forgiveness were needed.[101]

The Bible writer Jonah ben Amittai may have been one of the prophets inspired by ben Barachiah. The work attributed to him was decidedly put together by Talmudic committee and reflects the old-style Chaldeaic moral allegory. Chapter one concerns Jonah's decision to leave Israel by ship. He wound up lost at sea for three days and nights while the ship he was on disappeared into a storm. Interestingly, the deep-ocean diving equipment used to find sunken vessels like the historic Titanic are now being used to explore the Mediterranean floor for ancient ships. New evidence is quite literally coming to the surface as archaeologists harvest underwater treasure troves.

The expression "swallowed by a whale or sea monster" is obviously ancient code for being lost at sea. The prayer in chapter two of the book of Jonah says nothing about a whale or large fish, and may actually be an excerpt preserved from the apocryphal book of Jashar. The main thrust of chapters three and four in the edited allegory deals with forgiveness, a new concept for the Mosaic material theocracy. In the very last sentence, one can almost hear the expression "forgive them for they know not what they do." This popular expression is attributed to the later prophet Joshua ben Joseph in the gospels, and may have found currency in the new age of prophets. The moral ascendancy of forgiveness gained strength while Uzziah was on the Judean throne. The kings in Jerusalem began dying in their beds from natural causes.

Jeroboam II escaped the assassin's blade, but his son Zechariah did not. Zechariah came to the throne at Samaria in Jeroboam II's twenty-ninth

---

100. 2 Chronicles 24:20-22.
101. 2 Kings 14:25-27.

year of rule. After six months as co-regent, he was murdered by Shallum ben Jabesh, who usurped the co-regency, leaving Jeroboam unharmed. After all, the Israelite king was protected by prophetic sanction.[102] Clearly the words of the prophets were treated as if they had been spoken by God himself. Their power had risen beyond the realm of mortals.

Menahem ben Gadi, who was at Tirzah, marched to Samaria and supplanted Shallum in the co-regency. What the situation was at Samaria is not stated in the text, but my new chronology indicates ben Gadi was co-regent for twelve years before his solo reign of ten years. In the year that Uzziah died, Menahem's successor Pekahiah, who was in a co-regency with his father for two years, was murdered and replaced by Pekah ben Remaliah. Menahem continued to live as king because he delivered one thousand talents to King Pul, or Tilgath-pileser III. Pul's annals tell us, "I received tribute from Menahem of Samaria, like a bird, alone he fled and submitted to me." This indicates Menahem was an exile at the Assyrian court for a time before he returned to Israel. Whether a state of civil war existed between the two Israelite capitals is not stated. However, the Assyrian records appear to indicate such a situation was likely. Perhaps Menahem came to some kind of an accommodation with Pekah, ending their dispute. However, ben Remaliah did succeed Menahem for a solo reign of some ten years. Nearly all of his rule was spent preparing for the inevitable.

In 734 BC, Tilgath-pileser marched south, capturing the northern territories of Naphtali around the Sea of Chinnereth, sending its population into exile, and replacing them with settlers from elsewhere. Known by his Babylonian name Pulu, the Assyrian king invaded Philistia, laying siege to its cities and extending his land bridge along the Mediterranean to the border of Egypt. While campaigning in that region, he accepted embassies and tribute from other rulers, including those who wish to become kings. One of these was Hosea ben Elah, who made his approach sometime around 732 BC. He proposed to supplant Pekah ben Remaliah at Samaria. It is possible the situation of Menahem ben Gadi played a part in Tilgath-pileser's decision. In any case, the Assyrian invader accepted ben Elah's proposal and made him Israel's king.

The prophet Hosea ben Beeri is one of the first two Deutero-Classic prophets whose work has survived. Writing sometime in the latter half of Jeroboam II's reign, Hosea added what we call "street theater" to his words. He lived what he said. The prophet purposely married a prostitute named Gomer. He had three children by her; two sons and one daughter. His first son was named Jezreel to remind Israel of Ahab's sin against Naboth. His

---

102. 2 Kings 10:30.

next child was a daughter he named Lo-ruhamah, as a signal that Israel's end was close. Only Judah would survive the coming retribution. His third child was a son called Lo-ammi to advertise that God had rejected Israel.

Using his wife Gomer as the object of denunciation, Hosea repudiated her and his children in public. "Upon her children also I have no pity, because they are children of whoredom, for their mother has played the whore; she who conceived them has acted shamefully."

In typical Deutero-Classic style, the words of condemnation then turn into hope for the future.

> Therefore, I will now allure her, and bring her into the wilderness, and speak tenderly to her . . . . On that day, says the Lord, you will call me, "My husband," and no longer will you call me, "My Baal." . . . And I will have pity on Lo-ruhamah, and I will say to Lo-ammi, "You are my people"; and he shall say, "You are my God."

The Deutero-Classic writings are a continuation of the material theocracy with forgiveness and restoration at the end. This style derives from the Deutero-Classic formula contained in the book of Deuteronomy. Between chapters twenty-seven and thirty, Moses sets out the blessing and the curse.[103] Mounts Gerizim and Ebal were respectively the mountains which symbolized the blessing and curse. In chapter thirty-one, verse sixteen, the book of Deuteronomy predicts Israel will inevitably fall under the curse. Moses then composes two songs which Israel must know intimately. The first, in chapter thirty-two, is the "Song of the Curse," followed by the "Song of the Blessing." The blessing always follows the curse. This is the Deutero-Classic formula. It is the source of inspiration for most of the prophetic works in the biblical collection. In the hands of the new age disciples of ben Barachiah, it was a poetic format based on transgression and forgiveness and leading to restoration.

However, forgiveness only follows from repentance and a sincere effort to correct the transgression. Repentance must produce a demonstration of change. In Hosea's work, the Israelites have placed themselves beyond recovery.

---

103. See also Leviticus 26.

Their deeds do not permit them to return to their God.

They made kings, but not through me; they set up princes, but without my knowledge.

Your calf is rejected, O Samaria. My anger burns against them. How long will they be incapable of innocence?
For it is from Israel, an artisan made it; it is not from God.
The calf of Samaria shall be broken to pieces.

I will destroy you, O Israel; who can help you? Where now is your king, that he may save you?

Every evil of theirs began at Gilgal; there I came to hate them.

I gave you a king in my anger, and I took him away in my wrath.

Your love is like a morning cloud, like the dew that departs early. Therefore I have hewn them by the prophets. I have killed them by the words of my mouth, and my judgment goes forth as the light.
For I desire steadfast love and not sacrifice, the knowledge of God rather than burnt offerings.

Although the "Song of the Curse" composed by Moses would fall on them, it would be only for a time. To symbolize the exile that would overtake Israel, Hosea purchased a slave woman for fifteen shekels and some barley and wine. The prophet instructed her not to have relations with anyone, including himself. This "dry spell" would recall Israel to her senses and "afterward the Israelites shall return and seek Yahweh their God, and David their king; they shall come in awe to Yahweh and to his goodness in later days.

This is how the Book of Hosea finishes off in the last chapter. The blessing would follow the curse in due course. Israel would be redeemed when it turned its attention to the law and its fulfillment in Israel. Then:

His shoots shall spread out; his beauty shall be like the olive tree, and his fragrance like that of Lebanon.
They shall again live beneath my shadow, they shall flourish as a garden; they shall blossom like the vine, their fragrance shall be like the wine of Lebanon.

Using the Deutero-Classic formula with some street theater techniques to draw the public's attention to his message, Hosea recounted some of Israel's history with succinct references and personal observations made in his own day. Presenting it all together in the poetry of prosaic language, he created a work worth preserving by other prophets, who no doubt used it themselves, raising it to an authority. The prophecy of Hosea is a truly timeless work. Many of the foibles and attitudes described by Hosea ben Beeri are clearly visible in humankind the world over. We today readily recognize what we read in the pages of his book. Though we can discover some of the past through historical study, there are many things we will never know. The book of Hosea cuts through evidence and non-evidence by connecting the ties that bind humanity together through common experience.

Amos was a contemporary of Hosea ben Beeri who was a Judean from Tekoa. The city was also one of the king's fortresses, and Amos worked as a shepherd and "a dresser of sycamore trees." He was not a member of the community of prophets, but an outsider who took it upon himself to journey to Jeroboam's court by way of Bethel, just over the Judean border. From the priest Amaziah at the sacred center of calf worship, word arrived in Samaria of Amos's presence. The self-styled prophet or seer had predicted that Jeroboam II would die violently.[104] However, the brief account of Jeroboam's reign indicates he died of old age like his forebears. It appears Amos missed the mark on that occasion.[105] However, he was a literate man who understood how to use the Deutero-Classic formula. His references indicate he was a worker of the land, and the reader can hear the influence from the book of Job in his composition.

The introduction and chapter nine of the book of Amos tell us a devastating earthquake occurred in Israel in his day. Geologists have confirmed there was such a cataclysm along the Carmel mountain range. We hear earthquake language in Isaiah and Micah.[106] Geologists estimate the time period was circa 750 BC. This was the year Uzziah died, chronicled

---

104. Amos 7:10-15.
105. Amos 7:1-9.
106. Isaiah 6:4; Micah 1:3-4; Zechariah 14:5.

in Isaiah 6. Two years before the earthquake would place Amos's work in the last year of Jeroboam II's reign, 752 BC. It would appear the book of Amos was written in two parts. Chapters 1 through 7:15 was written before the earthquake, and chapter 7:16 to the end was written after the cataclysm.

The passage in Amos 8:9-10 is referenced in the synoptic gospels as a prophecy fulfilled by the death of Jesus Christ, but John's gospel makes no mention of it. Since he was there at the time, it would have been mentioned in his history. John's gospel is the only history worth trusting, and his account essentially contradicts many of the early Christian notions, including the application of Deutero-Classic passages.

Hosea 11:1 is another popular application that misses the mark. Jacob-Israel was not the firstborn of Isaac. Rather, Jacob made a dubious purchase from his brother Esau and then deceived his father to acquire the blessing of the firstborn. Later he spent a night wrestling with a prophet to acquire recognition for his claim to be an adopted son of Elohiym. This was a contentious issue between Jacob and his older brother, but Esau forgave Jacob and Jacob acknowledged Esau as his master.[107] This makes Obadiah's work a piece of hate literature. The passage in Hosea 11:1 applies only to Israel in Egypt. The account of Jesus's flight to Egypt is probably bogus, considering a move to Nazareth was all that was needed. What better place to hide than under the enemy's nose? Who would bother looking in Nazareth?[108]

Amos recognized the injustice done to the Edomites by two of Judah's kings.

> On that day I will raise up the booth of David that is fallen,
> and repair its breaches, and raise up its ruins, and rebuild
> it as in the days of old; in order that they may possess the
> remnant of Edom and all the nations who are called by my
> name, says Yahweh who does this.

It is not difficult to appreciate that the Israelite prophets could see the rise of Assyria. For years it had been occupied with internal troubles, but new solutions had been found. Conquered lands were repopulated after the locals had been exiled far away from their homeland. Interestingly, the biblical record places King Pul ahead of Tiglath-pileser. He should actually come after. When the Babylonians gave the Assyrian monarch the name Pulu, it was well into the middle of his reign. Perhaps Tiglath-

---

107. Genesis 33:4-11.
108. John 1:46.

pileser reminded them of a previous Assyrian ruler. Was King Pul an earlier monarch?

It was well within the grasp of the prophetic viewpoint that Assyria would be the one to punish Israel. The massive earthquake near Mount Carmel that destroyed Megiddo and other towns close by seemed to confirm their pronouncements. To Elijah, Yahweh was not in the earthquake, but to many he was. The term "Harmagedon" comes from this time. It is derived from the phrase "Har-megiddo." Earthquakes were nothing new in Palestine. Indeed, the temple and other constructions were built to withstand earthquake.[109] At this time, however, the area north of the River Kishon was in Assyrian hands. Between Mount Carmel and Mount Gilboa, the Valley of Jezreel and the plain to the northwest were protected by the fortress of Megiddo, built by Solomon. Its destruction by the earthquake symbolized the end of wicked Israel. It was as if God himself had opened the gate to the Assyrian invader on their border.

On the Judean throne sat King Uzziah, a student and disciple of Zechariah ben Barachiah. The new age prophets had a royal patron. Uzziah succeeded in throwing off the Philistine and Arab yoke, making both subject to his will. Judah was autonomous again. He rebuilt the walls destroyed by Joash of Israel and mounted defensive siege engines on Jerusalem's ramparts. The military was re-equipped, and the kingdom's defensive footing was strengthened. He built lookout towers in the wilderness areas. Uzziah, it is said, was a lover of the soil. He increased the water supply with many cisterns and probably made improvements to the kingdom's agrarian base. With Uzziah, Judah entered into a second golden age.

But all was not well among the people he ruled. The prophet Isaiah ben Amoz began his work during the Judean king's last years. Chapter six is dated to the year of his death in 750 BC, three years after the city of Rome was founded. His work is directed to the Judeans, and his words echo the mentor of his soul, Zechariah ben Barachiah. Isaiah is very much a new age prophet in the fullest sense of the phrase.

According to Isaiah, the people of Judah had missed the whole thrust of the sacrificial altar in front of the temple. "What to me is the multitude of your sacrifices?" said Yahweh. If people sought justice and did what was right, they would prosper, not by declaring their iniquity by piling sacrificial victims on his altar and spilling enormous amounts of blood. If Israel did what was right by their God, only the minimum would be required. Instead, Jerusalem had become a slaughterhouse.

---

109. 1 Kings 7:10-12.

Under Uzziah's rule, Judah had become wealthy again, but it had also produced arrogance and injustice. Judah was a latter-day Sodom and Gomorrah. Social justice had been repudiated among them. The Judeans preferred to spend the wealth on their own indulgence.

Isaiah also took aim at the religious community and their hangups. He specifically criticized those who said, "Let him make haste; let him speed his work that we may see it; let the plan of the Holy One of Israel hasten to fulfillment." Instead of dreading God's wrath, many of the self-righteous religious wanted to see their kindred destroyed, and on their schedule. Shrewd in their own sight, these hypocrites often called evil good and good evil. What they called light was often darkness, and darkness they proclaimed as light. "The lamp of the body is the eye," said a famous rabbi.

> If your eye is simple or healthy your whole body will be bright. However, if your eye is not healthy then your whole body will be darkened. If the light in you is actually darkness; then how great is that darkness.

Although proclaiming love for their fellow man, the self-righteous harbored a deep desire to see their brethren consigned to oblivion. They were ever-resourceful to invent reasons why they could not do right.

Yet in the true voice of the Deutero-Classic formula, there would come a day when all wrongs would be righted. In Isaiah we find the counter to the ideal of Zionism, which elevates Jerusalem above a material mountain to be Yahweh's throne. This is a new feature among the new age prophets in the material theocracy.

> For out of Zion shall go forth instruction, and the word of Yahweh from Jerusalem. He shall judge between the nations, and shall arbitrate for many peoples; they shall beat their swords into plowshares, and their spears into pruning hooks; nation shall not lift up sword against nation, neither shall they learn war anymore.

This swelling idealism gives us an indication of how prosperous Judah was under King Uzziah. Rising expectations created new plateaus, including the notion of a Jerusalem more grandiose than the material city they lived in. Even Uzziah's expectations reached beyond his station. He decided he could be his own priest and entered the holy part of the temple sanctuary to make an offering at the altar of incense in front of the curtain separating the holy from the Holy of Holies. This act was prohibited by religious law, and the priests went in after him to bring him out. In the process, it was discovered the king was leperous. Because he was a leper, Uzziah was excluded not only from the temple precinct, but his own palace. He was isolated in a separate house. His son Jotham took over the palace and ruled as his co-regent.

When Uzziah died, Israel was shattered by a massive earthquake. In Judah, Jotham continued in his father's footsteps, but the populace could not be reformed. He warned against the Ammonites in the east and subjugated them into paying tribute. Assyrian activity in Aram and Israel continued while Jotham extended Judah's building program and defensive measures. Toward the end of his rule, the kings Rezin and Pekah ben Remaliah attempted to war against Judah, so Jotham placed his son Ahaziah, or Ahaz, on the throne in Jerusalem and based his defensive operations from Lachish.

We do not hear from Isaiah until Ahaz comes to the throne. Samaria and Damascus were then becoming more of a threat to Judah, wanting to replace him with their own ally named ben Tabeel. Unlike his father and grandfather, Ahaz was a pagan and a somewhat timid soul. If there was one constant Ahaz could have taken comfort in, it was the survival of the Judean monarchy. He would become the thirteenth king in the dynasty of David ben Jesse. Isaiah tried to calm the fears of Ahaz by telling him he would produce a fourteenth successor. The successor's name, Immanuel, meant "God is with us." Surely, after a dynastic succession of fourteen kings, Ahaz would realize it was something of a miracle.

But Ahaz knew the history of his forebears. Polytheist or Yahwist, religion was no guarantee of his own safety. Perhaps the Davidic dynasty would continue, but being Yahwist had not prevented Jehoash and Amaziah from being assassinated.

> Look, the young woman is with child and shall bear a son,
> and shall name him Immanuel. For before the child knows
> how to refuse the evil and choose the good, the land before
> whose two kings you are in dread will be deserted.

Ahaz had no faith in the Yahwists and devoted his petitions for salvation to Baal, offering the god the firstborn of his sons in sacrifice at ben Hinnom. But the tide had turned in the north, and Assyria was pressing its interest southward. Damascus and Samaria needed resources to defend their domains. The Baal deity never came to Judah's aid, and Ahaz suffered defeat when his father's army was badly crushed by the northern coalition. Ahaz lost three sons to the army of ben Remaliah.

While Assyria was campaigning in Philistia, the Edomites revolted and invaded Judah. Ahaz sent envoys to Tiglath-pileser asking for help. The Assyrian king complied and helped himself to all Judah's treasures. About this time, Hosea ben Elah approached Pulu in a conspiracy against Pekah of Israel. Pulu granted Hosea's petition, making him king in Samaria and ending the rule of Rezin in Damascus.

Isaiah performed the same public demonstration with his children as Hosea ben Beeri had, but Isaiah was not as harsh in his treatment. His son by the prophetess he named Maher-shalal-hash-baz as a sign that Damascus and Samaria would fall to the Assyrian before the boy could talk clearly. Then Isaiah published his prophecy concerning Ahaz's successor.

> Because this people has refused the waters of Shiloah that
> flow gently, and melt in fear before Rezin and the son of
> Remaliah;
> therefore,
> the Lord is bringing up against it the mighty flood waters
> of the River, the King of Assyria and all his glory;
> It will rise above all its channels and overflow all its banks;
>
> It will sweep on into Judah as a flood, and pouring over, it
> will reach up to the neck; and its outspread wings will fill
> the breadth of your land, O Immanuel.

Immanuel is clearly Hezekiah, the son and successor of Ahaz. Immanuel came to the throne in Ahaz's fourteenth year of rule as co-regent, and some three years later his father left for Lachish. Hezekiah was a devout Yahwist and better suited to rule at Jerusalem. Ahaz ruled at Lachish for some eleven years. Judah was a de facto divided kingdom.

In Hezekiah's fourth year and Ahaz's seventeenth, Shalmaneser V invaded Israel, laying siege to Samaria for three years. Hosea ben Elah had betrayed his predecessor and had made an alliance with King So of Egypt. This event may have been the campaign of the Libyan pharaoh Sosenk inscribed on an archway at Karnak. All the Assyrian garrisons were removed and tribute suspended.

Samaria fell to Shalmaneser's successor, Sargon II, in 722 BC. The Israelites were exiled to the north and the land was resettled by others. The curse of Moses had fallen on the kingdom of Jeroboam ben Nebat, which was never to rise again. At Lachish and Jerusalem, the two kings of David's house continued preparations for what was sure to come.

While the siege of Samaria was in progress, Ahaz would have paid tribute to Shalmaneser V, acknowledging him as his overlord, and then attended Sargon II in the same manner. Judah probably took part in the siege by providing supplies and troops. Ahaz would have been part of Sargon's military victory over Egypt in 720 BC at Raphia. Assyrian power had conquered to the border of the pharaohs' kingdom on the Nile.

To upset the pocket of Philistia, Egypt sponsored a coalition around the city of Ashdod to the west of Jerusalem on the Mediterranean coast. In 713 BC, Sargon's military marched into Palestine. Hezekiah, then early in his solo reign, would have joined him with troops and supplies, pledging his loyalty. Yet there was another land bridge that had not been conquered by the Assyrians. Edom, Moab, and Ammon, east of Judah, provided a salient that could possibly close the Philistine pocket if Judah could be persuaded to shift her loyalty. From Isaiah's words, it appears Egypt was ruled by the Ethiopians at the time.[110] The Assyrian tribute was heavy on Judah, and Hezekiah relented to the Egyptian diplomats and ceased paying tribute.

Assyria's peace with its neighbors was broken early in Sennacherib's reign. Merodach-Baladan had revolted in Babylonia. He had united an anti-Assyrian alliance of Chaldeans, Elam, and other Aramean groups, including Judah. Taking Babylon with Elamite troops, the usurper held on to Babylonia until 703 BC. The collapse of the northern revolt led Hezekiah to shift his loyalty to Egypt. Hezekiah made preparations for a long siege by digging out the tunnel of Siloam, giving Jerusalem a reliable supply of water.

In 701 BC, Sennacherib invaded south into Philistia, clashing with Egyptian forces near Elteken. The Ethiopian dynast Shabaka was defeated. According to Herodotus, Shabaka withdrew to Egypt, leaving Judah to its fate.[111] In the meantime, Sennacherib had bypassed Jerusalem and destroyed Lachish, subduing most of Judah before laying siege to the religious stronghold of Yahweh.

While Sennacherib was subjugating Hezekiah's kingdom, a new king had come to the throne named Sethôs according to Herodotus and Taharga according to the biblical record. This pharaoh had difficulty raising an army and the reason given by the Greek historian may indeed have been the cause. Relying on volunteers, he marched them to Pelusium on Egypt's border. Hearing of the Egyptian approach, Sennacherib marched down to

---

110. Isaiah 20:3-5.
111. Book 2:139-141. See also 2 Kings 19:9.

meet him. Both the account in Herodotus and the biblical record state that the Assyrian host was disastrously defeated by a miraculous event, but the miracles cited differ. Neither is plausible. A plague is the most likely cause of mass destruction on the level described.

Herodotus tells us he saw inscriptional evidence of this event commemorated by the pharaoh. Armies dying of plague was not an uncommon event in the ancient world. Modern ambulances and medical treatment for armies did not begin appearing until the mid-nineteenth century in Europe and North America. Hezekiah's illness may have resulted from the contagion.[112] The number given at Isaiah 37:36 is not plausible for the Assyrian army, but may account for the number of troops and locals who died. The number actually was derived from the formula in Leviticus 26:8 and then extrapolated based on the number of defenders in Jerusalem or survivors in Judah. This was the same method used by the Maccabean historians, who referred to this event in their account.

Hezekiah died shortly afterward, escaping Assyrian retribution. Judah had been effectively subjugated by Sennacherib and his successors, and Jerusalem could now be almost ignored by an invader. Jerusalem could still be taken by siege, but its importance had shifted to that of a religious center. Its military significance had been considerably diminished.

The prediction in Isaiah 8:6-8 reveals something of the mechanics of probability. It had been forecast that the king would have a son, Immanuel, and he would see the invasion of Assyria into his kingdom up to the neck of Jerusalem. Isaiah then had a document drawn up of the prophecy against Damascus, Samaria, and Jerusalem. This document is recounted in chapters seven and eight with the heading, "Belonging to Maher-shalal-hash-baz." The document was attested to by two witnesses. Then Isaiah and Mrs. Ben Amoz conceived and bore their son Maher-shalal-hash-baz, a name which means "The spoils speeds, the prey hastens."

When Sennacherib invaded Palestine and sent Rabshakeh to intimidate Hezekiah, the king had a legal document given to him by Isaiah to assure him the prophets of Yahweh were his supporters. They could tell him, "And he shall not come into this city, shoot an arrow there, come before it with a shield, or cast up a siege rampant against it." When the prophecy came true, Isaiah ben Amoz rose in stature and could begin commanding the king. The balance of power at court shifted.

> Bind up the testimony, seal the teaching among my disciples.

---

112. Isaiah 38:1, 21; 10:16.

I will wait for Yahweh, who is hiding his face from the house of Jacob, and I will hope in him. See, I and the children whom Yahweh has given me are signs and portents in Israel from Yahweh of Hosts, who dwells on Mount Zion.

But there will be no gloom for those who were in anguish. In the former time he brought into contempt to the land of Zebulun and Naphtali, but in the latter time he will make glorious. The way of the sea, the land beyond the Jordan, Galilee of the nations. The people who walked in darkness have seen a great light; those who lived in a land of deep darkness—on them light has shined.

Based on this prophetic success, the community of prophets could go to the Israelites in exile and the new settlers to the north and engage in evangelistic work to promote the worship of Yahweh. Hezekiah supported their efforts. The God of Zion was a teller of oracles that came about as predicted. Powers would rise and fall at his command. Kings mighty and fearsome could be broken and torn, but those who loved God could rise in glory.

Until this period of Israelite history, most predictions and prophecies had been largely self-fulfilling. The distinguished prophets would predict into a well-organized system that could deliver and then carry it out under suitable conditions. In time, they developed a track record to impress a largely illiterate and superstitious populace. This type of organized community was typical in the ancient world and not exclusive to the Israelites. As a polytheistic society, they fought among themselves for the supremacy of their own particular deities. Each had a record of successes and failures. The biblical corpus, if viewed properly, can tell us much about pagan societies in general.

However, the spectacular and dramatic success of Isaiah's prophecy in Isaiah 8:1-8 had an enormous impact on the community of prophets in particular, and was to gradually create what came to be known in the post-exile age as the Jew. The standard of what constituted a genuine prophecy or oracle had been raised. The prediction had been legally witnessed and tied to the lives of two high-profile children. Some thirty-five years later, all events had taken place as predicted. The new age prophet was now in the mainstream and the conclusion quite clear. Zion was the holy city of Yahweh and now inviolate.

The book of Isaiah is a collection of works under ben Amoz's name. Most compositions belong to other authors. Each of Isaiah's prophecies is introduced with his full name. Only fifteen chapters can be directly attributed to him.[113] The history in chapters 36-39 could have been written by Isaiah but were likely composed by someone else, perhaps one of his sons or contemporaries. These chapters can be collected into one book under the prophet's name and renumbered one through nineteen. In this way, we can distinguish what belongs to the prophet and what cannot be secured. The remaining chapters, from 14:28 through 19 and 21 through 35, can and should be collected under a second book called 2 Isaiah and then renumbered.

Second Isaiah is a most interesting book and parts of it may have been written by ben Amoz, although there is no evidence to suggest it is so. Chapters 28 and 29 contain passages used by Jesus and his disciples.[114] Chapters 24-27 give us a glimpse of the apocalyptic tone we will hear in the later prophets. Zephaniah, who wrote during King Josiah's reign, may well have been inspired by this section. It hints at the Christian book of Revelation.

The books of Isaiah also launch a group of Gentile prophecies of dubious veracity. Most disturbing is the venomous tone and language used. Like Obadiah, much of it is pure hate literature toward non-Israelites. Such vitriolic sentiment and high-handed rhetoric are a direct contradiction of Mosaic law and principles. Sad to say, Bible readers and others have allowed themselves to be infected by such hate materials, only to produce in themselves and others the tragic end result that cultivated enmity invariably yields. Much of the anti-Gentile works are of dubious origin, and some are entirely bogus with no basis in historical fact. Written by anonymous authors, these works were included in the Bible under the names of others to lend distinguished stature to literature they never produced or sanctioned. This practice was also true of other works that are among some of the Bible's best literature. The author of Isaiah 40-66 is unknown, yet is happily preserved for readers today. Likewise, the authorship of some of the psalms is unknown. However, the anti-Gentile hate literature found in the Bible differs in one important respect. The writers offer no hope of salvation to these non-Israelite nations. The conclusion is as savage as the expressions used in the exposition. It ends with a void that remains unresolved. These texts should have been removed long ago. Why have they not?

---

113. Chapters 1 through 14:27 and chapter 20.
114. 28:16; 29:13, 19.

There was, of course, a cause for the anti-Gentile hatred evidenced in Isaiah. Israel was a vassal kingdom from early times. Its years of autonomy were few. The first suzerain was Egypt, whose pharaoh viewed himself as well above the common cut.[115] When Solomon married the pharaoh's daughter, she enjoyed freedom and prominence in Jerusalem, and through her the pharaoh ruled at ben David's court. It was a marriage of convenience for both. Regardless of the biblical tone used to describe his reign, Solomon was a vassal and client king.

All suzerains become hated over time.[116] The Assyrians were particularly cruel and heavy-handed, pushing Judah into poverty while Ahaz and Hezekiah reigned.[117] Those Judeans not taken into exile were left to a bare existence and their hope of better things to come. They imagined an ideal Israelite paradise where there was a wasteful abundance of all good things. The land would be filled with rotting corpses of all their Gentile enemies, and any who survived Yahweh's holocaust would become their willing slaves.[118] There would be a sufficient supply of Edomites on hand for Israel to indiscriminately slaughter at their whim.[119] All Israel's righteous who had died would receive a resurrection[120] and those with disabilities would be cured.[121] The Mosaic law and Yahweh's worship would be perfected in Israel, and Jerusalem with its temple precinct would become the center of the earth. Everyone would travel to the holy city every year for the three festivals. There, Israel would instruct them, and each male twenty years and older would leave behind the temple tax. This was the vision conceived by the new age prophets for humanity's future. It appears to be the same today as it was then.

Like his grandfather, Manasseh became a pagan. Since Lachish had been destroyed, Manasseh included polytheistic deities inside the temple precinct at Jerusalem. The gods of Assyria had to be accepted. Hezekiah could reject them and did so, escaping retribution for his rebellion by dying shortly afterward. Manasseh was in a different position, however. He came to the throne at age twelve and in a co-regent rule which would have been supervised by Assyrian officials. He had no choice but to comply with his suzerain's demands. In 678 BC, the city of Sidon revolted against Esarhaddon (681-669 BC), the new Assyrian king-an event that would see

---

115. Isaiah 31:3.
116. Isaiah 19.
117. Isaiah 19:4.
118. Isaiah 14:2; also chapter 24.
119. Isaiah 34; Deuteronomy 2:4-8.
120. Isaiah 26:19.
121. Isaiah 29:18-19; 35:5-6.

increased Assyrian involvement in Manasseh's kingdom. The Judean king was about age thirty-five at the time.

Esarhaddon laid siege to Sidon and took the city by assault. However, Tyre also revolted against his suzerainty in spite of Sidon's fall. Both cities had economic ties with Egypt, but Tyre resisted a long siege because it was located on a promontory on the Mediterranean coast. The city could be supplied and reinforced by sea. Tyre was Egypt's thorn in Assyria's side.

Esarhaddon invaded south, finally taking Memphis in 671 BC. The Ethiopian dynast Tirhakah fled south to Thebes while the Nile delta capitulated to its new suzerain. The Assyrian king selected twenty-two local princes to run the government and then returned to Nineveh. Tirhakah began intrigues among the local princes, provoking unrest in the delta. Esarhaddon responded with another military expedition, but he died en route in 669 BC. His son and successor Ashurbanipal took up the reins of power and continued the campaign south. Tirhakah withdrew once again to Thebes. The new suzerain retained the local princes as rulers but created garrisons manned by his own troops to establish his control.

But Tirhakah continued his intrigues among the rulers. Ashurbanipal heard of it from his garrison commanders and raised one of the local princes named Necho to be a rival pharaoh. Necho would act in Assyria's interests. This ploy forced Tirhakah's nephew and successor Tanutamen to enter Thebes, where he was proclaimed Egypt's savior and new pharaoh. Organizing an army, he marched down river, investing the capital Memphis that was defended by Assyria's client pharoah. The city fell to Tanutamen's forces, and Necho died in the fighting.

Ashurbanipal mustered his troops and journeyed into the delta, taking Memphis and forcing the new pharaoh to fall back on Thebes. Chasing him up the Nile, the Assyrians invested Thebes, which fell to Ashurbanipal in 663 BC. Tanutamen fled to Napata, where he remained, ending Ethiopian rule in Egypt.

Before returning home, the Assyrian king raised Necho's son Psamtik or Psammetichus (663-610 BC) to be his pharaoh and the founder of the twenty-sixth dynasty in Egypt. By 654, he had gained complete control over the Nile kingdom, making an alliance with Lydia and using Ionian and Carian mercenaries to expel all the Assyrian garrisons. Yet he remained an ally of Ashurbanipal, sending him troops to fight Babylonian and Median threats to Nineveh.

It was probably during Ashurbanipal's journey home that Manasseh and other Palestinian kings along the coast, including in Tyre, were taken captive to prevent possible political intrigue. While in his Babylonian prison cell, Manasseh became an open Yahwist. We begin to see a pattern emerging among the later Judean kings that was largely ignored by the Bible writers. This pattern developed into the Babylonia period with inevitable results for Jerusalem.

Micah was a contemporary of Isaiah. His work can be described as a mini-Isaiah. Many of the main elements contained in Isaiah are found in the seven chapters of Micah's lament and prediction that Jerusalem will suffer the same outcome as Samaria, but at the hands of Babylon. Micah is not anti-Gentile to the degree that Second Isaiah is, but it is there also.[122] Chapter four of Micah contains the first three verses of chapter two of Isaiah. The question is, who duplicated who? Was Micah the basis for Isaiah, or was Micah a later synopsis? One can reasonably assume Habakkuk's was inspired by Micah. Although introduced as an oracle, Habakkuk's three-chapter work is a lament that confirms past prophecy. Micah to a large degree is also a lament at the sorry condition of Judah brought about by the Assyrians.[123] Everything produced in Judah was being sold to pay the tribute. Poverty had greatly increased crime and betrayal. All that was left to the faithful of Yahweh was faith itself: the hope their God would restore their fortunes.[124]

Josiah was one of the great Judean kings whose life and reign resembled those of Jehoash ben Ahaziah in many ways. His father, Amon ben Manasseh, ruled two years before he was assassinated, bringing Josiah to the throne at the tender age of eight. Like his predecessor, his rule was guided by a regent and greatly influenced by priest and prophet. Like Asa ben Abijam, the great-grandson of Solomon, Josiah supported widespread reforms that included an enlarged kingdom. During his reign, Judah and Benjamin encompassed Manasseh and Ephraim to the north and Simeon to the south. In 639 BC, the year Josiah was crowned king, Ashurbanipal had destroyed Susa in Elam, ending a protracted war that included Babylon. The Assyrian king then turned his military against the Arabs, who had helped the Babylonian usurper Shamash-shum-ukin (652-648 BC) and his other allies: Psamtik of Egypt, Elam, and other Aramean tribes. In his later years, Cyrus the Persian sought an alliance with Ashurbanipal against the Medes. We owe a debt to this Assyrian monarch for the great library he created at Nineveh, discovered in the 1940s.

The first year of Sin-shar-ishkun of Assyria was the year Jeremiah began his career as a prophet to Jerusalem. Zephaniah was a contemporary of Jeremiah. The following year of 626 BC, Nabopolassar became king

---

122. Micah 4:12-13.
123. Micah 7:5-7.
124. Habakkuk 2:1-4.

in Babylonia, ending the anarchy there and ending Assyrian control at Babylon. Josiah became an ally of Nabopolassar, throwing off the Assyrian yoke.

Josiah now began major religious reforms, making worship of Yahweh compulsory in his kingdom. He had consulted a local prophetess named Huldah, the wife of Shallum ben Tikvah, keeper of the royal wardrobe. She assured Josiah the Mosaic curse would fall on Judah just as it had on Israel. Josiah responded by renewing the covenant with Yahweh at Jerusalem, opening the east gates of the temple and having the population swear an oath much like Asa ben Abijah did. All pagan altars, idols, and priests were removed, along with the high places that had returned. The ark of the covenant was placed inside the Holy of Holies, where it remained. In the eighteenth year of his reign, at age twenty-five, Josiah held the greatest Passover since the time of Moses.

But the prophets were unrelenting. The prophetess Huldah did not revise her earlier prediction, and the prophets would not alter theirs. The short but succinct book of Zephaniah held out no reprieve. Judah would go into exile and Jerusalem would fall. The message of Jeremiah was the same. But the people of the kingdom had considered Jerusalem inviolate since the days of Hezekiah. All was well.

The book of Jeremiah gives the reader an insight into the daily itinerary of a working evangelical prophet. Jeremiah composed some twenty prophecies spoken publicly and gave prophetic interviews with kings Jehoiakim and Zedekiah. His written prophecies delivered in the public forum were segmented into groups of two, three, and six, usually began with "Thus says Yahweh," and at times ended with "says Yahweh." Each segment had its own continuity and at times was punctuated with "thus says the Lord," requiring a certain amount of discretionary perceptiveness from the reader. The determining factor was that each segment was self-contained as a miniprophecy inside a larger one. The rabbinic Jews have given the reader no help in this respect, and Christendom's scholars have failed to smooth out the scriptural obstacles.

In fact, beginning with Isaiah and Jeremiah, the scriptural canon is in need of serious reconstructive surgery. The first half of Jeremiah is laid out chronologically, but the last half was put together by a drunken Talmudic committee. Too much Mogen David got in the way. It is so badly out of sequence that one can only wonder at the rationale behind such seemingly slovenly work. And what of the great theological doctors of the Christian church? They can postulate intricate theologies but can't recognize when something simple is needed, like the repair of the disheveled book of Jeremiah.

Or were they captivated by superstition and the fundamentalist notion that the Bible is the irrevocable word of God? All Scripture may be inspired by God, but how much of it actually belongs to God? Would God actually take credit for such a sloppy construction as is found in Jeremiah? Is God responsible for the hate literature contained in the canon?

When Jeremiah and others say, "thus speaks Yahweh," it is not God speaking. It is Jeremiah ben Hilkiah and others putting their words in Yahweh's mouth. They used Mosaic law, the Deutero-Classic formula, and extant religious literature to form a comprehensive whole. The prophets had extraordinary power over Israel and used it for good and evil.[125] This was an evolving material theocracy. It was not that difficult for observant individuals to see changes in the political landscape and possible future effects of those changes. Jeremiah could see Babylon rising in the north. It was the key to King Josiah's independance. The Babylonians and Assyrians shared only a dialectic difference in their close similarity.

The material theocracy could be used by God at various times, but it was a man-made society, inspired by God but not belonging to Yahweh. The Mosaic covenant was uniquely elevated, and the Judean dynasty was one of a kind. But the notion that Yahweh said this and that at every corner and every twist and turn is pure nonsense. The prophets, carried away with their growing power, were free to let their imaginations soar in many directions, and gave Yahweh full credit for all the mistakes and evil they created.

Now Jeremiah was telling them the theocracy they had created did not represent Yahweh, and that their God was not pleased with the "work of their hands." The law given to Moses on Mount Horeb would remain, the temple shrine would stand as a symbol, and the Judean covenant would be supported by a reformed priesthood and community of prophets. The rest would be scrapped as junk. A successful theocracy was not one of outward piety, nor could it be brought about by compulsion. It was born from a willing spirit and cultivated in the heart. People performed the law because they understood the reasons and experienced the effect. The material world was a dangerous place, but humankind was given dominion over it. A world at peace was ruled by people who lived at peace among themselves and with God.

To fully appreciate the life of an itinerant prophet requires a complete reconstruction of the book of Jeremiah. Each prophecy and its subsections should be laid out in the following manner.

---

125. Jeremiah 5:31.

Prophecy One (1:11-3:5)
Day One (1:11-19)
Segment One

> The word of the Lord came to me saying, 'Jeremiah, what do you see? And I said, 'I see a branch of almond tree'. Then Yahweh said to me, 'You have seen well, for I am watching over my word to perform it'. Yahweh spoke a second time, 'What do you see?' I replied, 'A boiling pot tilted toward the north'. Yahweh then said: 'Out of the north disaster shall fall on all the lands' inhabitants. For now I am calling forth the tribes and kingdoms from the north and they shall place their thrones at Jerusalems gates. Against it's walls and all Judahs' cities they will come. For they have forsaken me worshipped other gods made with their own hands and I will utter judgments against them for their wickedness. But you, prepare yourself; stand among them and say publicly what I command you. Do not fear them or I will break you in their sight. Today I have made you a fortified city with iron pillars and bronze walls against Judah, it's king, princes, priests, and the population in this land. They will oppose you but not prevail because I Yahweh will deliver you from their hand."[126]

Jeremiah was assisted by his servant, Baruch ben Neriah, and possibly other prophets such as Huldah and her colleagues. They would set up their symposium in a gateway or square where people continually passed by, and repeat at regular intervals each prophetic segment from morning till evening. While his servants helped him deliver the prophecy, Jeremiah may have had a table nearby with pen and ink, composing the next segment. The prophet was not married, so he had time also in the evening. The next day they would assemble in the same location and repeat the next segment.

---

126. It's quite possible the early apostolic church followed the classical model we see in Jeremiah. To maintain doctrinal continuity, new disciples may have simply read from the apostolic letters in public.

Day Two (2:2-3)
Segment Two

> I remember the devotion of your youth, your love as a
> bride, how you followed me in the wilderness, in a land
> not sown. Israel was holy to Yahweh, the first fruits of his
> harvest. All who ate of it were held guilty; disaster came
> upon them, says Yahweh.

As on the previous day, this rather short segment would be repeated
throughout the day until the evening. This method would be used each day
until all six segments had been delivered. No public speaking was done on
the Sabbath.

The following was how the first prophecy was broken down:

Day Three (2:4-13)
Day Four (2:14-22)
Day Five (2:23-29)
Day Six (2:30-3:5)

The following week, this same prophecy would be repeated in a new
location, perhaps at the opposite end of Jerusalem. Each week this prophecy
would be moved to another location until Jeremiah was satisfied the message
had been sufficiently delivered. Then his little group of evangelists would
deliver the second prophecy, segment by segment.

This next prophecy was segmented into three, covering the same
amount of ground in half the time.

Prophecy Two (3:6-4:4)
Day One (3:6-10)
Day Two (3:11-25)
Day Three (4:1-4)

Once these prophecies had made the rounds in Jerusalem, could take
them to the other Judean towns. Jeremiah and his group of prophets may
have needed to leave Jerusalem for awhile and gradually work their way
back. The longer segments in the third prophecy may indicate the Judean
countryside was a safer place.

Prophecy Three (4:5-6:30)
Day One (4:5-26)
Day Two (4:27-5:17)
Day Three (5:18-6:8)
Day Four (6:9-15)
Day Five (6:16-21)
Day Six (6:22-30)

No doubt in their travels, the prophets took time out for necessary business and rest along the way. They may have taken a longer break at the end of their first tour because the fourth prophecy was to be spoken at the temple entrance. This could have been their first appearance in that location. Festival time would have been very busy in a temple precinct and city filled with people.

Prophecy Four (7:1-10:25)
Day One (7:1-20)
Day Two (7:21-8:3)
Day Three (8:4-9:6)
Day Four (9:7-16)
Day Five (9:17-26)
Day Six (10:1-25)

After one week inside the temple precinct, it was time to head out into the Judean countryside again for a second preaching tour. Obviously, Jerusalem and its temple needed another break while Jeremiah and his itinerant prophets continued breathing elsewhere. It's entirely possible that Jeremiah's fame was attracting other prophets to the fold who believed in what he was doing and wished to be a part of it. By the end of his second tour, his disciples would have grown in number; of course, so would his enemies.

Prophecy Five (11:1-12:17)
Day One (11:1-8)
Day Two (the covenant read)
Day Three (the covenant read)
Day Four (11:9-23)
Day Five (12:1-13)
Day Six (12:14-17)

By this point, ben Hilkiah would have become a well-known name in Judah. He gave leave to his disciples and absented himself for a while. He journeyed to Babylon, and somewhere near the Euphrates River, he buried his underwear. Then Jeremiah and his servant Baruch traveled in Mesopotamia among the Israelite communities and preached to them for a time. When his Babylonian tour ended, he returned to the Euphrates and dug up his ruined underwear. Returning to Judah, he used the cloth as a prop to illustrate the words of his sixth prophecy.

Prophecy Six (13:1-27)
Day One (13:8-11)
Day Two (13:12-17)
Day Three (13:8-27)

On this domestic tour, Jeremiah moved faster, covering the same amount of ground in half the time. Airing his dirty underwear in public probably was perceived as an insult. The third segment was directed at the king and queen mother. Obviously Jeremiah had gained a higher profile, able to attract the royal family.

The next three prophecies are shorter. Each is delivered in one day and then moved to the next location. The seventh prophecy (14:1-10) was occasioned by a drought, and Jeremiah and his colleagues observed there was no repentant disposition among their countrymen. Indeed, other prophets were telling the Judeans that all was well and there would be no invasion from Babylon. Therefore, Jeremiah delivered his eighth prophecy (14:17-22) calling Israel to repentance, but to no avail. The ninth prophecy followed (15:1-21). The first segment was followed by a personal lament from Jeremiah (15:10-18) before it closed with the third segment (15:19-21).

Prophecy Ten (16:1-17:18)
Day One (16:5-17:4)
Day Two (17:5-18)

With prophecy ten, Jeremiah's life and routine became more precarious. His next location was at the people's gate in Jerusalem, through which the kings of Judah and their entourages passed. The prophet had become more than a royal curiosity.

The eleventh prophecy was very simple. The Israelites were to restore the Sabbath, doing no work and carrying no burdens.

Next, Jeremiah went to the potter's house as the setting for his twelfth prophecy, which compared Israel to a clay pot.

Prophecy Twelve (18:1-19:15)
Day One (18:5-17)
Day Two (18:19-23, lament)
Day Three (19:3-13) at Potsherd Gate

Sometime about the first day of the twelfth prophecy, the opposition to Jeremiah broke out into punitive violence. Plots and charges against the prophet were openly contemplated by his enemies. The second segment was another of Jeremiah's laments as he appreciated the growing threat to his life. The third segment was delivered at the Potsherd Gate, opening out into the Valley of Hinnom, also called Topheth, where Baal worship was practiced along with human sacrifice of innocent children as first fruits to Baal. Jeremiah used an earthen water jug as a prop and broke it halfway through the segment.

> Here the word of Yahweh, O kings of Judah and people of Jerusalem. I am going to bring special disaster on this place that will tingle everyone's ears who hears of it. These people have forsaken me, making this place a profanity by offering innocent blood to Baal, burning their children as offerings at Baal's high places which you continually build for him. I did not command nor decree this abomination, nor did it ever enter my mind or heart. Therefore I will give this place a new name. It will be called the Valley of Slaughter because I will end the plans of Judah and Jerusalem, and fill this place with their dead bodies. The birds and wild animals will feed on their flesh. Anyone passing by this city will express horror at its disaster. During the siege of this city, the people will become cannibals, eating the flesh of friend and neighbor.
>
> [Jeremiah breaks the jug.]
>
> So will I break this city and its inhabitants and it will never be mended. In Topheth you will bury the dead until there is no room left. I will make this city like Topheth, defiling the houses and palaces of Judah's people and kings who

offered libations to other gods and to the whole host of heaven.[127]

From Topheth, Jeremiah went to the temple precinct and inside the courtyard, where he pronounced,

> Thus says Yahweh of hosts, the guide of Israel: I am now bringing upon this city and its towns all the disaster that I have pronounced against it, because they have stubbornly resisted and have rejected all the words I have spoken to them.

Pashur ben Immer, the chief officer of the temple, was listening to Jeremiah. He approached the prophet, slapping him in the face, taking him into custody, and locking him in the stocks located in the upper Benjamin Gate. To pass the time, Jeremiah composed another prayer to lament his plight (20:7-18). The next morning, he was released and told never to enter the temple area again. Jeremiah uttered a prophecy over Pashur.

About this time, the fortunes of Assyria were turning, and in 616 BC Nabopolassar defeated Assyrian forces near Harran. Sin-shar-ishkun entered into a treaty alliance with Psamtik of Egypt. In 614 BC, the Medes took Tarbisu, northwest of Nineveh, and then turned south, capturing Ashur. The Babylonian king arrived too late to help, but concluded an alliance with King Cyaxares of Media.

In 612 BC, both kings laid siege to Nineveh, which fell during the summer. In the west, Ashur-uballit II centered the Assyrian resistance at Harran. Nabopolassar moved on the city, taking it in 610 BC. Ashur-uballit II fled to Pharoah Necho II at Riblah in Hamath. King Josiah attempted to oppose the Egyptian force at Megiddo but was defeated and killed in the fighting. The pharoah then descended on Jerusalem, taking Josiah's son and successor Jehoahaz hostage and imposing tribute on Judah of one gold talent and one hundred talents of silver. Necho II put Eliakim on the throne, whom we know as Jehoiakim.

Against this background, Jeremiah went down to the palace and requested an audience with the new king. There he delivered his thirteenth prophecy to Jehoiakim, admonishing the king to "act with justice and righteousness, and deliver from the hand of the oppressor anyone who has been robbed. And do no wrong or violence to the alien, the orphan, and the widow, or shed innocent blood in this place." Concerning his brother

---

127. Isaiah 30:33.

Shallum ben Joash, who was also Jehoahaz, Jeremiah told the king he would never return home. From Riblah, he would be carried to Egypt and die there.

At Riblah, Pharaoh Necho II and Ashur-uballit II marched to Carchemish on the Euphrates. Egyptian forces and Babylonian troops fought each other in 607 and 606 BC, but Nabopolassar's army could not dislodge the pharaoh and his Assyrian ally. Finally in 605 BC, the Egyptian army succumbed to a surprise attack at Carchemish on the Euphrates by the Chaldean forces of Nebuchadnezzer, the crown prince. The book of Daniel places the Babylonians at Jerusalem in Jehoiakim's third year of rule, which was 606 BC—the previous year. The crown prince made Jehoiakim his vassal, taking the best of Judean society into exile with him. Jeremiah made no mention of it, but then his work doesn't mention a lot of useful things, such as the pharoah's visit to the capitol.

The prophecy of Egypt's conquest in pseudo-Jeremiah chapter forty-six never happened, but the prediction is pre-ambled byhas a preamble that contains a prosaic description of the battle of Carchemish couched in oracular style.[128] The anonymous writer may have witnessed the ignominous defeat of Necho's forces, and gave it as a reason why the prophet believed the Babylonians would ultimately conquer Egypt. The pharoah's intelligence sources had no information or indication that Chaldean forces were coming from the east. There was certainly no reason to expect them to come from the south. This may have been a large part of the surprise. Although bogus prophecy cannot be accepted as genuine, the material can still be useful history in other ways. It comes under the heading of strange knowledge.

Nebuchadnezzer pursued the remaining Egyptian forces southward and caught them near the Orontes River at Hamath, annihilating most of them. The pharoah and his elite corps escaped to Riblah. Necho may have evacuated his garrison there and any troops in the area. He would have had to return home with a respectable army in tow.

In the summer of 605 BC, Nabopolassar died and Nebuchadnezzar was crowned king in Babylon. After securing his grip on power, which the book of Daniel alludes to in chapter two, Nebuchadnezzar II consolidated his hold on Syria, the "land of Hattii." In 601 BC, Nebuchadnezzar II fought an indecisive battle with Egyptian forces in Palestine.

The first year of Jehoiakim's reign in 610 BC saw a growing confrontation between the city of Jerusalem and Jeremiah. The prophet had openly appeared in the temple during one of the festivals and spoke to all the

---

128. The authentic book of Jeremiah ends at 43:7. The contents from 43:8 to the end of chapter 51 are pseudo-Jeremiah.

Judeans present. The priests and prophets arrested him, and ben Hilkiah was presented in front of the city officials at the New Gate.[129] He was on trial for his life. Jeremiah's defense was that he spoke from Yahweh and would do no less. He was innocent and did not deserve to die.

Some of the elders came to the prophet's defense by citing the example of Micah from Moresheth. Although the prophet had said uncomplimentary words against Judah, King Zedekiah never had him killed. Based on this defense, the city officials acquitted Jeremiah, and Ahikam ben Shaphan helped the prophet escape mob justice.

However, Jeremiah was not safe. Jehoiakim had chased another prophet into Egypt and brought him back in chains. Uriah ben Shemaiah had prophesied, with similar words, the same thing Jeremiah had, and the king murdered him on arrival.

At this time, Judah was a vassal to the pharaoh, with extradition privileges. The only escape route was into Babylon. Jeremiah took a route to the east along the king's highway or perhaps some other route, in any case avoiding the pharoah. Perhaps Jeremiah was given an audience with the crown prince Nebuchadnezzar, who would have been co-regent while his father was in the west with Pharaoh Necho II and Ashur-uballit near Carchemish. Jeremiah may have told the crown prince that Yahweh would give him the kingdom of Judah and that Nebuchadnezzar was to punish them for their disobedience. Jeremiah and Baruch would have impressed Nebuchadnezzar with Judah's long dynasty of four hundred years.[130] Jehoiakim ben Josiah came from an unbroken line of kings descended from David ben Jesse. But Yahweh would give the crown prince leave to conquer them. This could have given Nebuchadnezzar the idea to take Jerusalem by the inland route and then attack the Egyptians from the south.

Indeed, Jeremiah would have accompanied him there. To openly continue his prophetic activity in Judah and Jerusalem would have required a protective watchdog at court,[131] particularly when we hear what Jeremiah said concerning King Jehoiakim in the first half of his reign.[132] The king's desire for revenge was obviously restrained from another quarter.

---

129. Jeremiah 26.
130. Although we see dynasties that lasted four hundred years or more in Egypt, these occurred at a time when Egypt's power was unrivaled. The Judean dynasty survived during troubled years that could have cut it short and almost did on some occasions.
     Old Kingdom   2780-2181 BC   (600 years)
     New Kingdom 1567-1085 BC   (482 years)
131. 39:11-14.
132. 22:18, 19.

The death of Uriah proved Egypt was not a safe haven for ben Hilkiah. In addition, the Rechabites appeared to be in the city prior to the fourth year of Jehoiakim's reign.[133] Sometime between his fourth and fifth year of leadership, Jehoiakim placed his son Jehoiachin, or Coniah, on the throne as co-regent.[134] The signal was obvious. Jehoiakim was about to rebel against his Babylonian suzerain.

In the meanwhile, Jeremiah continued to prophesy in Babylon's new vassal state while Pharaoh Necho went from defeat to defeat. The Judeans were treated to the spectacle of a humiliated nation passing through their country. It may well be that King Jehoiakim was compelled to place his son on the throne with himself as a symbol to Necho of his loyalty. To Nebuchadnezzar, it was an act of rebellion and declaration of war. The king of Judah and his son Jeconiah were caught in the middle. The consequences were entirely predictable.

The remaining text of Jeremiah becomes disorganized from chapter twenty through chapter forty. Why the redactor did not trouble to organize a more plausible sequence is unknown. Perhaps he wished to create a sense of confusion and disorder in the reader to mimic the times. Whatever the reason, I have attempted to organize a plausible chronology useful to our understanding.[135]

Jeremiah's message was becoming sharper in Judah. King Nebuchadnezzar II of Babylon would come into their kingdom to destroy it. Judah and the nations around her would serve the king in Babylon for seventy years. In the case of Judah, this seventy-year period began in 609 BC.[136] However, Daniel 9:25 makes it reasonably clear that Jerusalem was destroyed for forty-nine years and not seventy. The period of sixty-two weeks began the restoration from 537 BC, requiring the reader to calculate backward for the seven weeks. Interestingly, Daniel makes a reasonably accurate calculation. Sad to say, some modern-day eschatologists have stumbled in their understanding of this prophecy.

---

133. 35:11.
134. 22:24.
135. Chapter   20/26/35-36:8/25/36:9-32/22:18-24:10/27-28:17/21/37-38:28/
     29-34/39-43:7.
136. Jeremiah 25:10; 29:10.

Prophecy Thirteen (26:1-6)

Prophecy Fourteen (35:1-19) The Rechabites

Prophecy Fifteen (25:1-38)
Day One (25:1-14)
Day Two (25:15-31)
Day Three (25:32-38)

The new political reality at court once again would threaten ben Hilkiah and his servant Baruch and all those loyal to his cause. After escaping the death penalty, Jeremiah was unable to appear inside the temple precinct. Like Zechariah ben Barachiah, he would have been stoned to death. Consequently, he gave copies of his works to Baruch, who read them in the temple precinct in Jehoiakim's fifth year of rule. The priests and prophets who heard Baruch making Jeremiah's pronouncements actually let him finish, indicating they had had a change of heart in 604 BC. They interviewed Baruch with a new civility and then informed him that Jehoiakim would have to see the scroll. However, they advised Baruch to take himself into hiding along with Jeremiah, and to keep their whereabouts secret.

Clearly Jeremiah still had friends at court. One of them may have been the young priest Ezekiel ben Buzi, who was about twenty years of age at the time. The only possible refuge was at the court of Nebuchadnezzar II. After allowing ben Hilkiah and Baruch sufficient time to escape, the priests handed over the scroll to the king, whose servant Jehudi read it to him in the winter palace. As Jehudi read, Jehoiakim cut off the completed portions and threw them into a brazier. Hearing of this in Babylon, Jeremiah rewrote another scroll, making additions,[137] and sent it to ben Josiah. Jerusalem prepared for another siege.

In 603 BC, Nebuchadnezzar II was having some difficulty of his own with the Chaldean priests.[138] To his new intelligentsia at court, he proposed a riddle for anyone to solve. He had been troubled by a dream he couldn't understand. He had summoned the Chaldean priests and prophets to tell him the dream and its interpretation. When all had arrived, they asked the king to relate his dream and they would give the interpretation. There followed an awkward silence. His majesty wanted more from them this

---

137. Prophecy Sixteen (22:18-30).
138. Nebuchadnezzar II may have discovered an assassination plot against himself and decided to use this as an opportunity to flush out the conspirators. The priests could have duplicated what Daniel did, but probably did not think Nebuchadnezzar would be around much longer.

time. He then made a decree. They would tell him what the dream was as well as its interpretation, or suffer the consequences. But the oracle priests could not relate what the dream was. How could they interpret something they didn't know?

However, Belteshazzar, whom we know as Daniel, knew the king was impressed with the Judean dynasty of David ben Jesse, and that Nebuchadnezzar's concern was for his own dynasty. Whether the king actually had a dream or not was essentially unimportant. Belteshazzar knew what Nebuchadnezzar wanted to hear.

Jeremiah and Baruch were already at court, and Belteshazzar no doubt had copies of ben Hilkiah's work.[139] Belteshazzar decided to relate a dynastic dream and construct something plausible over a seventy-year period. Whatever it was, Nebuchadnezzar decided Belteshazzar was his creature at court, and Belteshazzar became part of the king's new intelligentsia.

The prophecy in the book of Daniel, chapter two is an example of history written in oracular style. It simply chronicles the dynasty of Nebuchadnezzar II. If it was a genuine oracle then only those who witnessed those events could say for sure. For us today, there is no evidence it was genuine.

However, it is useful history. The head of gold, said Belteshazzar, was the Babylonian king himself. He would be the most illustrious patriarch of all his lineage. With this spectacular prophetic display and Belteshazzar as his watchdog at court, Nebuchadnezzar could eventually bring his son Amel-Marduk forward as his successor.

The king could now turn his attention to the needs of his growing empire. Aramean-Syria was firmly consolidated under his power, and in 601 BC he invaded south into Samaria. Jehoiakim had sent word to Necho II in Egypt, who sent an army to confront the Babylonian forces, possibly somewhere in Philistia. The battle fought was indecisive and both withdrew. The Egyptians went home while the Chaldeans laid siege to Jerusalem.

After two years, King Jehoiakim died, leaving his teenage son King Coniah as sole ruler. Jeconiah had been installed as co-regent at age ten and had co-ruled for eight years. He proposed to surrender. Nebuchadnezzar left his court at Babylon with Jeremiah and Baruch in his entourage, receiving the city and its young king in the spring of 598 BC. At ben Hilkiah's request, Jehoiakim's body was buried in a common graveyard.[140] Jehoiachin and the royal family, along with the best of Judah's military and elite, were taken into custody and exiled to Babylonia. Among them was the twenty-six-year-old Ezekiel ben Buzi. These Judeans were the basket of good figs

139. Daniel 9:2.
140. Jeremiah 22:18-19.

portrayed by Jeremiah, who probably had a hand in selecting the best talent Judah could offer.[141]

Jeremiah and Baruch remained in Judah and Jerusalem, protected by Babylonian officials at court. It must have chagrined many in the now impoverished kingdom to see Jeremiah and his servant back on the streets, prophesying without obstruction.

King Zedekiah, Jehoiakim's brother, was the new king from 597 BC, raised by Nebuchadnezzar. Jeremiah's next prophecy singled out the prophets for denunciation and also included the new king and his court. The remnant were bad figs!

Prophecy Seventeen (23:1-24:10)
Day One (23:1-15)
Day Two (23:16-40)
Day Three (24:1-10)

Jeremiah also prophesied directly to Zedekiah and the remaining kings of Edom, Moab, Amon, Tyre, and Sidon to submit to Nebuchadnezzar. He portrayed this with an actual yoke, telling them to put their necks under it.

In Zedekiah's fourth year of rule, 593 BC, the prophet Hananiah ben Azzur opposed Jeremiah, saying the king of Babylon would be broken in two years. Jeconiah and the other exiles would be returned. Clearly a new rebellion was in the offing. To symbolize his prediction, Hananiah removed the yoke from Jeremiah's shoulders and broke it inside the temple precinct, where Jeremiah was now allowed under escort. Jeremiah then told ben Azzur the yoke of wood would be replaced by one of iron.[142]

Judah once again had broken with the king of Babylon, forming an alliance with Psammeticus II (595-589 BC) of Egypt. Jeremiah pleaded with the king to end the rebellion and submit, but Zedekiah instead asked Jeremiah to support his cause. However, among the exiles in 594 BC, a new society was being created. The old material theocracy was coming to its end in Judah. The priest Ezekiel ben Buzi at age thirty was to spearhead the continuation of the new age prophets, and later Belteshazzar would join this apocalyptic age. After some eight hundred years, the genuine oracle would emerge that could be measured and proven. All oracles are prophecy,

141. Jeremiah 24:1-5.
142. Jeremiah 27-28:17.

but not all prophecies are oracles. Humanity was about to see the colossal difference between the two.

In Jerusalem, the people had prepared for a siege, and Jeremiah and Baruch had also taken refuge inside the city. They continued to prophesy among the defenders. When Zedekiah sent Pashur ben Malachi and the priest Zephaniah ben Maaseiah to ask Jeremiah for his prayers on behalf of the city, perhaps he hoped that Yahweh would perform a miracle for them. The prophet's response was they should leave the city and surrender to Nebuchadnezzar, who probably came with the army. Jeremiah advised the King to "execute justice in the morning and deliver from the hand of the oppressor anyone who has been robbed," and to place his neck under the yoke of the king of Babylon.

However, the arrival of Pharaoh Hophra (588-569 BC), also known as Apries, promised salvation to the city, The Babylonian army raised the siege to confront the Egyptian army. Jeremiah and Baruch attempted to leave the city via the Benjamin Gate but were arrested, and Jeremiah was beaten and thrown into prison. After some days, King Zedekiah sent for ben Hilkiah and asked him what the outcome for the city would be. Jeremiah told him the Babylonians would return and take the city. Jeremiah protested his arrest and imprisonment and used the opportunity to needle Zedekiah about the prophets who said Nebuchadnezzar would never lay siege to the city. He asked the king to release him from the prison. The king had him confined in the court of the guard with a daily ration of one loaf of bread and water. However, Jeremiah continued to advocate for leaving the city among the king's soldiers, who became nervous over their future prospects. Four of the king's officials approached Zedekiah and told him Jeremiah was inciting a mutiny among the defenders. They wanted the prophet to die. The king handed Jeremiah over to them. They threw the prophet into a cistern which was in the court of the guard and left him to die.

However, an Ethiopian eunuch named Ebed-melech and Zedekiah had Jeremiah retrieved from the cistern and returned to custody in the guards' courtyard. The king knew Jeremiah was on friendly terms with Nebuchadnezzar and that the prophet's favor may come in handy. To reinforce his clever ploy, the king swore an oath to shield Jeremiah from harm. Again, ben Hilkiah admonished the king to surrender, but Zedekiah explained that he could not because his enemies at court, the "Judean party," had already deserted to the king of Babylon. He might be handed over to them while in custody. Jeremiah tried to assuage the king's fears but to no avail. Zedekiah would risk his own devices.

While in custody, Jeremiah spent his time to writing. He sent a letter to the exiles in Babylonia and continued to compose prophecy, but turned his attention from the curse of the Deutero-Classic formula to the restoration of Israel. His servants and associates not in custody stood in the public places and delivered a much needed message of hope. To symbolize this, Jeremiah purchased his cousin's field at Anathoth in Benjamin while in custody.

Prophecy Twenty (30:1-31:40)
Day One (30:1-17)
Day Two (30:18-31:1)
Day Three (31:2-14)
Day Four (31:15-22)
Day Five (31:23-34)
Day Six (31:35-40)

Toward the end, Zedekiah made a promising gesture by freeing any in the city who were slaves. However, the gesture turned ugly when those individuals were enslaved again shortly afterward. To Jeremiah, this was the last straw. Zedekiah would fall into the hands of the Babylonians and his enemies, and ben Hilkiah would not admonish him further.

Meanwhile the forces of Nebuchadnezzar had withdrawn to confront Pharoah Hophra's forces. What actually happened is not known, but there is no mention of a battle in any of the ancient records. Perhaps the kings held a conference to resolve their differences. It is my opinion they did. The last battle fought between the two armies had been inconclusive. Both forces mauled each other and the Chaldeans withdrew. It was a technical win for the pharaoh and his forces. The Babylonians needed their forces to take Jerusalem, and Nebuchadnezzar was loath to risk a loss at this juncture. To the Egyptians it mattered little who actually won or lost. The prestige of the pharaoh would remain intact if he spent his force to prevent an invasion over his border. If he took the city and sustained too many casualties, he could fall victim to a patient pharaoh. How to resolve the impasse?

Pharaoh and Jerusalem could wait, but Nebuchadnezzar could not. It is my view that both parties decided to deny an advantage to the other. Babylon would maintain its prestige by punishing a rebel, but the city would not be used as a stronghold by either party. Jerusalem would be razed to the ground and the land made insignificant. It would become a no-man's-land for both kings. When the destruction was completed both parties would withdraw and leave the other in peace.

Once this agreement had been concluded, the siege of Jerusalem continued and Nebuchadnezzar returned north, where he waited at Riblah in Hamath. On Tammuz 9, 586 BC, Jerusalem fell to the Babylonians and was destroyed a month later. Zedekiah tried to escape but was taken captive on the plain of Jericho. He was bound with chains and sent to Riblah. Nebuchadnezzar slaughtered all the Judean nobles and each of Zedekiah's sons while ben Josiah watched, then had him blinded and sent to Babylon. It was an ignominious end for an obstinate man.

Jeremiah found himself a prisoner of the Babylonians, but Nebuzaradan, the captain of the king's bodyguard, released him from Ramah. He could go to Babylon if he wished or anywhere else. Jeremiah went to Gedaliah ben Ahikam, who had been made governor of Judah at Mizpah. He ended up in Egypt, however.

5

THE ORACLE IN THE WEST

The Lydian king, Croesus (560-546 BC), came to his throne in the same year as Nerglissar in Babylon. Croesus in Asia Minor was in a tripartite treaty with Media and Babylonia. The treaty had been signed by all three kingdoms after the Assyrian power had fallen by 610 BC.

The treaty moved the natural frontier of Lydia back to the Halys River in the west to resist any threat Sardis could pose to the other two. The kingdom was situated on the Anatolian plain at a higher elevation than Mesopotamia, making it a natural fortress. Interestingly, the Delphic oracle of Apollo had predicted that Gyges, who murdered his master Candaules, would suffer retribution for his crime in the fourth generation. Herodotus also recorded in his history that Croesus son of Alyattes was the fourth-generation descendant. The community of prophets in Asia Minor and Greece used similar methods as the Israelites in the Near East.[143]

When the Alcmaeonid family of Athens was expelled by the Pisistratids, the exiled Alcmaeonids used their wealth and influence to win the building contract for the temple complex of Apollo at Delphi. They followed up by using their goodwill with the oracle center and its amphictyon of twelve tribes to persuade the Spartans, through the oracles Delphi would give them, to expel the Pisistratid tyrants. The oracle of Apollo did this by advocating the rule of democracy in Athens. The oracles given to the Lacedaemonian Pythians had this underlying theme.

The Spartan kingdom had been ruled by a dual monarchy and their respective courts for years. The notion of a government including representatives from the *demes* may have been viewed as suspicious but not altogether strange. In fact, the human race has always been ruled by

---

143. Herodotus 1:13-26.

a type of loose democracy. No monarch, regardless of how dictatorial or cruel, can maintain rulership without the tacit approval of the population at large. When the public perceives a king or monarch has turned against them, the aristocracy can solicit their aid to bring the tyrant down. The oracle of Apollo was now advocating the next step: a formalized body of representatives lawfully constituted to advocate their own interests to the king. In time, this was to include those on the periphery.

The town of Delphi was located on the north side of the Corinthian gulf, south of Mount Parnassus. The deity Apollo is believed to have originated in Asia and been transmitted to the Greeks through Asia Minor.[144] In the Aegean world, this deity is most recognized in his role as Phoebus the Sun god and as a *logion* or oracle teller.[145] He was the dutiful son of Zeus, the Indo-European sky god. Apollo was the brightest part of Zeus's day. Phoebus was the patron deity of truth and prophecy. He was a skilled musician and archer. Delphi had eclipsed the remote oracle center of Zeus at Dodona because of its more convenient location by land and sea. Incidentally, the shrine of Zeus at Dodona was an excellent example of the "wind as God."

The amphictyon of Delphi was a league of twelve tribes to guarantee the independence of the Apollo oracle center.[146] They met twice a year in the spring and autumn for religious rites and political discussion. Membership or expulsion was decided by vote. Each tribe had two votes. The Amphictyonic League fought three sacred wars in its history. The first war in the sixth century BC was fought against the Criseans. In the fifth and fourth centuries, the last two wars were against their own Phocian tribe. After the second war, the Phocians were expelled and replaced in the league by a group of Delphian officials. In 582 BC, the Pythian Games took place every four years instead of eight. The highlight of the games was the selection of the best song to Apollo by a poet and cithara musician.

---

144. The argument between Agamemnon and the prince Achilles reveals the dispute as one of authority and religious difference. There was consternation in the Achean camp because of the plague among the army that began with their animals. Agamemnon was a devotee of Zeus, but the deity Apollo had a strong following in the camp. The commander-in-chief of the allied forces, Agamemnon, was determined to assert the deity Zeus over Apollo. Since he couldn't do that, he equalized the situation by taking Achilles's consort Briseis in place of Chryseis, the daughter of Apollo's priest Chryses.
145. Phoebus means radiant. See the prayer of Chryses in the Iliad.
146. The tribes included the Ionians, Dolophians, Thessalians, Acniares, Magnetes, Malians, Phthiotics, Achaens, Dorians, Phocians, Locrians, Perrhaebians, and Boeotians.

The first site of the Delphic oracle was the shrine of Poseidon, Apollo's uncle. The *megaron* or interior of the temple was divided into three main aisles by eight columns on each side. The altar of Apollo occupied the center and Poseidon's was to the right. Behind a brightly shining throne, attended by celibate women, burned an aromatic fire known as the eternal flame. From the temple's megaron, the Pythian priestess descended into the *adytum*, where the oracles were received. This inner sanctum was obscured by a heavy, sheer curtain. The Most Holy was furnished with a golden statue of the deity with Phoebus's armor. Branches of fresh laurel and the Omphalos, or earth's navel, were found there also. The celibate Pythian priestess sat on a tripod above the oracle cavity of exposed ground in the adytum. The exposed ground in the Most Holy sanctum recalled the Pythian's ancient past as the priestess of Ge, the earth goddess. It was also considered to be the burial site of Dionysius/Bacchus. Various aromatic substances were burned in the oracle cavity, producing "vapors of ecstasy" inhaled by the Pythian priestess. Only on the seventh day in nine months of the year did the Pythian priestess imbibe the sacred fumes and speak in a tongue known only to the male prophets who attended her pronouncements. She would throw her head back or to one side and say, "thus says Apollo." The prophecy was copied, translated into poetic text, and then given to the client and their *proxenos*.[147]

The toxic fumes emitted through the fault fissures were from a hydrocarbon gas called ethylene that causes a light-headed, euphoric state. It signaled the god was present.

It is also believed the Pythonese spoke as a ventriloquist through her genitalia. Ventriloquism literally means "belly speaker." It was a feature of oracles in the ancient world and believed to be the spoken word of divinity. In later antiquity, mechanical devices were also employed to awe the audience.

The Greek word for seer or prophet is *mantis* and comes from *mainein*, meaning frenzied ecstasy. Today many employ what is called psychomaintein by gazing into a mirror that does not reflect their image. This was the process Macbeth fell victim to. Plato concluded there were four kinds of madness that belonged to the divine: erotic madness personified by Eros and Aphrodite; poetic madness granted by the Muses and viewed as genius; ritual madness introduced by Dionysius and his maenad female companions; and prophetic madness. Ritual madness was distinct from prophetic madness because ritual madness was accompanied by excessive drunkenness and frenzied dancing. From this display, the festival of

---

147. Proxenos meaning someone known both to the oracle and the client.

Dionysius developed, featuring dramatic performances and comedy that gradually became modern Greek theater. Prophetic madness, introduced by Apollo's oracle, gave way to ecstatic utterances comparable to the modern phenomena of speaking in tongues.

Oracle centers connected together in the ancient world like an early, albeit primitive, Internet, a network on which information was king. In my opinion, Herodotus may have been a fabric merchant, but he was also a traveling representative for the Delphic oracle.[148] Plutarch was a prophet there in later years. The information gathered by the Greek historian would have been invaluable to the oracle of Apollo. Ancient kings were appreciative of good information from sources independent of their courts. The Lydian king Croesus was among them and was instrumental in raising the reputation of the Delphic oracle to its highest level. He wished to break the tripartite agreement with Babylon and Ecbatana in Media by crossing the Halys River and recovering Lydia's former frontier. Sometime about 547 BC, he consulted the oracle at Delphi before he made his decision.

Previously he had sent envoys to the main oracle centers at Dodona, Abae, and Siwa in Lybia, among others. Delphi was the only one who correctly answered his riddle. Each group of envoys had left Sardis on the same day, and each oracle center was to tell them what Croesus was doing on the hundredth day. The envoys sent to Delphi brought back the following response from Apollo's Pythia.[149]

> I've counted the grains of sand in the extent of the sea;
> The deaf-mute struggles to speak and I hear their words.
> I know the voice of the dumb.
> The sensations of hard-shelled tortoise cooked under bronze
> Beneath it lies bronze and the flesh of lambs.

Croesus was doing exactly that. The Delphic oracle was good. However, considering the ritual rites leading up to the actual oracle, which only took place on the seventh day of the month, the oracle could expand or contract as it wished.

The ritual purification began with bathing the Pythonese at the Cassotis springs. Afterward the priestess was escorted to the temple by Delphian dignitaries, where offerings were made at the Hestian altar. Water was then sprinkled on a goat kid to determine if Apollo was present. If the goat

---

148. Herodotus 7:152.
149. Herodotus 1:47.

kid did not suitably tremble, the whole enterprise halted till the following month. In fact, any interruption of the process could abruptly end the consultation, and clients would have to wait till next time. Of course, the local merchants and innkeepers didn't mind.

Consequently, the temple and its personnel could take the time required to discover what they needed to know when they needed to know it. If you wished to consult the future, you had to wait till the oracle caught up to it.

Croesus, of course, was pleased with the Delphic response as well as the one from Amphiaraus. What the latter said is not known. "Should I go to war with the Persians?" he asked both. "Whom should I make an alliance with?" Both oracle centers advised him to seek a Greek ally, and if he went to war, he would destroy a mighty empire. This last part was ambigous enough that it should have caused him a pause. Which empire? Babylon, Media, Persia—or perhaps his own? Instead, he decided he would achieve a great victory over Persia. He asked Apollo a third time, "Will my kingdom last a long time?"

> When sits on the throne of Media; a mule is king.
> Then soft-footed Lydian,
> Flee by the river Hermus
> Wait not! Fly with great haste nor blush to behave like a coward.

Herodotus tells us Croesus was most happy with the latter response. He concluded Media would never be ruled by a mule but gave no consideration to the statement's possible symbolism.

He next turned his attention to selecting an ally and decided on the Lacedaemonians, who accepted his invitation. While preparing his military campaign, Croesus was approached by a sage named Sandanis, a fellow Lydian, who counseled the king that he had everything to lose and nothing to gain from the rugged Persians, who had nothing to lose and everything to gain from a war. But the Lydian king wasn't listening. The oracle favored his action, or so he thought, and besides Astyages, held captive by Cyrus the Persian, was his brother-in-law.

Crossing the Halys with his army, Croesus subjugated the Syrians of Cappadocia. Hearing of Lydia's treachery, Cyrus mustered his troops and marched them into Lydia along a route north of Babylonia that eventually became the Persian royal road.

The armies clashed in the district of Pteria inside Cappadocia, but the battle was costly and inconclusive for both sides. Croesus withdrew to his capital to raise a new army and call his allies to his aid—the pharaoh

Amasis and Nabonidus, who was in North Arabia at the time. He called an assembly within five months of the dispatch of his envoys. Then he disbanded his remaining troops.

However, Cyrus had followed Croesus to Sardis. Caught by surprise, Croesus tried his best to put an army together around his cavalry and marched them out to the plain near his city. Cyrus unloaded his camels and, placing riders on them, positioned them in front of his infantry. Horses are afraid of camels, and the Lydian riders were forced to fight on foot. Gradually the Persians pushed the Sardian troops into retreat.

Cyrus then laid siege to Sardis. Some fifteen days later, the city fell. In the interim, Croesus had sent word to Delphi. The oracle's reply must have felt like revenge on Alyatte's son.

> Lydian, you magnificent necessary yet, simple Croesus of vast domain. Fear to ever hear in your palace the voice you have longed for best that silence remain on your sons' lips.
> Ah! Tragedy on the day he should utter a sound.

As it turned out, the great empire Croesus destroyed was his own. The tripartite treaty had been broken, and the Medes, subjugated by their suzerain, the Persian Cyrus the Great, had filled the vacuum.

The oracle of Apollo had given Croesus a very cautious, uncommitted answer that could have applied to anyone. The only way the oracle could have failed was if the war with Persia was a stalemate, a 75% probability of success measured against a 25% probability of failure. Those would be good odds at the local casino. Underneath the international power struggle, Delphi had a score to settle with Gyges, one of Croesus's forebears. The Lydian king paid handsomely for the manipulation of his own doom. At the end of it, Apollo's fame and the reputation of his oracle center climbed to its highest level.

The Persian presence in Asia Minor was to have unexpected future repercussions for the eastern Mediterranean world. The conquest of Lydia and Babylonia in October 539 BC significantly increased the wealth of Media and Persia. The royal road was a great inspiration to a future Rome, and the standardized coinage of Lydia was adopted by the Persians for their silver currency, which was the standard royal medium of exchange. Greek mercenaries were used by Egypt and then Babylon, but in the Persian period their presence became more of a permanent feature in the eastern Mediterranean. Greek culture came with them, and the Persians particularly liked their dramas and comedies. Political intercourse with the perfidious

Europeans introduced a reality the oriental mind-set was unaccustomed to. Yet Greek mercenaries were the best fighters in the Middle and Near Eastern world at that time. Their leaders also understood the business side of warfare. Legendary wealth and conspicuous extravagance attracts all kinds, and the increasing hoard of Persian gold was a constant lure to the adventurous.

6

THE APOLLO OF GOD EMERGES

The book of Ezekiel, once redacted, is the divorce decree of Israel's material theocracy. While Jeremiah and Baruch were ducking insults and prophesying among the bad figs in Judah, the good figs were up north working out sleeping arrangements with the Babylonians. One of the exported figs was the priest Ezekiel ben Buzi, who lived near the Chebar canal. Ezekiel was a priest who, probably at least, knew of Jeremiah's work among the old material theocracy in Judah.

After almost eight hundred years, Yahweh was about to speak about the end result produced by the nation from the impetus given to Moses at Mount Horeb. After some eight hundred years of silence, the national deity took a position between the old, dying Israelite society and the new, emerging Jewish reconciliation in exile.

The language of the oracle is precise and legalistic, yet simple to understand. Each of the six oracles to Israel were dated by Jehoiachin's exile to the day. The six oracles were perfected by the addition of a seventh oracle written by another prophet at a future date. The result was an oracle whose contents span some two thousand years into the future from 594 BC, contents which can be measured and proven to be authentic. The Apollo of God emerges as prediction beyond the human pale.

However, before we begin our examination, we must perform a corrective procedure with the redactor's scalpel. Moving to the end of chapter twenty-four, we collect the seven Gentile oracles between chapters twenty-five and thirty-two in our left hand and then make an incision with the scalpel in our right hand, deftly removing said contents and placing them into the apocrypha. Like pseudo-Jeremiah, they are bogus oracles yet useful history. In addition we need to remove verses 1-20 of chapter thirty-three. They are a repetition of verses in chapter eighteen. Consequently, the verses in what is now chapter twenty-five need to be renumbered. Chapters thirty-three through forty-eight also need to be renumbered twenty-five through forty.

With this simple surgical procedure, the original scroll of Ezekiel is restored to good health. Of course, the dedicated Bible reader may require extensive therapy and shock treatment, and many may never recover. Nevertheless, the functional continuity of Ezekial's work, hidden for centuries, is wonderfully returned to the land of the living while the physician struggles to at least appear humble in the midst of unrelenting accolades from every possible quarter.[150]

Ezekiel, like Jeremiah, was an itinerant evangelical prophet who journeyed among the Israelite exiles in Babylonia. His work was organized along similar lines as Jeremiah's, and he engaged in some theatrical portrayals as well. Jeremiah's preaching was spread over some forty years among a larger population in a smaller area. Ezekiel engaged in five speaking tours over an eight-year period. His territory was a larger area with a smaller population. For three of his eight years, Ezekiel was silent, waiting for a sign to the Israelites. His first four tours took place between Tammuz 594 and Sivan 590 BC. His fifth tour began about Tebeth in 586 BC and lasted some six to nine months. It dealt mostly with the blessing and restoration part of the Deutero-Classic formula. About 573/2 BC, his final oracle envisioned the restoration of the temple in post-exilic Jerusalem.

To begin the "seven times" of Jerusalem's end, Ezekiel envisioned a spectacular, surrealistic picture he was already familiar with. Some modern interpreters have interpreted this vision as flying saucers, rocket ships, and God only knows what else. In fact, the surreal image was more down to earth than most imagine. Ezekiel had been among the exiles taken by Nebuchadnezzar in 598 BC. When Jehoiachin succeeded his dead father, his court signaled the Babylonian army outside its walls that they intended to surrender. Word was sent to Babylon notifying the king, who traveled to Jerusalem with his entourage to receive the city.

Ezekiel's vision closely resembled what he saw upon the arrival of Nebuchadnezzar at Jerusalem. It was the Babylonian king's private coach. The coach was a four-wheeled carriage with a dome-shaped roof, containing an altar and whatever else. Above the dome was another platform on which a throne was placed. In all probability, there was a staircase of some kind to access the top platform. Wherever Nebuchadnezzar went, he had a chapel

---

150. We will encounter a similar adjustment in the oracle of Jesus Christ, where the content must once again be shifted to be understood.

and throne room to elevate his dignity as ruler. It was no doubt a large transport drawn by oxen, with surreal representations artfully crafted on it.

The vision Ezekiel saw was much more grandiose and colossal, with some differing features, but after four years in Chaldea, the vision, albeit overwhelming, was not strange. The priest ben Buzi knew what it represented. The four cherubic figures beside each wheel looked very similar to the winged bull carved from limestone that guarded the throne room of Sargon II, who received the city of Samaria in 722 BC. In Ezekiel's vision, the figure stood upright and had three additional heads representing the Chaldean spirits of chaos: a lion on the right, a bull on the left, and an eagle behind. No doubt these same spirits of chaos were artfully crafted on Nebuchadnezzar's royal throne carriage, perhaps on each corner.[151]

What Ezekiel was seeing was the return of Nebuchadnezzar's royal coach and his army to destroy Jerusalem. The more spectacular vision indicated this was judgment from Yahweh and the human form on the throne was Nebuchadnezzar, God's instrument. As Ezekiel would also have known, the human form did not represent almighty God because of the prohibition in the Ten Commandments. The splendor of Nebuchadnezzar's court at Babylon and on the road was awe-inspiring, but what Ezekiel saw was much more spectacular and colossal in appearance. It was the kind of glory only Yahweh could bestow. (1:4-28)

Ezekiel was given an official commission to speak to Israel, as Isaiah and Jeremiah had. Israel's descendants had become impudent, stubborn of heart and with hard foreheads like a prostitute. Ezekiel wrote down what he saw and heard and took it to the exiles. He began his itinerant prophesying at a place called Tel-abib, where he sat stunned for seven days. (2 & 3) Ezekiel was Yahweh's secretary and traveling spokesman. The response to the message was the responsibility of each Israelite, and Ezekiel was not to interfere with those decisions, as the community of prophets had interfered in the past. Coercion was no longer an acceptable method. Each person decided for him—or herself. Those who were repentant and turned to Yahweh would be forgiven of their past iniquity, provided they maintained their repentant course. God would forgive them. The priests and prophets was no longer judge, jury, and executioner. Their only responsibility

---

151. However, in this case these four living creatures were the same ones we see in the book of Revelation at God's throne. Naturally this has led eschatologists to erroneously postulate that the throne on the chariot is also the throne of almighty God. This throne belongs to Nebuchadnezzar II, albeit employed in almighty God's service for the required period of time and the specified task allotted. These four living creatures represent the four disciplines of earthly power: military, economic, political, and legal.

was to put the message before each Israelite and then get out of the way. Each person's relationship to God was a matter between the individual and Yahweh alone. (3:16-27)

In his first speaking tour, Ezekiel used some street theater. The prophet made a brick wall of suitable size and thickness to represent Jerusalem, and then raised a sleeveless arm against it in a threatening gesture while he read his prophecies against Judah and its people. His food and drink were measured out, and his cooking fuel was dung. He shaved all his hair off by thirds and disposed of it in three different ways. He lay on his left side for 390 days for the sin of Israel, and on his right side for forty days for Judah. Perhaps he displayed a scorecard of some kind. Each prophecy, except in rare instances, began with the expression "The word of Yahweh came to me." (4-5:4)

Prophecy One (5:5-17)
Prophecy Two (6:1-14)
Prophecy Three (7:1-9)
Prophecy Four (7:10-27)

His first speaking tour allowed him one day per location, including travel time, for a total of 430 days, less the Sabbath in each week. The year 594 BC must have had an intercalary month, Veadar. There were various ways he could possibly have shortened the above time frame to cover the same fourteen months plus one. By the summer of 593 BC, he had completed his first task.

About that time, Ezekiel envisioned the religious apostasy at Jerusalem's temple compound, idolatry and sun worship among them. (8:1-18.) Ezekiel also saw the sack of Jerusalem in advance. In his vision, six warriors with weapons entered through the north gate, accompanied by a seventh man wearing linen and carrying a writer's case with pen and ink. They approached the temple and waited near the bronze altar in front of the temple door. Ezekiel also knew the north side of Jerusalem was considered its weakest point. The landscape rose to a higher level outside the walls on the north side. Invaders almost invariably approached from that direction.

Inside the temple, the glory of Yahweh, represented by the miraculous *shekinah* light, rose above the cherubim fixed to the ark of the covenant in the Holy of Holies. It moved from its traditional place to the temple threshold near the altar, filling the courtyard. Yahweh ordered the man in linen, wearing no armor, to mark anyone righteous in the city who cried out concerning the population's iniquity. Yahweh then ordered the six warriors to go through the city killing all who were unmarked with pen and ink.

Meanwhile the surreal carriage Ezekiel had seen earlier took a position on the south side of the temple. When the man in linen returned from his completed task, he announced it. The man on the cherubic throne ordered him to fire the city and burn it to the ground.

As the cherubic carriage left for the east gate, the glory of Yahweh moved to a position above it. They left the city together. At the east gate, the officials of the city assured each other that the Babylonians would spare them to continue running the affairs of the city. However, Ezekiel heard that all twenty-five would be slain. (8:1-11:13)

The second speaking tour took eleven months between Elul 5, 593 BC through Ab 9, 592 BC.

Prophecy Five (11:5-25)
Prophecy Six (12:1-7)
Prophecy Seven (12:8-16)
Prophecy Eight (12:17-20)
Prophecy Nine (12:21-25)
Prophecy Ten (12:26-28)
Prophecy Eleven 13 (against the prophets)
Prophecy Twelve (14:1-11)
Prophecy Thirteen (14:12-23)
Prophecy Fourteen (chapter 15)
Prophecy Fifteen (chapter 16)
Prophecy Sixteen (17:1-10)
Prophecy Seventeen (17:11-24)
Prophecy Eighteen (chapter 18)
Prophecy Nineteen (chapter 19)

Ezekiel's third preaching tour was his longest, lasting from sometime in the month of Ab 592 BC or thereabouts till Tebeth in 590 BC. Like Jeremiah in Judea, Ezekiel was finally confronted by the elders among the exiles, but Ezekiel rejected them after telling them their history. Yahweh had abandoned them, and he would no longer accept rebels who refused to acknowledge the Almighty as their king. Only those who approached him willingly and free of transgression would be called Israel. They had to come to him out of the wilderness of the nations, loathing the evil they had done and seeking the Lord's holiness.

The material theocracy had come to the final curtain and the hand of the destroyer had been prepared. (21:8) Ezekiel finished his prophesying with the allegorical Oholah, who symbolized Israel, and her younger sister Oholibah, who symbolized Judah. Both had played the whore in Egypt before Moses cleaned them up and brought them out into a new land flowing with milk and honey. Oholah, who lived in Samaria, lusted after the Assyrians clothed in blue, and had many of them as lovers. Her sister, who lived in Jerusalem and witnessed her sister's end, not only continued with her Assyrian lovers but lusted after the Chaldeans, who painted themselves in a bright reddish-orange on their walls. There would be no forgiveness this time. No rescue would come like before. Their lewd idolatry had defiled them all beyond redemption. The end had come.

On Tebeth 10, 590 BC, Nebuchadnezzar's army began the final siege of Jerusalem at the half point in the "seven times." Ezekiel wrote down two more prophecies and delivered them to the exiles over a six-month period between Tebeth and Sivan 10 or thereabouts, and then rested. On his return, his wife died, which was viewed as a sign to the Israelites. Ezekiel became speechless for the next three years.

Among the exiles in Babylonia, Ezekiel broke his threeyear silence when word arrived that David's city had fallen. It lay in ruins. More exiles were on their way.

Chapter twenty-five in redacted Ezekiel tells how the prophet's work would continue among the Israelites in the wilderness of the nations. The community of prophets would still have a function in the restored theocracy, but it would be a more passive one. They would warn the wicked, but not by killing them if they refused to change as had been done in the past. God would judge and execute, and the prophets would give warning. Israel would be a new creation. The Israelites would love God of their own free will and not because they were threatened. They would worship not because they were descendants of Abraham but because Yahweh had proved who he was. He was Yehovah of Armies, the Most High among the nations, the Giver of life. God could also take away from those undeserving. To the exiles he would stand up as the great Shepherd of his people. God would seek out his sheep and rescue them from human shepherds who fed themselves at the expense of the flock. (See Ezekiel 26:22-24; 26:28; 33:22-24; 33:28.)

New Israel would inherit the blessing while Old Israel would continue under the curse. The balance of Ezekiel's message to the increasing number of exiles was one of restoration. It was now time to focus on healing the wounds and determining who was New Israel and who was not.

To illustrate the creation of New Israel, Ezekiel came to be in a valley of dry bones belonging to deceased Israelites. There he witnessed a dramatic resurrection of "dem bones" and their complete restoration to life. The time would surely come when the scattered nation of Israel would be gathered back to their devastated homeland. Israel would receive a miraculous resurrection from the dead, and the once-divided nation would be united again. The stick of Joseph and Judah would be bound together and never again broken. They would live together on the mountains of Israel, albeit in a much smaller land base than before. King David ben Jesse would be restored to Jerusalem in that one of his descendants would ultimately claim the kingship. The east gate would be opened in Jerusalem above the mountains, and the covenant renewed for all time. They would do well with God at his sanctuary and receive everlasting peace and security. (25-29) or (33-37)

Pseudo-Ezekiel (chapters 25-32) is a collection of Gentile oracles that were carelessly inserted into the original scroll and have no place in Ezekiel's work. They are seven in number, and two were never fulfilled in history. Nebuchadnezzar never conquered Egypt, and the pharaoh's kingdom was never depopulated for forty years.

These pseudo-oracles contrast significantly with the Gentile prophecy in Ezekiel 27. However, the Bible writers preserved the pseudo-isolation of Edom by setting it apart under one chapter. In actual fact, the prophecy included Mount Seir and the mountains of Israel together in one prophecy. Chapter 27 included the first fifteen verses of chapter 28. Consequently, the prophecy in chapter 27 should be renumbered verse one through thirty. Chapter 28 begins at verse sixteen and should be renumbered one through twenty-three. After renumbering, we have a more accurate picture. The prophecy was against the religious practices of both nations. Israel and Edom were kindred, and the prophecy treated them that way. Just as Israel had no right to the land of Edom, the Edomites had no right to the land of Israel. Their hatred for the Israelites was understandable, considering King David's commander Joab practiced genocide against them and Samuel and Saul did the same to the Amalekites. Genocide is an evil act. Neither party had the right to the other's land, which both violated in their past.

The excessive hate literature against Edom came about when Jehoram ben Jehoshaphat's punitive campaign to Edom failed and his kingdom was conquered by the Arabs, Philistines, and Edomites in coalition. The Edomites took their revenge on the Judeans in particular by returning the genocide on them. "Because you cherished an ancient enmity and gave over the people of Israel to the sword at the time of their calamity, at the time of their final punishment;—. It would appear the Babylonians used Edomite mercenaries to sack Jerusalem.[152] The Judeans kept the flame of hatred alive by slaughtering the Edomites again in another genocide under Amaziah ben Joash. This accounts for the venomous hate literature against Edom in the Bible, which spills over against other Gentile nations. In time,

---

152. Psalm 137:7.

Edom did become a desolate land like Israel, because both were guilty of genocidal hatred.

Old Israel could readily see the sins of others against itself, but it could never bring itself to see the evil it perpetrated against others. This was why Old Israel would never see the blessing of God but live under the curse all its days. New Israel would reconcile its differences with other nations and put away old hatreds, becoming teachers to the Gentiles and serving their interest. Old Israel maintained old enmities and created new ones. Today, the western Christian nations make themselves guilty of crimes against humanity when they condemn ethnic hatred and genocide among themselves, yet condone it in others. Regardless of anyone's particularism, genocide is genocide and an evil act by evil people.

The prophecy about Gog of Magog is based in the ancient age of Noah's descendants. In verse seventeen, the question is asked, "Are you he of whom I spoke in former days by my servants the prophets of Israel, who in those days prophesied for years that I would bring you against them?" This is, of course, against Babylon, but there are elements in this prophecy that never took place around 539 BC. This is a prophecy that reaches far back into the so-called postdiluvian era and then propels itself beyond the present day well into the future. The tribes mentioned in Ezekiel are the sons of Japheth and his brother Ham.[153] The chief prince of Meshech and Tubal was their patriarchal father Japheth. Magog was the brother of Meshech and Tubal, as was Gomer. Togarmah was the son of Gomer and the nephew of Magog. The prince of Put, Cush, Parsis,[154] and Canaan was Ham. The Shemitic house had received the blessing of Noah, which had major political ramifications in post-diluvian society.

The Elamites, Assyrians, and Arameans were Shemites. Who was Gog? As near as can be determined, Gog means a remote region or mountainous region. Magog means "land of a remote or mountainous place." In the context of Ezekiel, these are the Hamitic Persians descended from Parsis. In the biblical, post-diluvian age, Gog appears to be associated with the Hamitic Nimrod, the son of Cush. He was the first mighty warrior to conquer western territories, making Babel one of his major cities. It would appear Nimrod made an alliance with the Japhetic tribes of Meshech, Tubal, and Magog. Perhaps it wasn't an alliance at all but a conquest of the Japhetic tribes by a Hamite. In Ezekiel's day, the Medes, descended from Madai, a Japhetic house, dominated the Hamitic Persians for many years. Prior to the fall of Babylon, this traditional role was reversed, making the Japhetic tribe

---

153. Genesis 10.
154. Persia.

subject to the Hamitic Persians before an invasion was made westward into Babylonia and Lydia. Extrapolating backward tells us the same situation had a parallel in that particular ancient world.

An examination of the single Shemite chronology adds an incredible dimension to the conquest from the east. Individuals in the first four generations from Shem lived for an average of four hundred and fifty years. Nimrod belonged to the third generation, as did Togarmah. Magog, Tubal, and Meshech belonged to the second generation from Shem. The first four generations witnessed their children and grandchildren to the twelfth generation die of old age well before they did. Generations five through twelve, in most cases, did not see their parents or grandparents die.

The psychological impact of this dynamic would have been enormous. Generations five through fifteen would have viewed their ancestors as the immortal gods. For someone like Nimrod, his godlike stature among the later generations created a power dynamic that elevated him to supreme rulership in the Mesopotamian ancient world. Once Nimrod had become the head chieftain of Meshech, Tubal, Magog, and Togarmah, he invaded Shemitic territories in the north and west belonging to Elam, Asshur, and Aram, making his capital at Babel on the Euphrates River.

The confusion of human language at Babel must have an allegorical meaning because the Mesopotamian and alluvial people and the surrounding nations down into Canaan spoke the Aramaic tongue with only dialectic differences. The ancient Aramean world was a big place that encompassed many national groups, including the Israelites. Language changed through distance, isolation, and the human penchant to playfully evolve expression in all its various forms.

As noted earlier, the notion of a global flood survived by Noah is an allegory based on an event that probably took place locally. However, the oracle in Revelation 20:7-9 makes mention of this distant history and indicates that this early rebellion will take place a second time on a much larger scale in the future. The fact that the flood is mentioned in two oracles is significant. This gives credence to chapters ten and eleven in Genesis. It obviously gives us a brief account of the Aramean world and the consolidation of power in the hands of tribal monarchs circa 4000 BC or thereabouts. The date given for the creation of the world is likely the time when the Aramean world began to emerge.

In that ancient age, we see the birth of polytheism based on ancestor worship. The "brave new world" of the post-diluvian generations entertained an optimism that collapsed in the face of diminishing life expectancy. This controversial upheaval in the human psyche destroyed the fabric of a unified society. Instead it produced a fragmented and disillusioned humanity

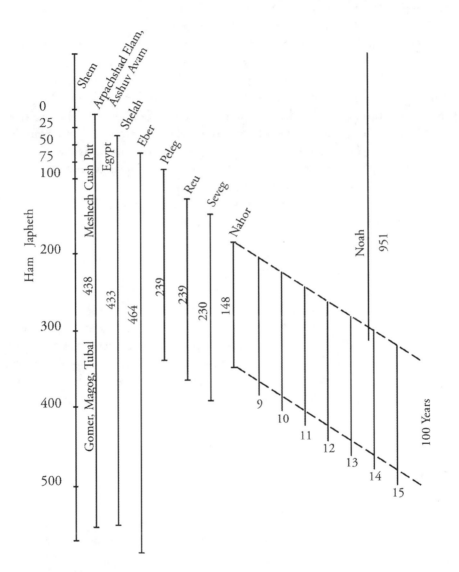

Plate A

that preferred polytheistic tribalism. The oracle in Ezekiel projected this same tragedy far into the future, when the human race will once again be confronted with a serious threat to its well-being and sense of security.

After some twenty-one years as an itinerant prophet, the fifty-one-year-old priest Ezekiel wrote down his last and sixth oracle in Jehoiachin's twenty-fifth year of exile. Jehoiachin was then forty years of age. From chapter thirty-two to forty of redacted Ezekiel, the prophet envisioned a restored Israel. The new temple was situated on a very high mountain in the middle of the New Israel. Ezekiel took this visionary oracle on his last speaking tour among the exiles before he retired. It was part of the hopeful message structured according to the Deutero-Classic formula that Israel would be restored to its patrimony in the future. The year of the last vision was 569 BC.

The boundaries of New Israel were west of the Jordan River and the two eastern seas from the Hethlon road near the border of Damascus in the north, to the Wadi of Egypt, through Meribath-Kadesh, to Tamar in the south. The land was divided into equal strips from east to west with seven tribes to the north and five in the south. In the middle of the land, between the tribes of Judah to the north and Benjamin in the south, was a strip of land twenty-five thousand cubits wide.[155]

The prophet Daniel had predicted Egypt would be invaded following the battle of Carchemish. But Nebuchadnezzar had been unable to repeat his success from 601 BC, and it must have irked him that he had been forced to back down in the face of two successive opportunities to destroy the pharoah's power. It took the Assyrians some time to conquer Egypt, and with a larger stronger force he would duplicate their achievement as well. It was simply a matter of time. It was on this premise that the writers of the pseudo-Jeremiah and Ezekiel based their predictions. This would require extensive preparations, and the pseudo-oracles indicated Nebuchadnezzar would circumvent Judah and invade via the king's highway, turning west through the Negeb and possibly picking up mercenaries on the way. This would require placing the crown prince Amel-Marduk on the throne in a co-regency with himself. Royal contracts extant place Amel-Marduk in a co-regency at least one year ahead of his succession. There is only a relative consensus for a longer co-regent period. Daniel chapters 2 and 4 indicate there was.

In chapter four, Nebuchadnezzar approached Belteshazzar and asked him to interpret a recent vision. He recalled a great tree with branches and foliage reaching into the heavens. However, a "watcher" commanded

---

155. A cubit = 45.7 centimeters or 18 inches.

the luxuriant tree be chopped down and ruined and the remaining stump banded with copper and iron straps. It would be "wet with the dew of heaven" and a period of "seven times" or seven years would pass by. This is the second appearance of the "seven times." In the first instance, the "seven times" was a strict seven years, and that was usual. The next appearance of this measurement involved a more expanded time frame. (In Dan. 7.)

The North American Adventist movement begun by William Miller in the early nineteenth century made liberal use of the prophet Daniel's writings. Their eschatologies incorporated various interpretations of the "seven times." William Miller's interpretations for the 1840s ended in a deep and profound failure that resounds in the Adventist movement to this day. Sad to say, failure engenders more failure. Adventist eschatologists continue to extrapolate Daniel's writings into more grandiose scenarios. The fact is that Daniel's work in chapters two and four is down to earth and local, except perhaps in one instance.[156]

If the statue seen in chapter two were a true representation of the "march of world powers" as history records, it would have a much different appearance than the one described by Belteshazzar.

Successive empires were defeated by their predecessors. Where and when did the Anglo-Americans defeat the Romans? In what year or years? In what battle or battles? The notion of the Anglo-American power as the feet of mixed clay and iron is ridiculous. The Roman empire fell long before the Anglo-Americans showed up. The Americans would never take credit for defeating the Roman empire unless they thought they could get away with it.

What Daniel meant was simpler and closer to home. The statue in chapter two has a direct connection to the tree in chapter four. The head of gold was Nebuchadnezzar. The silver arms and breast indicates two rulers of the same kingdom, a characteristic not found in the Persians. Their kingdom was superior to the Babylonians. The silver kingdom was a joint rulership of Nebuchadnezzar and his son Amel-Marduk. That this is so can be seen in chapter four. The dynasty "stump" is only banded with copper and iron straps, corresponding to the statue's copper belly and thighs followed by the legs of iron. The silver band is missing! This can only mean the silver kingdom was in progress while Nebuchadnezzar was alive.

The largesse of the symbolism suggests a long co-regency. While the king was suffering from his illness, Amel-Marduk would have taken the reins of government. Once a co-regency was established, it could not be

---

156. The seven times is supposed to be the forty-nine years (7 x 7) followed by a Jubilee year, or 586-537 BC (Daniel 4:17).

The Seven Times

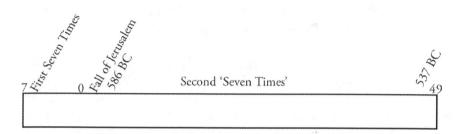

then follows 62 weeks or 434 years + 9 (8.68) years for the 50th jubilee = 443 yrs then comes 1 week. (3½ + 3½)

Nebuchadnezzar II   43 yrs   – 605 BC-562
Evil Merodach 572 [10]   2 yrs   – 562-60 BC
Nerglissar   4   – 560-556
    (Labashi-Marduk 2 mos.)
Nabonidus   17   – 556-539
    Belshazzar – co-regent
    at Babylon   553-539 BC

2 Kings 24   605-19 yrs = 586 BC.

undone. The joint rulership lasted at least ten years. Extant evidence only documents one year, but scholars suspect longer. Two years into his solo reign, Amel-Marduk was assassinated and replaced in 560 BC by Neriglissar, a son-in-law of the great king Nebuchadnezzar II. His kingdom was the belly of bronze and the copper band on the dynasty stump. The two copper thighs represent the co-regent rule of Neriglissar and his son Labashi-Marduk. The kingdom of iron legs was the joint rulership of Nabonidus, who came to the throne in 556 BC and elevated his son Belshazzar, another son-in-law of Nebuchadnezzar, to the co-regency in 553 BC.

Nabonidus left his son at Babylon while he marched the best of his army south into the North Arabian desert, taking control of the oasis town of Tema and the rich caravan trade that came to it. The feet of clay mixed with iron symbolized the same two rulers in a weakened state. This corresponds to the band of iron on the dynasty stump.[157] One image connects to the other in a seamless fashion.

The seventh oracle of Ezekiel is contained in the book of Daniel. Daniel 7 is the first instance of a provable oracle that spans some two thousand years once it is connected to the six oracles of Ezekiel.[158] Daniel 7 can be measured and established as genuine and beyond the human pale. This is not the case with Daniel 2. Like it or not, there is no way to prove whether the statue is a genuine oracle or simply a history of the Neo-Babylonian dynasty written in oracular style. If it was genuine, then only those familiar with its contents at the time could say so. We today cannot. Faith is an admirable quality, but it is not an endless journey. The courage of one's convictions must eventually end in positive results. Faith must lead to perfect belief.

Some six years before Lydia fell to the Persians, Belteshazzar envisioned the seventh oracle of Ezekiel as recorded in Daniel 7. It was 553 BC, and Belshazzar, the natural son of Nabonidus, also known as Labyuetus, had been raised to be co-regent at Babylon. The prophet envisioned the next four kingdoms to follow Babylonia. The Neo-Babylonian empire was depicted in surreal terms in Daniel 2 and 4 and in the first two oracles of Ezekiel. The Persian power was pictured as a lion sporting two great eagle's wings. Each wing symbolized the two main conquerors, Cyrus and his son Cambyses, who conquered Egypt in 525 BC.[159] The lion then stood on its feet and was given the heart of a man. This was the period of the

---

157. Isaiah 7:4; 11:1.

158. This is now the second reconstruction we've made to Ezekiel. We will see it reappear in the oracle of Jesus Christ.

159. The lion can't be Neo-Babylonia because the country's last king, Nabonidus, continued conquest into North Arabia to gain control of the trade in spices and luxury goods. The wings of the eagle symbolize military conquest.

Zoroastrian kings of Persia, who never worshipped idols or built temples. From Darius to Darius III, the Achaemenid royalty were monotheists who worshipped Ahura Mazda, the supreme god. The world was divided into two camps of good and evil, and the devotees of Ahura Mazda championed good thoughts and good deeds. The doctrine of an eternal hellfire comes from them. Fire was sacred to the Persians, who did build fire altars in their domain. Birthday celebrations come from them as well.

The fall of Babylon was good news for the exiled Jews, and Cyrus decreed they could return to their patrimony in Palestine and build a new temple to the Most High. Cyrus installed a Median satrap named Darius, who became de facto king of Babylon for at least one year, possibly two. He was an aged man and probably died in the second year. He is the Darius the books of Zechariah and Haggai date their prophecies to. Although satrap Darius the Mede was viewed by the Babylonians and Jews as the ruling king, it is only at the beginning of Zechariah 7 that we find ourselves in the reign of Darius the Persian.[160] The temple had been built and the seventy years of Jeremiah had long passed by.[161] Although Ezra tells us the work was frustrated, it nevertheless went forward to completion.[162]

The reason for the restoration, as the Persians saw it, was as prelude to the invasion of Egypt. Judea was conquered without a fight by simply repopulating it. Cambyses, the son and successor of Cyrus, could not be opposed to a loyal tenant in Palestine while he was satrap at Babylon for ten years. Nor could he object to a loyal ally at his rear when he invaded and subjugated Egypt in 525 BC. It wasn't actually the temple building that anyone was opposed to. It was the rebuilding of Jerusalem and the traditional loyalty of Israel to Egypt that worried them. It was a legitimate concern, considering the geography and Israelite history. To the king of Persia and his successors, what they had in mind for Egypt precluded any worry about Judea.

---

160. Zechariah 7:2-5.
161. From Zechariah 7:2-5 and Ezra 1:1 it would appear there were two interpretations of Jeremiah's seventy years current in the post-exilic period. See Zechariah 1:12.
162. Ezra 4:4-5; 5:5.

7

THE POST-EXILIC WORLD

The Jews were released in the spring of 538 BC and the temple foundation was laid the following year. The prophet Zechariah, who used the sacred calendar, counted the satrapal rule of Darius the Mede from the end of October 539 BC.[163] In his first chapters, he refers to the satrap as simply Darius. The introduction of his prophetic book is dated November 538 BC, and the bulk of the first six chapters belong to February 537 BC.

The prophet Haggai used the civil calendar and also began his work in February 537 BC, finishing it by June of that same year. It appears Darius the satrap died sometime during the following four months. Zechariah began his seventh chapter in the fourth year of Darius the Persian, who was king in 518/17 BC.[164]

A strict reading of Jeremiah's seventy-year prophecy reveals an alternative understanding. According to some, the seventy years counted from 586 BC would end in 517 BC. The contents of the prophecy could apply to this period if one was unaware of Jeremiah 29:10 at that time. The contents indicate the temple construction was well beyond the foundation stage and was nearing completion, or was at least in use.[165] The building work on the second temple would have been much slower than the seven years King Solomon took to construct the first. His father had helped with considerable advance preparation, and the alien conscripts available to

---

163. Zechariah 1:1-12.
164. Zechariah 1:1-7; 7:1.
165. In fact, the temple was completed on February 13, 516 BC, in Darius's sixth year of rule (Ezra 6:15). The city of Jerusalem would have had to have been rebuilt prior to Xerxes's invasion of Greece to complete Jewish appeasement, and the city's walls completed. The invasion of Greece tells us Judea was fully able to defend against Egyptian counterattack (62 weeks).

Solomon were a more numerous workforce. The post-exilic Jews had to be content with limited resources, though the stones and rubble of the first temple were available for use nearby.

The conversation with Zechariah and the words of Sharezar and Regem-melech indicate they understood the seventy years of Jeremiah's prophecy had just ended in 517 BC. However, Jeremiah chapter twenty-nine and Zechariah chapter one, verse twelve make it clear the seventy years began when the crown prince Nebuchadnezzar made his first military appearance before the walls of Jerusalem early in Jehoiakim's reign. The halt in the temple building by royal officials and the promise in Zechariah that Zerubbabel would finish the house in his lifetime prompted some to conclude the seventy years of Jeremiah actually began to count from 586 BC, when the temple was destroyed. Both interpretations are plausible.

Bible readers do themselves and others a great disservice when they conclude the Bible writers were infallible. They were not. This fundamentally ridiculous idea comes from the fundamentalists' cherished notion that Scripture is the sacred word of almighty God.

The story of Cain and Abel may be an allegorical reference to the destruction of Israel and Jerusalem by their "brothers," the Aramean Chaldeans and Edomites.

Isaiah chapters two and three bear the hallmark of early Judiaism but were misappropriated by Christians. The suffering servant of chapter 53 was Israel in exile.

All Scripture may be inspired by those who believe in God, but very little of it belongs to God. The faith displayed by many is admirable, but the reasons they give and the supports they use to bolster its existence are becoming more ridiculous as time goes by. The fundamentalists are going the way of the dinosaur and deservedly so.

In the post-exilic world, we see an effort on the part of the Bible writers to incorporate the blessing part of the Deutero-Classic formula into their restoration. Yet the restoration of Israel and its temple as outlined by Ezekiel in the sixth oracle never took place. Little Judea and its temple at Jerusalem were more to be pitied than admired. Indeed, the prophecy of Daniel from chapters seven to twelve indicates that post-exilic Judea was not going to inherit the blessing spoken of in Ezekiel and Daniel 7. Daniel 9 between verses 24 and 27 indicates the Jews would rebuild Jerusalem in a troubled time. The anointed of Israel would be cut off and the temple destroyed. War and desolation would overtake them.[166] Daniel was praying for just the

---

166. This understanding coordinates well with the first three plagues in Egypt before Moses led the Egypto-Arameans into Canaan. The seventh plague,

opposite, as were most devout Jews, but what Belteshazzar envisioned was a future that meant their prayers would go unanswered over the long term.

Yet the stubborn and stiff-necked Israelites and Jews would try to force the notion on the dedicated Bible reader that God's blessing would prevail for their material theocracy. This effort reached the ridiculous in the Maccabean period and in the apocryphal books. In the post-exilic period, Jews and later Christians in the first century and beyond would console themselves with the idea that the blessing of God was within.

What Jews and Christians can't seem to realize was that a new theocracy came about unperceived by Old Israel. There was a modicum of renewal in the post-exilic period, and the Jew was a dedicated Yahwist who loathed idolatry. Jews were lifelong students of Scripture and Mosaic law. In order to merge the law covenant into the modern world, they developed the Talmudic tradition to explain current applications of Mosaic law. However, Talmudic legalese wasn't the answer either. The creation account in Genesis was a product of Talmudic legalese. It was determined that the law of the Sabbath and the six working days of the seven-day week was also observed by the Most High. After all, God must follow his own law. Consequently, the two main creative epochs were divided into six creative days and a Sabbath.[167]

Actually, there was no such thing as six creative days and a Sabbath rest day for God. Days 2-4 were simply a chain reaction proceeding from the first "Let light come to be." The removal by whatever means of the thick, black gloom covering the planet exposed the surface waters to the sun's direct light. The rest can be explained with simple science leading directly to the second creative epoch. If we use the same criteria for the so-called first four days, then we arrive at more than seven. What is interesting about the creative account is that it demonstrates the correct steps in the scientific process were known some twenty-five hundred years ago. That is remarkable.[168]

---

as stated, was the first miracle of almighty God that was a sign of his intervention in human affairs. The eighth plague of locusts signaled that Israel would be plagued by invasions from outside its borders during all of its existence, which was certainly true. Although Exodus tells us the Egypto-Arameans were not affected by these plagues, that notion is not credible. They were.

167. Genesis 1:1-19 and 1:20-2:3.

168. It would appear the small, religiously rigid state of Judea was being influenced by the scientific thinking of others, probably the Greeks or the Persian Magi or both.

Using Talmudic legalese to create six creative days and a Sabbath, whether that was a period lasting thousands of years or one literal week, is erroneous and falls short of the mark. Today we have solid evidence of the planet's' prehistory denied by dedicated Bible readers for almost two thousand years. To support their ridiculous views, fundamentalists argue against reason and science in an attempt to defeat both with blind faith.

The era of faith is at an end. Faith must be transferred onto perfect belief. Faith is not an endless journey. It must eventually arrive at tangible results that are proven. Perfect belief is assured expectation ultimately realized in fact.

Politically, the post-exilic nation of Judea became divided by two diasporas, one in Egypt and the other in Babylon. As the Persian empire continued after the Egyptian conquest of Cambyses, the loyalty of Judea became suspect when two political parties emerged around the high priest, favoring its diaspora. Egypt was always a worry to the Persian kings. The return of the Jews to Palestine and the reconstruction of their Yahwist temple was enough to secure Jewish loyalty, but as time passed it became necessary to have Jewish representatives at court to ensure their loyalty was maintained. This began with the Jewess who became Queen Esther and continued in other personages, such as Ezra and Nehemiah.

Egyptian aspirations for national independence and the unsettling conditions that arose in Jerusalem from the influence of the pro-Egyptian party served to strain relations with Persepolis. Inevitably, Egyptian money on the one side and Persian on the other produced a corrosive, corrupting influence in Judea. The advent of the Hellenistic kingdoms only exacerbated the growing problems of the two factions. The politics of Xerxes were reiterated by the Roman hegemony, which tied Judea to the state by the treaty of 161 BC.

8

THE DELPHIC ORACLE: THE GREEK INFLUENCE

The reign of the Persian Achaemenids Darius and his son Xerxes represent the zenith of Persian power. Their involvement with the European Greeks was to change the course of history. The root cause was the struggle of Athens to rid itself of the Pisistradid tyranny.[169] The Spartans, gradually massaged by the Delphic oracles, also attempted to dislodge the ruling Pisistradid by sending a task force by sea, commanded by Anchimolius. But its defeat by Thessalian cavalry at Phalerum brought out a larger army by land commanded by King Cleomenes, who blunted the Thessalian mercenaries. He then marched into Athens, capitalizing on some unexpected good fortune and taking the city. The Pisistratidae were expelled and a democratic council put in place.

A power struggle developed between two political competitors named Isagaras and Cleisthenes. The latter divided the four tribes of Athens into ten and made himself popular with the common folk, rising to a dominant position in the early democracy. Determined to hold on to his fading power, Isagoras appealed to Cleomenes to remove his opponent. Cleomenes sent a letter to Athens demanding Cleisthenes and his supporters leave the city. Cleisthenes left of his own volition, but his supporters remained. The Spartan king returned to Athens with a small entourage and expelled some seven hundred families. The democratic council was dissolved and Isagoras was made ruler. This angered the council, which besieged Cleomenes and Isagoras in the Acropolis for two days. On the third day the Lacedaemonian king and his entourage, including Isagoras, made a truce and left Athens.

---

169. Herodotus 5:62-73.

While he was in the Acropolis, he laid his hands on the oracles of Apollo, who were kept in Athena's temple. He was deeply hurt over the contents when he discovered the oracle's subterfuge and the Lacedaemonian feeling in Delphi's pronouncements. The dual Spartan kingship then allied themselves in common cause against Athens and marched their forces to Eleusis to engage the Athenian army. However, the Corinthians and one of the Spartan kings, Demaratus, withdrew their ranks from the field, forcing Cleomenes to quit the campaign also.

Meanwhile the Athenian council had sent envoys to the Persian satrap Artaphrenes at Sardis in Asia Minor to propose an alliance. They were told an alliance was possible if they were willing to offer Darius "earth and water" as tokens. This they agreed to, and Artaphrenes accepted the "tokens of submission" from them, after which they returned to their city. After reporting to the council their embassy's success, they were shocked to discover that earth and water were tokens, not of an alliance, but willing subjugation. Persia had now become the suzerain and Athens the vassal.

On the death of Isagoras, the dual monarchy of Sparta summoned Hippias of Sigeon, the son of Pisistratus, to become tyrant of Athens. This move was defeated by the persuasive eloquence of the Corinthian Socleas, leaving Hippias without a supporter. He journeyed to Sardis and complained to Artaphrenes. Hearing of his appeal to the satrap, the Athenians advised him to reject any of Hippias's claims. The Persian satrap then returned word to the effect that the future of Athens depended on the acceptance of Hippias as ruler. The council refused. Hearing this news, Aristagoras of Miletus spoke to the council, reminding them Miletus was an Athenian colony and proposing a war with Persia. Athens responded by voting twenty ships to support the Ionian revolt in Asia Minor against Persian rule. The rebels attacked Sardis and destroyed most of the town. On this act, word was sent to King Darius that the Ionians had revolted and were in alliance with Athens against Artaphrenes.

The first order of business for the Persians was to quell the revolt in Ionia. Off the coast of Milesia, they assembled a land army and six hundred ships. The Ionians decided not to fight the Persians on land and mustered a navy of three hundred and fifty warships off the island of Ladé near Miletus. The Persian fleet won the contest and reduced Miletus to slavery.

Wintering at the fallen city, the navy followed up in the spring by reducing the islands of Chios, Lesbos, and Tendos, then moving on to the Hellespont. The towns on the eastern side of the straits had been taken by the land forces, and the navy began its attack on the Chersonese side. The following year, Darius sent his young son-in-law Mardonius with additional forces into the Aegean. Stopping in Ionia, he allowed the natives to institute democratic government.[170] Proceeding to the Hellespont, he transported his land army to the Chersonese and conquered Thrace, Macedonia, and the island, gaining possession of the gold and silver mines in the area. Persian control of the Hellespont gave them access to the flow of wheat from the lands north of the Euxine (Black) Sea. It was a very successful campaign. Darius followed up by sending his heralds into Greece demanding earth and water. Many complied, paying the great king tribute.

Standing the lion up on two feet after its wings were plucked out represents Darius and Xerxes, who acquire the "heart of a man" by adopting the monotheistic view. Daniel 7:4.

Whenever the Persians moved their forces inside or outside their empire in massive numbers, they had to be continually aware of possible revolts from within. Egypt and Babylon were troublesome spots. Darius's bid for power involved him in numerous revolts between 521 and 518 BC. Consequently, when a storm near Mount Athos destroyed half the Persian fleet in 492 BC, the king and his commanders were compelled to withdraw the bulk of their military to a safe position before the rebel elements discovered what happened. This served to confuse early reports while the fleet repaired its damage in Cilicia. By the time an accurate report was in rebel hands, it was too late for a revolt.

The loss of half the fleet made the Greeks competitive at sea. Any rebel faction with ships of its own would be quick to conclude an alliance with them. To maintain a grip on their new possessions in the north Aegean, the Persians would have to rebuild their navy.

In 490 BC, the Persian host returned to Aegean waters under the command of Datis the Mede and Artaphernes. This time they sailed from Samos across the Icarian Sea to Naxos and then to Delos, which was said to be Apollo's birthplace. There he made an offering to the god and sailed to Eretria. They laid siege to Carystus on the southern tip of the Euboean island. In Eretria, the city's populace was divided between those who advocated fleeing to the mountains and those willing to surrender. After a six-day siege, the city was betrayed into Persian hands.

From there, they sent a task force to Attica, led by Hippias, the son of Pisistratus.[171] In the battle of Marathon, the Persians and Athenians achieved partial victories at first. The Persian center defeated the Greek center, but the flanks had an opposite outcome. The Athenian wings then united to defeat the victorious Persian center. The survivors boarded their ships and withdrew, leaving seven vessels behind. The fleet sailed to Athens,

---

170. Herodotus 6:43-49.
171. Herodotus 6:94-119.

dropping anchor off Phalerum just as the victorious Athenian army was returning. After a standoff, Datis and Artaphernes decided to quit Attica and sailed back to Asia with their Euboean exiles in tow. The great king was aged at this time and died some three years later. Perhaps they had received word Darius was suffering from ill health, or possibly that a revolt was in the offing. Whatever the case, they did not return the following year because Egypt did launch a revolt. The Persians would not return for another ten years.

Although much has been made of the Athenian victory at Marathon, the Achaemenid expedition was not a total failure. By comparison, the Greeks lost considerable ground. The defeat at Marathon and the loss of seven vessels near the mouth of the Charadra was nothing more than the cost of doing business for the Persians. The best part of the Greek world was already in Persian hands, and it is doubtful the great king had any interest in what was left, other than hiring their mercenaries and keeping them in line with suitable punishments. It may actually have been better for Hellas had the Athenians lost the battle. Darius may have concluded Athena's miscreants had been suitably chastised before he died in 486 BC. His son and successor may have decided the same. But it was not to be. The old Achaemenid monarch died, leaving a promise unrequited to his successor Xerxes.

In the spring of 536 BC, Belteshazzar saw a vision that almost killed him. He was visited by three entities. In chapter eight, Daniel tells us the vision he saw circa 550 BC was the same as the one above.[172] Consequently the oracles from Daniel 7-12 came about through supernatural visitation and not through dreams, as the text erroneously says. The above chapters are the only part of Daniel's work that is genuine. Chapters one through six are a mixture of history written in oracular style and history that is not. Chapter three is pure Jewish propaganda and never happened. It is typical of Aramean/Chaldean literature designed to present a moral lesson. Although Daniel was the chief priest in Babylon, he is missing from the account. His presence would have been required. If he was present, then it means he apostatized and was therefore undeserving of the divine accolades he received.[173] This piece of propaganda was constructed to impress the Persians. Fire was sacred to them. The thrust of the story was the Almighty of Israel can and does rescue from fire. This bogus children's story is, amusingly, believed by many Bible readers today. The first six chapters of Daniel belong in the apocrypha, with the exception of chapter four.

---

172. Daniel 8:1, 15-18; 7:1; 10:5-19.
173. Daniel 10:11, 19.

The alien beings Belteshazzar saw were probably seraphim. The term *seraph* simply means "flying serpent." These were actual creatures seen in the desert and had a characteristic copper color. The copper serpent was one of Israel's sacred poles inaugurated by Moses.[174] These snakes came to represent otherworldly creatures of divine essence that were coppery in appearance and had a serpentine quality to their manifestation. Not that they actually looked like serpents, but their humanoid form was startling in some way. Cherubs, on the other hand, were similar in appearance but were less powerful than seraphs. The term *cherub* applies to whatever God gives life to, whether animate or inanimate. Once its function has been accomplished, it disappears. What that actually means is difficult to say. Does its life form change or does it terminate? God only knows!

Once Daniel was revived and given the sensibility to understand what he was seeing, the seraph Gabriel dictated an oracle that was to span some six hundred years into the future and contain more detail than Ezekiel's seventh oracle. Many historians regard Daniel 11 and 12 as history written in oracular style because of its accuracy. This, at first, appears plausible until one realizes the oracle is measurable, and the long-range flourishes at the end couldn't possibly have been oracular history written as it happened.

When the Ptolemaic pharoahs came on the scene, they sponsored the translation of the Hebrew/Aramaic Bible into Greek for the Jews in Alexandria and abroad. This translation is called the Septuagint. It represents a legal milestone enabling the oracles in the Old Testament to be measured. We now have a tool to confirm Daniel 10-12 is a genuine oracle with all the classical features.

> There shall rise in Persia
> Three more kings
> The fourth King will amass
> much more wealth than
> his predecessors
> When he becomes mighty
> because of his treasure
> He shall set his eye on
> the Kingdom of Greece.

This fourth king is Xerxes[175] (486-465 BC), the son of Darius Hystaspes and his queen Attosa, the daughter of Cyrus the Great. Xerxes was born

---

174. Numbers 21:8-9; John 3:14.
175. Xerxes means "warrior."

after Darius had made his older brother king. Persian law stated no king could go to war without a designated successor. In this case Darius decided to follow Spartan custom and made Xerxes his successor instead of his oldest brother.[176]

However, Egypt revolted in 487 BC while preparations for the expedition to Greece were underway. Darius Hystaspes died the following year, and Xerxes decided on an expedition to Egypt first. He put down the revolt in 485 BC and gave the governance of the Nile kingdom to his brother Achaemenes.

Mardonius, the cousin of Xerxes, persuaded the great king to mount an expedition to Greece in the wake of the Egyptian success. Mardonius entertained hopes of becoming satrap in Europe. Herodotus gives us a fairly detailed account of this expedition from beginning to end.[177] How the native of Halicarnassus came about some of his information is somewhat curious. He was born some four years before the invasion of Greece by Xerxes. (ca. 484-425 BC) His *History* received a monetary award from the Athenians in 445 BC, and he was a member of the Periclean society. Herodotus was a friend of Sophocles and knew Thucydides, who authored the *History of the Peloponnesian War*. He lived among those who were able to recall the events they lived through, and there were probably documents he or others had access to. Plutarch's *Lives* also contain accounts of the invasion as it featured in the lives of Themistocles and Aristides, but Herodotus gave it the most comprehensive treatment. Also important to the invasion and our understanding of the political manipulations at court is the biblical book of Esther.

The meeting that took place between the council of Persian nobility and the king is the most curious aspect of Herodotus's account.[178] Xerxes announced his intention to conquer Greece and punish the Athenians. Once mainland Greece had been subdued and Athens burned, his force would extend its conquest to the Peloponnesus. Mardonius, the great king's cousin, spoke first and supported the war. But Artabanus, the uncle of Xerxes and son of Hystaspes, broke the silence of consent among the others and opposed the expedition. Artabanus reminded the king of past follies, adding that the element of the unknown can undo the most carefully laid plans. By contrast the most foolish of plans could succeed by mere luck. Artabanus

---

176. Herodotus 7:3.
177. Herodotus 7:8-9:106.
178. How did Herodotus become privy to what follows? Although the Persians cowed the Greeks into submission, it would appear the word "conquest" meant only that. It would have been a campaign intended to bend the Greek world to the Persian will without actually occupying Greek lands.

counseled that the great king should not elevate his pride to the point of insolence, making him a target of divine retribution. The Greeks may have been perfidious, but they were good fighters when the need arose.

Xerxes was determined to proceed, however. Still, his uncle's words followed him, leading to doubts about the enterprise. That night, he saw in a vision a tall, good-looking man who spoke over him. "Have you changed your mind, Persian? Will you not lead your host against the Greeks, after gathering together your levies? There is not one among you who will approve of your conduct. What you have decided during the day should be followed." The following day he assembled his council, announcing his change of mind and apologizing to his uncle for his impetuosity. His council cheerfully welcomed his change of mind.

Then that evening, the same vision appeared, threatening the king with swift humiliation unless he took the planned expedition forward. Frightened, the king called in his uncle Artabanus and related his vision to him. The brother of Darius repudiated the dream, but that night he also experienced the vision and heard the threats to himself. Artabanus immediately changed his mind and decided to support the expedition to Greece. The council was convened a third time, and it was agreed the invasion would go ahead as planned.

That night, Xerxes had a third vision wherein he saw himself wearing a crown of olive branches which spread out to cover the whole earth. While he was watching, the olive garland suddenly vanished. The magi interpreted the dream favorably and the preparations for the war went ahead to completion.

These, then, were the influences that launched a massive invasion of Europe along the Persian royal road to Sardis in Asia Minor.

One of Xerxes's main concerns was keeping Egypt inside its borders. Once the Persian host had crossed into Greece, the Egyptians could mount a revolt against the great king and link up with the Babylonians and the Ionian Greeks to his rear. Together with the Spartans and Athenians, this possible coalition could cause considerable difficulty for Xerxes and his huge force. Consequently, the Persian fleet included the Egyptian and Phoenician navies that numbered two hundred and three hundred respectively. It also required a marriage alliance with one of the provinces in Palestine in order to provide a trustworthy buffer state to blockade an Egyptian land army and keep the east coast of the Mediterranean open to the great king's expedition.

Judea owed much to the crown. Darius Hystaspes had ordered the decree of Cyrus the Great to be honored with no interference from anyone.

This enabled the temple to be completed and the city of Jerusalem to be rebuilt. David's city was no longer the threat it once was. The Jewish religion that had emerged from exile in post-Babylonian Palestine was now monotheistic. Darius Hystaspes had made Zoroastrianism the official religion of the Persian court, which was also monotheistic. Ahura Mazda was the supreme deity, and the new religion was non-idolatrous and built no temples. Only fire was sacred to them. This religious compatibility and the location of Judea near the Mediterranean, with access from two main roads, made the Jews an ideal choice for a defensive barrier to internal troubles.

Xerxes held an empire-wide beauty contest so he could choose the Jewish candidate. Esther, or Hadassah, became his new queen between the third and fifth year of his rule. With the alliance between Moses and Zoroaster complete, the military campaign to Greece could move on.

In 482 BC, the Babylonians rose in revolt for the last time. The Persian general Megabyzus was dispatched to put down the insurrection. In a few months, the city of Babylon was recaptured and its great idol Marduk destroyed, along with the Esaglia, the great ziggurat, and other temples. The city's walls and fortifications were torn down and its estates confiscated and given to Persians. The title "King of Babylon" was struck from the royal titulary. Babylon and Babylonia never recovered from Xerxes's punitive actions. Both gradually declined. By 480 BC, the only Persian concern was the Egyptians. By revolting when they did, the Babylonians actually helped the Greek expedition go forward with more confidence.

With news that a huge Persian force was moving over land to the Hellespont, accompanied by a fleet of some twelve hundred vessels, the Greeks were forced to settle their differences in the late spring of 480 BC. A general alliance was formed by Sparta, which headed the Greek congress. This was an alliance of thirty states, each having a single vote. The alliance had the power to send and receive embassies and the power to recruit. Judicial proceedings could be launched against anyone for any infraction. It was decided the Spartans would command the land forces and the Athenians the navy. The slow movement of the Persians gave the Greeks more preparation time.

En route, Xerxes and his Magian priests observed an eclipse of the sun. The Magi appeased the king by telling him Apollo had been eclipsed by the Persian moon. This positive omen encouraged the king to continue his expedition. At Delphi, the Pythian priestess Aristonice was telling the Greeks who inquired of her,

Fools! What are you doing here!
Leave your dwellings
And fly away from here
The heights of your cities won't save you.

Though she plies her
cunning tongue with
an army of clever words
Then shall freedom arise
For Greece on the eastern horizon
Brought on by far-seeing
Zeus and noble victory.

It was far-seeing Themistocles who urged the Athenian democratic council to build ships to war against Aegina, contributing to their struggle with Persian might. Although Athens sent envoys to Gelon of Syracuse in Sicily, he could not come to their rescue because his country was being invaded by Hamilcar from Carthage. Persian diplomacy and gold had a long reach.

The slow progress of Xerxes's forces from Sardis contributed to saving the southern Greeks. The pass at Thermopylae wasn't forced until August, and Athens was burned in September. The campaigning season was nearing an end. The Greeks had profited as well by Xerxes's choice of advisors. The exiled Spartan king Demaratus had counseled the great king well, but Xerxes instead heeded the advice of his courtiers. The Persians settled for a punitive expedition and left Mardonius behind with a sizable rear guard. Returning to Asia via the Hellespont, he beached the transport fleet at Mycale near Samos Island. The good advice of the Pythoness came to fruition when the Athenians crossed the Aegean the following year and destroyed the abandoned transport ships at Mycale.

Are the oracles of Apollo from Delphi and Bacis genuine? There is actually no way to determine one way or the other. The oracle of Bacis of Euboea appeared to come closer to the mark, as this example indicates: "When a man not speaking Greek throws his papyrus yoke on the sea / Don't forget to move your goats from Euboea."

This fit the description of the Hellespont bridges, but it assumed the Persian host would occupy the island of Euboea as they did prior to the fight at Marathon. This never happened. The bleaters were better off at home.

The oracle of Apollo at Delphi appeared to give the Lacedaemonians some good advice when it said,

Hear now your fate you dwellers of Sparta's spaces;
Will your glorious city be razed to the ground by Perseus'
sons?
Perhaps that will not happen.

Yet those inside the borders of Lacedaemon did actually escape. If we postulate Salamis as a victory for the Athenians, then we must also accept the outcome at Actium as a great victory for Cleopatra and Antony. The escape at Dunkirk by British troops would mean a great defeat for Germany in World War II. Of course such is not possible. We can't have it both ways. It's one or the other. In the same way the German resistance to the allied invasion of France on June 6, 1944, produced an occasional victory for Hitler's troops, such as "Operation Goodwood." However, those occasional victories did not translate into winning the war. Our ancient historians and those who love them want to defy that obvious logic and believe the opposite.

Xerxes never intended to conquer Greece. He only intended to punish the Athenians. In her speech to the Persian king in the immediate aftermath of Salamis, Queen Artemesia's words (as crafted by Herodotus) make this point clear.[179] Since Athens was now in flames, the great king's promise to his father Darius was now accomplished. There was no need to stay any longer. Since Mardonius was the one to suggest remaining to conquer Greece, let him stay and cover the Persian withdrawal. Perhaps he will be killed fulfilling that task and suffer the king's punishment at the hands of the Greeks.

But Xerxes had a much larger aim. He also punished the Greek world for not reining in the Athenians themselves. In the wake of Salamis, the Athenians did not teach themselves humility, indulging in defiant behavior after joining the Delian League. But the Spartans were watching. They had learned the Persian lesson. With the help of Persian money, they finished the task Persepolis started.

The use of ambiguous language can say much about an oracle. At first the reader is puzzled, and it may sound like nonsense. In the end, a proposed oracle may simply emerge as a collection of ambiguous nonsense. The oracles of Apollo at Delphi and Bacis at Euboea give us two different sounds. The oracle of Euboean Bacis uses ambiguity in a more positive way, revealing its clever meaning at the right time when ambiguity becomes recognizable fact. The Delphic oracles are reasonably clear but are decidedly tainted with uncertainty.

---

179. Herodotus Bk 8; 100-103.

They came closer to human prediction than divine. Most of its prediction is advice more than prophecy. Herodotus relates another source of prophecy from the oracles of Battus.[180] These pronouncements appeared to work in the short term but reduce to typical human advice. Over the longer term, they failed as oracles. Such assessments must be qualified by the recognition that ambiguity understood by one generation can be completely lost to successive ones.

The defeat of a small Persian rearguard force at Plataea and the destruction of their abandoned transport fleet at Mycale ended the Achaemenid punitive expedition in the Greek world. Xerxes remained at court in the new capital of Persepolis, falling victim to palace intrigues.

About 474 BC, the Jews became involved in a confrontation between two court officials: Mordecai, the uncle of the new queen Esther, and a man of higher rank, Haman ben Hammedatha, an Amalekite hated by the Israelites. It was an age-old ethnic enmity, and Mordecai refused to obey the king's command to give obeisance to Haman. The curse of Moses followed Israel into the new era. Judea and its minimal restoration in the Near East was only a symbol of something greater that would transcend the material theocracy. Judea in the post-exilic period had fallen victim to old habits. New Israel was yet unborn.

The reign of Artaxerxes was a period of consolidation for the Achaemenids. The "Great Warrior" signed a treaty conceding the loss of his western territories to the Greeks and agreeing to stay out of the Aegean. Under Darius II Ochus (423-404 BC), the temple at Jerusalem continued construction until it was completed in the sixth year of his reign (417 BC).

Ochus also found himself in a unique position to settle the outcome of the Peloponnesian war. Although weak by land, the Athenians were strong at sea. The Spartans had devastated Attica, but the Athenians could be resupplied by their ships as they held out behind the fortifications protecting the city and their connected harbor at Piraeus. The war settled into a stalemate. In his enviable position, Ochus decided to continue the punishment of the Athenians begun by Xerxes. The great king agreed to an alliance with Sparta when he learned Pissutheres, his satrap at Sardis, had revolted with the help of Athenian mercenaries in 413 BC. Tissaphernes bribed the slay-for-pay army to withdraw, isolating the rebel satrap. However, the Athenian mercenaries added insult to injury by backing the son of Pissutheres in Caria.

---

180. Herodotus 4:157, 159, 201-205.

In Persia, the son of Ochus and the queen Parysatis, Arsaces, ran afoul of his mother when he protected his wife Stateira from a purge that overwhelmed her family. Parysatis decided to supplant Arsaces with her younger son Cyrus. At age sixteen, the queen had Cyrus made satrap of Cappadocia, Lydia, and Phrygia, where the western armies were mustered from Castolus. He was the one who delivered Persian gold to the Lacedaemonians for their fleet against the Athenians. This tipped the balance of the Peloponnesian war against Athens. In 405 BC, the new Spartan fleet destroyed the pride of Athenian power at Aegospotami and closed the Hellespont. Attica's supply lines were cut, and the following year they could no longer resist the Lacedaemonian stranglehold. Ochus died in the same year, yielding the Persian throne to Arsaces, who was crowned Artaxerxes II Memnon (404-358 BC)

In 401 BC, Cyrus marched his troops from Anatolia into Babylonia to contest the throne. At Cunaxa, near Babylon, he engaged his brother's troops in battle. Clearchus's Greek mercenaries defeated Artaxerxes's troops on their right flank, exposing the great king to attack. Cyrus took advantage of this opening and led an assault on the king's position, wounding his brother. But Cyrus was killed in the attempt, and his revolt instantly collapsed. Artaxerxes had the commanders of the Greek soldiers executed. Then he left, leaving the mercenaries at Babylon.

This began the epic *anabasis* of the heroic "Ten Thousand," recorded for fame by the historian Xenophon. With winter approaching and on the losing side of a rebellion deep in hostile territory, they elected new leaders, who marched them north into Armenia. They fought their way to the town of Trapezus on the Black Sea, arriving in the spring of 400 BC. This event was to have a significant impact on the thinking of other Greeks. The Egyptians and Persians were well aware that Greek mercenaries were the best fighters in the eastern Mediterranean world, particularly the Spartans. They were led by good officers and well armed. Their leaders understood the business of war. Yet they were always a hard-fighting contingent in foreign armies fighting for the causes of others. It would take a young Macedonian prince and his father who was a military genius to fully realize the potential of the legendary Ten Thousand.[181]

The reign of Artaxerxes II Memnon finally completed the long task begun by Darius Hystaspes and his son Xerxes. The revolt of Egypt since 404 BC would not allow the Persians to mount a major expedition to Greece as in former times. Once Greece had been reduced to one dominant

---

181. See "Artaxerxes" in Plutarch's Lives.

state, Persia could concentrate its efforts on reducing the Lacedaemonians to the same status as Athens.

In 394 BC, the Spartan fleet was destroyed near Cnidus, yielding the sea to Persia. Egypt saw what was coming. A garrison was located on the island of Cythera directly south of the Peloponnese. Athens saw this defeat as an opportunity to revive the old Delian League and made alliance with Egypt, the Greek cities of Asia Minor, and Eragaras. However, Antalcidas went to Susa and concluded the "kings peace" with Sparta in 388 BC. In 386 BC, Athens was also compelled to sign the same document, now known as the Peace of Antalcidas. Two campaigns against Egypt failed in 385-83 and 373 BC, giving rise to revolt in Asia Minor. Although some of the territories were recovered by treachery, others remained independent.

The reign of Artaxerxes II Memnon saw religious changes among the Persians. Artaxerxes II Memnon was the first Persian monarch since Darius Hystaspes to reintroduce idolatry and other deities. His own personal deity was Hera, the wife of Zeus according to Plutarch. This can explain his relationship with Parysatis, his mother.

Two other deities rise to prominence during his reign: Anahita and Mithras. The god Mithras was similar to Apollo and was the champion of Ahura Mazda. Mithras had a long life and survived into Roman times, becoming a deity popular with Rome's soldiers. Indeed, one can see the armaments of the later Roman empire in the east among the Byzantines who, like Mithras, were armed to the teeth.

The account of Nehemiah begins in the year 484 BC or thereabouts, some two years after the Peace of Antalcidas was effected in Greece. Egypt had revolted at the beginning of Memnon's reign and was still independent. It wasn't until 345 BC that Memnon's son and successor, Artaxerxes III Ochus, mounted a massive force by land and sea from Babylon into Egypt, sending Nectanebo into early retirement.

Nectanebo was the last of the native Egyptian pharoahs to rule the Nile kingdom. What part Egypt or the war with Greece played in creating the perception of little Judea as a threat is not given. However, the city and temple gates were torn down and burned, and part of the protective wall was taken down. Nehemiah asked his brother Hanani about "the Jews that survived, those who had escaped captivity and about Jerusalem?" His brother, along with his traveling companions, tell him the "survivors are in great trouble and shame." Obviously things were not very good in post-exilic Israel. Although Nehemiah labored to give the impression that the hand of God was actively moving events on a much lower level, it falls to the ground when historians tell us Artaxerxes II Memnon was generous to a fault in granting privileges and gifts to his loyal servants.[182]

The Jews in post-exilic Judea were staunch believers in Yahweh. The voice of Moses had proved a powerful instrument when the curse fell on Israel under the Assyrians and on Judah at the hands of Babylon and Egypt. As a result, the prophets who predicted the exile along with Moses proved to be servants of Yahweh, and Yahweh had proved to be a deity of his word. Baal and Asherah paled into insignificance. Idolatry and paganism had been sufficiently repudiated among the Jews restored to Judea. Consequently, the name Yahweh, meaning "the one who proves to be," gradually went out of use. It was replaced by the Most High, God, or the Lord. The book of Daniel and the seraphs he spoke with never used the name Yahweh. In fact, the Apollo of God only used the name Yahweh in the first six oracles of Ezekiel. From the seventh oracle on, it is never used. Modern scholars and theologians who say the name Yahweh went out of use because of superstition make an error. It went out of use because it no longer applied.

Although the name of God had risen to a higher meaning among the religious, the kingdom of Judea in Palestine did not adequately represent the newly acquired glory of their deity. In fact, the earthly kingdom had become a shell of its former self. The glorious temple of Yahweh built by Solomon had been built in a few short years, whereas the second temple, started by decree of Cyrus, wasn't completed until the reign of Darius II. The provincial boundaries of Judea were tiny by comparison to pre-exilic times. To the major powers of the eastern Mediterranean, Jerusalem was insignificant. It was nothing more than a tourist curiosity. The monotheism of the Jews had largely been protected by the monotheistic religion of the royal family. But now under Artaxerxes II Memnon and his successors, the cosmos was changing. The roof of heaven had new tenants.

Paganism was advancing a new challenge to religion-Greek philosophy. The wisdom and precepts of men and science vied with old, anthropomorphic notions. The cleansing of Israel of its idolatrous practices was timely indeed. It was now prepared to engage the new influences without the burden of excess baggage. Yet there was no escaping the realization among Jews, whether in or out of Judea, that the blessing they had expected to inherit was not matching expectations. It would be a fair assumption to advance that many Jews who remained in the exiled territories had already concluded there was in fact no blessing to be had in post-exilic Judea.

---

182. See "Artaxerxes" in Plutarch's Lives.

The empire of Persia reached its largest extent under Artaxerxes III Ochus. Egypt and Asia Minor had been restored. Greece was not a truly conquered land in the sense of other Persian territories, but Persepolis was the sole arbiter of Greek affairs if it chose to be.

In 356 BC, Ochus determined Persia would produce its army from local levies, and all satraps were ordered to dismiss their mercenaries. Most complied, but Artabazus, the satrap of Phrygia, did not. When his Greek mercenaries were defeated by Ochus's forces, he was forced to flee for his life. The Macedonian court at Pella granted him asylum. Philip II (359-336 BC) was some three years into his rulership, and the presence of Artabazus at his court must have created some excitement in the old Persian satrapy. Macedonia was an autonomous kingdom at this time and supplied Persia with silver for some of its coinage. Under Philip II, Macedonia began to show its wealth and power flowing from the king's peace of 388-386 BC.

"Another beast appeared, a second one, in appearance like
a bear.
It was raised up on one side."

This bear-like beast was the Greek world, rising up on the Macedonian side. The three tusks in its mouth were the members of the Corinthian League, which included the Greeks of Asia Minor. The Corinthian League was given the injunction, "Arise, devour much flesh!" Philip acted on that directive by invading Persian territory in Asia Minor. This excursion by his father on behalf of the Asian Greeks and the legend of the Ten Thousand inspired the young Alexander to obey the injunction. He and the Corinthian League did exactly that. His historical conquest of Persia is well known.

The year 324 BC was a difficult one for the Macedonian god-king. The inclusion and recruitment of Orientals into the military and administration was offensive to the Greeks and Macedonians, who saw their privilege begin to slip away. The soil of ambition was now sprinkled with the seed of resentment. He had also planned to replace Antipater with Craterus in Macedon. In the autumn months, his long-time companion and lover Hephaestion died, causing him considerable grief. Afterward he began to demand recognition of his divine status from all his subjects. The Orientals prostrated themselves, but his Greek and Macedonian veterans refused.

Claiming divine status did not have the same impact on the Greeks that it had on the Orientals. To the latter, it meant godhead and absolute power. Alexander was the sun king and sole arbiter of good and evil in the world. His life did not end at death. To the Hellenes, a divinity was a genius of insight and knowledge—a great knower. However, in a democracy, it gave no special rights.

Alexander departed the human sphere as one would not expect of a god-king. After a ten-day banquet, Alexander fell ill. After lingering for a time, he sensed his own mortality and, removing his royal signet ring, handed it to his senior commander Perdiccas with the words, "To the strongest." Thus did Alexander Amen pass from life to legend on June 13, 323 BC.

9

North and South

As I continued to watch a beast appeared like a leopard.
It had four heads and four great wings on its back.

Antipater in Greece and Macedonia claimed his right to rule by Alexander himself. Since Perdiccas had received the ruling signet from the dying king, Antipater used a Macedonian tradition to make his claim. Ptolemy also used an old Macedonian tradition: the one who buries the king succeeds him. He confiscated Alexander's funeral cortége and took the remains to Alexandria in Egypt. There, Alexander's body was openly displayed.[183] After laying down their markers, the three chose Lysimachus to rule Thrace. This important land bridge was rich in silver and gave Lysimachus enough wealth to defend his territory, but not enough to threaten any of the others. The Thracian king knew this and did what was expected of him.

In Egypt, Ptolemy eliminated Cleomenes as satrap and claimed the succession from the last native pharoah Nectanebo through Alexander, becoming the first Greek pharoah of the new Lagid dynasty.

There wasn't much to argue about in Greece and Macedonia. Antipater was fully ensconced in his power there. He also sat on the supply of Macedonian military recruits, who were highly prized among the other territories. They were the best fighters in the eastern Mediterranean at that time. Macedonia was also well endowed with a silver supply.

Perdiccas remained in Babylon, where he controlled Mesopotamia, old Assyria, and the eastern satrapies. His kingdom was the largest of all. The others instinctively knew that one day Perdiccas, or whoever succeeded him, would want to reunite Alexander's empire as he had left it. This would take

183. See "Cimon" in Plutarch's Lives (last five paragraphs),

some time, of course, as each man had consolidated his grip on power. But it would surely come.

Asia Minor was initially divided between Eumenes and Antigonus the One-Eyed. Alexander's natural son by Queen Roxane, Alexander IV, and Phillip Arrhidaios were held at Babylon.

By 320 BC, Perdiccas decided he was in a position to reunite the empire and began by invading Egypt. When his march reached the Nile, Perdiccas was assassinated. The remaining Diadochi[184] met at Triparadeios in Syria to repartition the empire. In Macedonia and Greece, Antipater was confirmed, as were Lysimachus in Thrace and Ptolemy in Egypt. Antigonus the One-Eyed took over Asia, and Seleucus Nicator was installed in the eastern satrapies at Babylon.

The next nineteen years of relative peace helped each ruler to consolidate his hold in each domain. Philip III Arrhidaios and his wife Eurydice were both murdered at Olympia's direction to secure Alexander IV as the rightful heir to the empire. However, she and the young heir were also murdered in 310 BC to prevent another contest. In Macedonia and Greece, Antipater died, leaving the throne to his son Cassander. With the progeny of the legendary warrior dead, Antigonus the One-Eyed decided he would be the one to reunite the empire and launch a new dynasty through his son Demetrius Poliorcetes. Antigonus opened hostilities by accusing Seleucus Nicator of treachery and marching on Babylon. Seleucus fled to Ptolemy at Alexandria.

> In my visions I now saw four chariots coming forward
> between two bronze-coloured mountains.
> The first chariot was drawn by red coloured horses.
> Then black horses followed by white ones.
> The fourth chariot was harnessed to dappled-greys.

A coalition was developed between the other three power blocks against the One-Eyed. In 301 BC, at Ipsus in Phrygia, Lysimachus, Cassander, and Seleucus Nicator, who had recovered Babylon with Ptolemy's help, now clashed with the One-Eyed's alliance with Poliorcetes and defeated them. Antigonus died in the fighting and his son Demetrius fled. Seleucus Nicator had successfully introduced the war elephant from India, which was a determining factor in the battle's outcome.

The two bronze or copper mountains represented east and west, Asia and Europe. Antigonus the One-Eyed and his co-regent son and successor

---

184. Diadochi means "successors."

Demetrius were in the middle, drawn by the horses of war. Seleucus Nicator became ruler in Asia while the other three remained as they were. The location of the black horses was moved eastward over the next twenty years by invaders from the north. The red horses would not be a factor any longer.

For a time Alexandria enjoyed hegemonic influence in the eastern Mediterranean world. The best intellects of the day journeyed to the new court there to seek the pharoah's favor. Many achieved it. Science, art, literature, mathematics, and politics all flourished in Alexander's city. The new Lagids managed to secure their dynasty by more perfectly aligning the earth's seasonal cycles with the will of heaven. By adding one extra day every four years, the Ptolemys created the leap year. Surely the gods were impressed now that heaven and earth had been perfected.

In later years, Julius Caesar imposed this Ptolemaic innovation on the world, calling it the Julian calendar. His relationship with Cleopatra and the calendar change were clearly designed to cast him as an Egypto-Roman god-king in the Hellenistic style. As Cleopatra saw it, her kingdom would become the richest and most powerful expansionist power the civilized world had ever known. Julius Caesar would be its king and she would be its queen. Their son Caesarion would succeed them. The new reform was not lost on Caesar's enemies.

> The chariot pulled by black horses journeys northward
> The white horses go behind the sea and the dappled-greys
> move southward.

In February 281 BC, Lysimachus was defeated and killed at Corupedium and Thrace fell to Ptolemy Keraunos. Clearly Alexandria had its own designs on reunification. Unfortunately, it was cheated of its prize when the Thracian domain was invaded by a massive hoard of Gauls from the north.

The same fate had befallen the Romans in 299 BC. The Samnites and Etruscans had allied themselves with the Gallic invaders against the Romans. The Umbrians and Sabines also took the field against the "Quirites," threatening the very existence of ancient Pallanteum. In 295 BC, the Romans defeated a combined army of Gauls and Samnites at Sentinum in Umbria. The war for Rome's survival ended in 290 BC. The Sabine territory east of Rome was annexed to the Roman state while the Samnites remained sovereign, entering into an alliance with Rome. The Gauls withdrew and went elsewhere.

Keraunos and his military were destroyed by the Gauls, reducing the Hellenistic kingdoms to three. Gradually Thrace was reclaimed and absorbed into the Greco-Macedonian kingdom while the black horses went to the north country. The Greco-Macedonian kingdom in the west "behind the sea" had been taken over by the successors of Demetrius Poliorcetes and came to be known as the dynastic Antigonids. The Seleucids at Babylon had moved their capital to Antioch on the Orontes River in Syria, becoming the "black horses" of Zechariah's oracle in the first six chapters. The Lagids had ensconced themselves at Alexandria.

The next verses were to prove extremely important to our understanding of how the movements of empirical power changed and who became who in relation to Zechariah's oracle and the supplemental oracle in Daniel 9:24 through 12:13. Zechariah 1 through 6 are also supplemental to the Apollo of God.

The old pharaoh who opened up the ancient solar calendar of 360 days and added five additional days proved to every Egyptian every year that he had performed the will of heaven. No one in Egypt was willing to dispute his claim to divine right. The orderliness of the seasons had been aligned by his command. The Ptolemies had done the same thing, but it was not that readily noticed. The prior action had ensconced pharaonic power for millennia while the Greek pharaohs lasted a mere three hundred years. Although they had performed the will of heaven, their claim to divinity was considerably diminished in quality.

> Then he cried out to me, 'Lo those who go toward the north
> country have set my spirit at rest in the north country.'

Keep this last verse near the front of memory. As we apply it to the unfolding of history into modern times, we will see it's power unfold. This last verse proves to be the most powerful in Zechariah's oracle. It is these later verses in the supplemental oracles that produce a long-range flourish that can be adequately measured to produce authenticity.

From Zechariah chapter six, we move directly to the last prophecy of Daniel (chapters 10-12). Many historians accept the accuracy of this oracle but believe it is history written in oracular style. As stated above, a genuine oracle always ends its life as recorded history. However, we can reasonably establish a fixed point near the end of the oracle, after which an oracular flourish extends well beyond the first century CE. This is also true of the seventh oracle of Ezekiel in the book of Daniel, chapter seven. The fixed point begins after verse seven. Verses eight through twenty-seven are all in the future. This legal milestone is established by the mid-first century CE.

The oracle of the king of the north and the king of the south documents the struggle between Antioch of the Seleucids and Alexandria of the Lagids. The main issue of contention was over Coele-Syria, meaning "Hollow Syria." It was located across the Lebanon and anti-Lebanon range between the sources of the Leontes River flowing south and the Orontes River flowing north. The city of Heliopolis was located on this high ground.

The struggle began with marriage alliances. Ptolemy married his daughter Arsinoë to Lysimachus in Thrace as a diplomatic flank attack on the Asian center. Old Seleucus Nicator countered this move by a marriage alliance with Demetrius in Greco-Macedon, taking his daughter named Stratonice to wife. Ptolemy found his diplomatic flank outflanked. The destruction of Thrace by the Gauls eliminated Ptolemy's advantage, and the absorption of Thrace into Greco-Macedon gave Seleucid Asia a strong right wing in the diplomatic position. This was also the style of the Seleucid military. Like Alexander III at Gaugamela, the Seleucid formations always positioned their strongest fighters on their right wing. This forced the enemy to place its strength on its left flank in order to defend the Seleucid attack adequately. The center was always occupied by the phalanx in the "open" or "closed" position. The Seleucid left was constructed to have weaker elements. This could be true or a deception.

In the west, the Romans helped the city of Thurii against the Luccinians north of them. To approach the city, they sailed their ships into Tarentine waters, violating old agreements between Rome and Tarentum. Suspicions gave way to actions when the Tarentines appealed to Pyrrhus, the king of Epirus across the Adriatic. Pyrrhus responded by landing a force of twenty-five thousand soldiers and twenty elephants. Roman forces were defeated at Heraclea in 280 BC located midway between Thurii and Tarentum on the coast. They were no match for the Macedonian phalanx and the skillful use of elephants. Cavalry was useless unless they were mounted on horses especially trained to operate near elephants. These animals required considerable time and expense to produce.

The following year, both forces clashed at Ausculum in Apulia farther to the north, and the Romans were wasted in the fight. But they were not defeated badly enough to accept Pyrrhus's offers of peace. Instead they applied to Carthage for an alliance and used the Carthaginian fleet to their advantage. Returning from Sicily, Pyrrhus once again engaged the Romans at Malventum[185] in 275 BC near Capua. Here took place the battle that

---

185. Later named Beneventum.

made his name a byword. Although he defeated the Romans, it cost him his army. Thus the term "Pyrrhic victory." Unable to continue, he sailed back to Epirus. His garrison at Tarentum surrendered in 272 BC.

The Hellenic kingdoms took note of this struggle in the west between Greek and Roman. Hycophrous's "Alexandria" treated Rome as a new, rising power in the western Mediterranean, and the poet Callimachus extolled Roman virtues. The historian Timaeus wrote a history of the war. The Ptolemies also took note of Rome and exchanged ambassadors with the city. This placed a new power on the diplomatic flank of Greco-Macedon and Seleucid Asia. Rome and Carthage were on friendly terms giving added value to the new alliance. Once these five main power blocks had settled into their respective positions relative to one another, the pursuit of their own self-interests would discover where the weaknesses lay in each. Who would prove the strongest?

> Then I saw a fourth beast appear with great and frightening strength.
> It had ten horns and was different from its predecessors.
> With sharp iron teeth it devoured and broke its enemies to pieces.
> It smashed what was left with its feet.

Rome's involvement with Italy in the south and its diplomacy in 273 BC with Ptolemy II brought Aeneas's city into the politics of Mediterranean trade. Sea commerce was to have a similar impact as the eastern caravan trade had in the Near East. In fact the two were coming closer together. The Mediterranean was like a huge shopping mall that inspired as much interest from the Arab traders and Philistine merchants as it did among the local businesspeople from one end of the sea to the other. Until this time, the Romans had been farmers with little involvement in trans-Mediterranean trade. But now they began to see its potential.

By far the most desirable luxury goods came from the east. Arab traders still had that monopoly. The North Arabian desert was like an enormous fortress wall protecting them. Only the Neo-Babylonian power and its geographic location proved to be in a position to exert any meaningful control on the Arabs' exclusive trade. It was Neo-Babylonia's last monarch, Nabonidus, who made that hidden fact a reality when he marched into the desert with his troops, capturing the oasis town of Tema. However, Babylon's control lasted a mere ten years before its grip was broken.

The Arab traders were still a power to be reckoned with. In 270 BC, their caravans still made the age-old journey through southern Palestine, and Egypt was their policeman. But their trade route into the eastern Mediterranean could shift northward if they wished, making the Seleucids rich instead.

In the years to come, it became obvious to any astute observer that someone had to police the Mediterranean. There was room for just one. Too many fingers in the honey pot left too little at the bottom. However, the lesson taught by the reign of Nabonidus suggested the Arab traders could not trust the Seleucids in Asia. Of all the powers in the Mediterranean world, they could ultimately control the caravan trade from Mesopotamia westward. Egypt was still the better constable.

In 270 BC, the king of the south was the strongest in the Mediterranean. Favored by the Arab traders, it was dominant in cultural influence and wealth and continued to possess the intrigue Egypt had long been famous for. On her left flank were the other traders of influence who limited the western Mediterranean to the city of Carthage and its ancient ties to Tyre. Italy to the northwest was coming under Roman domination and threatened the power in the Greek mainland. The Seleucid king of the north did not have in place the royal system he needed to manage its huge geographic territory. A dual monarchy was required to manage the eastern satrapies of Babylon and Asia Minor from Antioch. Its alliance with Greco-Macedon on its right flank had already sustained an inconclusive trial with the Romans. The battle for hegemony in the Mediterranean still belonged to the Egyptian Greeks.

A disturbance on Egypt's left flank came about in 264 BC when Rome went to war with Carthage over control of the Sicilian straits. The first Punic war (264-241 BC) saw a new sea power emerge in the western Mediterranean. Roman ships defeated the experienced Carthaginian navy off Mylae in 260 BC. Here was another surprise to the Hellenistic east. The attack on Carthage by land failed, but another naval victory off the Aegates Islands and the loss of Carthaginian sea power in the western Mediterranean forced the government in Carthage to capitulate to terms. They agreed to quit Sicily and pay Rome an indemnity.

In the east, the Lagids had concluded a marriage alliance in 253 BC, but the death of Ptolemy Philadelphus and Antiochus Theos in the same year produced two contending parties for the throne at Antioch. Ptolemy Euergetes lost his diplomatic bid to control the Seleucid empire when his sister and her son were murdered and the Third Syrian War, ending in 241 BC, left Seleucus Kallinikos, the grandson of Seleucus Nicator, on the throne.

About the time when Rome was capturing Sardinia, Kallinikos went to war with his younger brother Antiochus Hierax (239-236 BC), In this war of the brothers, Egypt backed Hierax, who was eventually driven out by Kallinikos. In 229 BC, Rome crossed the Adriatic and subjugated the kingdom of Queen Teuta in Illyria, creating a protectorate with liberal terms in order to bring piracy to an end on Italy's east coast. Most Greek states welcomed Rome's intervention, and Corinth admitted them to the Isthmian games. When Philip V of Macedonia came to the throne in 221 BC, he backed the Illyrian protectorate, which violated the treaty with Rome. In 219 BC, Illyria was returned to Roman control just in time, as Hannibal of Carthage had invested Saguntum, taking it after an eight-month siege. This action began the second Punic war (218-210 BC).

In the east, Antiochus III the Great was the Seleucid king from 223 BC. Ptolemy IV Philopater succeeded Euergetes in 221 BC. The next twenty years would be a dark period for the Egyptians and their Roman ally. Antiochus III embarked on the conquest of the Near East, but his efforts unraveled after the defeat at Raphia. Coele-Syria would remain in Ptolemaic hands.

> In those days the king of the south will have many enemies.
> Even the rebels among your own shall attempt to make a
> vision come true. But they will fail. The king of the north
> will invade south and take a strong fortress city
> The army of the south will fail against him.

After the victory at Raphia, Philopater decided to visit Jerusalem and offer sacrifice there. He made the offerings permitted to a Gentile, but then decided to enter the temple sanctuary itself and make sacrifice there also.[186] This caused an uproar in the city, and Philopater, in fear for his life, appears to have experienced an epileptic fit or similar condition during the excitement.[187] Needless to say, this angered Philopater, who turned against the Jews in his kingdom. In Philopater's action, the Jews also saw the fulfillment of a prophecy based on Daniel 7:19 and 8:9-10. However, as the oracle tells us, that was a misinterpretation. Nevertheless, Jewish loyalties turned away from Alexandria and shifted north to Antioch.

More seriously, Egypt was falling into a state of economic anarchy. Substantial revenues had been lost in the southern part of the kingdom and its silver currency was losing its value. Philopater was succeeded by an infant styled Ptolemy V Epiphanes, and his ministers ruled the country. Seeing his advantage, Antiochus III overwhelmed Coele-Syria and captured Sidon

---

186. 3 Maccabees 1:1-15.
187. 2:22-24.

on the coast. He engaged the forces of Epiphanes at Panion, inflicting a devastating defeat on them. Antiochus had in his employ the brilliant Carthaginian general Hannibal, whose armies had been defeated at Zama by the Romans, ending the Second Punic War. But now he had helped the Seleucid king acquire Palestine. This event was not unwelcome to the Jews, who gained easier access to the Babylonian diaspora. However, earlier eschatological aspirations came to an abrupt end. To conclude and consolidate his new gains, Antiochus the Great ratified the treaty with Egypt, giving his daughter Cleopatra in marriage to Ptolemy Epiphanes in 195 BC.

The weakness in the Egyptian center was offset when Rome destroyed the Seleucid right wing by defeating the forces of Philip V at Cynoscephalae in 197 BC. In 193 BC, the Roman commander in Greece, Flaminius, offered Antiochus full control of Asia Minor, including Pergamon, if he stayed in Asia. Antiochus declined. This particular decision proved fatal to Antioch. When the Seleucid king landed at Demetrias to aid the Aetolians in an uprising against Rome, the expected support never materialized as promised. He had been betrayed by his defeated right flank. His small army clashed with Roman legions at Thermopylae, but he managed to withdraw against superior forces of arms. In response, the Achaean League and Rome declared war on the Seleucids while Antiochus contemplated the result of his ally's treachery.

In 189 BC, Rome's legions stood opposite the Seleucid military at Magnesia-by-Sipylos in Asia Minor. The forces of Antiochus were drawn up in the classic Seleucid position. Antiochus's right wing opened the engagement by overwhelming the Roman left and defeating it. However, the Seleucid cavalry left the battlefield to confiscate the Roman baggage and supplies at their camp.

On the Roman right flank, Eumenes II of Pergamon lead a successful assault on the Seleucid left while Lucius Cornelius Scipio and his famous brother Scipio Africanus reorganized their shattered left flank. The Seleucid phalanx in the center was surrounded with no cavalry support and was slaughtered. The king of Syria had snatched defeat from the jaws of victory.

Antiochus paid a large indemnity to Rome. He was allowed a small army to police his kingdom, including ten ships. He was denied recruits from Macedonia and elephants. The Seleucid military had to rely on local levies. His younger son was taken hostage to Rome, and Hannibal the Carthaginian was to be surrendered. These terms were ratified at Apamea in 188 BC. The following year, Antiochus III the Great died. He was killed in Elam while looting a local temple to pay the Roman indemnity.

> Then shall rise in his place one who shall send an official
> for the glory of the kingdom; but within a few days he shall
> be broken, though not in anger or in battle.

This king is Seleucus IV, the son and successor of Antiochus the Great. The official he sent was Heliodorus, who came to confiscate the wealth of Jerusalem to help pay the Roman indemnity still in force. The great renaissance painter Raphael immortalized this event in one of his paintings, "The Expulsion of Heliodorus from the Temple." This work and others are perfect examples of the impact of Jewish religious bombast on western Christendom. Although a beautiful work of art, Raphael's painting nevertheless gives an erroneous impression to the viewer. The actual words of the prophecy were general in content, but the Jews insisted on turning the event into an apparent blessing granted them in the post-exilic world by the mouth of Moses.

The fact was that Seleucus IV ruled a much smaller kingdom in Syria that included Mesopotamia and Palestine. The eastern satrapies and Asia Minor were no more, lost along with their revenues. Yet the high priest Oniass II, the prince of the covenant, had prevented Heliodorus from expropriating the temple treasury, sending the king's official back to Antioch empty-handed. Seleucus was furious over this matter, and fearing for his life, Heliodorus assassinated Seleucus on September 3, 175 BC.

> In his place shall suddenly appear one hated by the
> covenant people.
> His power will be obtained by intrigue.

For twelve years, young Antiochus had been held in comfortable exile in Rome. He was not the person Daniel's oracle spoke about. The conventional wisdom is wrong. Royal majesty was conferred on young Antiochus by Rome. When his older brother died, his return to Antioch was expected. The person spoken of here is the senate of the Republic of Rome, which had abolished monarchy and the majesty that goes with it. Antiochus IV was their creature, and in a sense Rome came with him when he returned to Syria.

Antiochus in a deeper and more spiritual sense prefigured Rome in the centuries ahead. To the prophetic Jewish mind of the day, Rome symbolized the "throne of Satan" in something of a surreal sense. From the second century onward, religion in ancient Rome and around the empire saw more monotheistic elements develop locally. Not only did Christians practice monotheism, but the cult of Sol Invictus and Mithraism, derived from

Persian Zoroastrianism, introduced competing monotheistic forms to the Roman empire. Devotion to philosophy and primitive science was also a type of monotheism for those who rejected anthropomorphism. Just as Antiochus IV tried to impose a polytheistic system on a largely monotheistic society in his day, the Roman emperors attempted to do the same thing in later years. History should have taught them the lesson of Antiochus IV and the consequences that followed. Fortunately for the empire, Constantine the Great understood that lesson.

The Seleucid king Antiochus IV was a pawn in Rome's game of political intrigue. For twelve years in captivity, he came to know the power and might of the Roman system. His rule would be their rule. Rome was fully aware that Judea lay north of the rich caravan trade passing from Petra to Gaza. The Seleucid empire held the eastern satrapies and was Rome's major threat in the east. There was a potential new middleman in the rich caravan trade. The incendiary religious zeal and nationalism of the Jews was a powerful force that could be used to Rome's advantage if handled with clarity of purpose. Idumea had become a substantial part of the equation in southern Palestine, but Jerusalem loathed them. Better that Rome remained in the shadows.

In Jerusalem, the pro-Seleucid party was in the ascendancy because Antiochus III had pursued a generous policy of accommodation with the Jews. This also sent a positive signal to the Arab traders. The "prince of the covenant," the high priest Simon II the Just, had rebuilt the ruined city of Jerusalem with early Seleucid generosity. However, the temple treasury in time had fallen under the control of wealthy Jewish financiers. Joseph ben Tobiah had become the *prostatēs* or tax collector of Ptolemy Euergetes in his Syrian territory. In prior years the Tobiads had extended their control in Palestine, and during the reign of Antiochus Epiphanes their control included the temple's s and the office of the high priest itself. The high priest was also the governor of Judea.

On Simon the Just's death, his son was in line for the office as Onias III but his brother Jason supplanted him by offering Epiphanes more money.[188]. Compelled by the Roman indemnity, Antiochus accepted Jason's offer. In 171 BC, the Seleucid king demanded access to the temple treasury, but Jason actually refused. The pro-Seleucid party turned against Jason and sent a non-Levitical candidate for the high priesthood, a Benjaminite named Menelaus who offered Antiochus 300 talents more for the post. The king accepted. Jason refused to abdicate, causing civil strife. Menelaus did take the office from Jason, and in 170 BC Onias III was assassinated, ending

---

188. Ezekiel 40:46; 44:15-16.

the Zadokian line of high priests and rulers of Judea. Through their creature Antiochus, Rome had "broken the prince of the covenant."

> And after an alliance is made with him, he shall act deceitfully and become strong with a small party.

The second ending begins at verse twenty-nine in chapter eleven and continues through to verse forty-five. The first third of the second ending deals with Antiochus himself (verses 29-35.) The sixth Syrian war against Ptolemy VI Philometer was a great success for the Seleucid king. In the spring of 169 BC, he marched south, capturing Pelusium, destroying Ptolemy's army, and gaining control of Egypt. Philometer was toppled and his brother, Ptolemy VIII Euergetes, replaced him on the throne with Cleopatra II, his sister. With that, Antiochus took the money, raised the siege, and returned home. On the way, he entered Jerusalem, confiscating the city's wealth.

In 168 BC, Antiochus returned to Egypt, but it was not as it was before. An embassy from Rome sailed from Cyprus (Kittim) and ordered Antiochus to quit Egypt. When the Seleucid king hesitated, Popillius Laenas humiliated the Syrian monarch, forcing a withdrawal. In Judea, it had been rumored Antiochus IV was dead, and Jason ben Simon attempted to oust Menelaus from the high priesthood. Jason's success forced Menelaus and his Tobiad supporters to flee to Antiochus's successor. Realizing the king wasn't dead, they persuaded him Jerusalem was under the control of pro-Ptolemaic supporters. On his return to Antioch, the king sacked Jerusalem, slaughtering its population. Entering the temple, he confiscated all its wealth.

In 167 BC, a Mysian officer named Apollonius returned and tore down the city's walls, garrisoning the city with a fortress called the Akra. Temple services were abolished by edict, as was the Sabbath and circumcision. The temple was rededicated to the new "Syro-Phoenician Baal-Shamin," also known as Olympian Zeus to the Greeks. A widespread persecution resulted that led directly to the Maccabean revolt.

The military exploits of Judas Maccabeus are highly exaggerated in the historic accounts, and in some cases the accounts become ridiculous. Judas was not a military genius as some have suggested, only a rebel. His early success was due to his knowledge of the landscape, of which the Seleucids were ignorant. Also the Seleucid government was facing trouble elsewhere in the kingdom, and Judea could wait. This allowed Judas to rededicate the temple to Yahweh on Chislev 25 (December) 164 BC.

Antiochus IV died in 163 BC, while in the east a struggle ensued for the throne at Antioch. Antiochus V Eupator was supplanted by the son of Seleucus IV named Demetrius. The new king sent his military commander Bacchides south to install Alkimos as high priest in Jerusalem and to eradicate Maccabean support. Judas Maccabeus appealed to Rome in 161 BC for a treaty alliance, and the senate sent Demetrius a pro forma warning on Judas's behalf.

The Seleucid government now swung into action to focus on the Judean problem. Demetrius joined Bacchides and, at the head of royal troops, hunted Judas and the rebels down. When the rebels encamped at Elasa heard about it, many of them fled. Judas's cavalry was reduced from 3000 to 800. The number of infantry is not given. The Seleucid army in Judea was the right wing of the royal army, divided between Bacchides and Alcimus. Each had some ten thousand infantry, including archers, and one thousand cavalry. In the Seleucid army the right wing always contained the best troops, forcing the enemy to load their left to counteract its strength. This was their tradition from Alexander the Great, who always fought on the right wing. Judas attacked the Seleucid right, not because he was especially brave, but because he had little choice. The right wing fell back, bringing Judas and the rebels in pursuit. At a given signal, the left wing cavalry came in behind the pursuers. Once Judas was caught in this simple trap, the right wing turned, catching the so-called genius in between and killing all the rebels. To the military professionals of the Seleucid army, killing a military genius must have seemed all too easy.

When Alkimos died, the office of high priest was left vacant until 152 BC. The Seleucid kingdom was going from weakness to weakness. In that year, the brother of Judas Maccabeus, Jonathan, became high priest, inaugurating the Hasmonean dynasty in Jerusalem until 63 BC. In 143/142 BC, Demetrius II Nicator recognized Jewish independence, and Jonathan's brother Simon succeeded him as high priest of an autonomous Judea.

Demetrias's younger brother, Antiochus VII Euergetes Sidetes, was the last of the great Seleucid monarchs. In 131/130 BC, he took Jerusalem while Hyrcanus was priest-king and then marched his troops into Babylonia and conquered Media. In this last great anabasis, he moved from Media against Parthia, ruled by Phraates II Antiochus Sidetes, but was killed in action against Scythian mercenaries in 129 BC. Rapid decline followed his death, and the Seleucid kingdom was eventually confined to Syria.

In Judea at about this time, the "Sons of Light" movement began in the eastern desert among the community of prophets (100 BC-70 CE). By 83 BC, Syria was a political basket case and the disgruntled Antiocheres offered the throne to Tigranes of Armenia, who accepted. Fearing Syria would fall into the hands of the Parthians, Rome undertook to send one of its commanders named Lucullus to the east, engaging his legions with Tigranes, who suffered a decisive defeat. Lucullus resurrected Seleucid rule in 69 BC with Antiochus XIII Asiaticus.

During this period, piracy in the eastern Mediterranean was becoming an empire of its own. From Sicily to Palestine, the pirates were uniting into a coalition able to assemble a navy of some 1,000 ships. In Rome, Aulus Gabinius had proposed a piracy law granting consular imperium for three years. Pompey received the imperium, which gave him a huge force of ships, legions, and cavalry. In three months, piracy had been seriously crippled.

The success of this imperium of Pompey helped pave the way for the Roman emperors. In 66 BC, the "Lex Manilia" granted Pompey extended powers to deal with the Near East. Mithridates, a formidable enemy of Rome, was pushed back into Cappadocia and Pontus. Mithridates finally cured the senate's headache by committing suicide. In 64 BC, Pompey put an end to the Seleucid kings, making Syria a Roman province. In his new role as "king of the north," he marched his army south, taking Judea in 63 BC.

In 11:36-45 we focus on Rome once again. He is the one who exalted himself and considered himself greater than any god. He himself was conquered by the Hellenistic ideals of the Greeks, which were earthly and self-serving. He put his faith in fortresses, turning them into massive stone barricades called castles in the medieval period. His armies adopted the Persian god Mithras as their own, modeling their army in his style in the Byzantine period.

The Egyptians of ancient times regarded themselves as *Rōme* from the word *Pi rōmis* which means "true men." It also approximates the word "gentlemen."

> When the end comes the land of Egypt shall attack the northern King.
> But the King above the sea shall crush them with many ships, horsemen, and a huge army.

This is the war between Octavian the triumvar and Cleopatra of Egypt. The empire of Cleopatra and Antony included Palestine, Syria, Asia Minor, and Greece, which was Antony's jurisdiction under the second triumvirate. Cleopatra simply married it. Marc Antony, her new husband, then parceled it out among her children. Cleopatra ultimately achieved what her ancestor Ptolemy Lagus had desired: the unification of Alexander's old empire. All that remained was Mesopotamia and Parthia in the east.

But full reunification was not to be. In 64 BC, Rome became the king of the north when Pompey took Antioch away from the Seleucids by the power of the Lex Manilia. In 63 BC, he marched south and took Judea, sacking Jerusalem on the Sabbath. Greece, Anatolia, Syria, and Judea in Palestine then belonged to Rome, and Judea was given to Herod the Idumean to govern.

The beast usually identified with Rome is the she-wolf. This was the form Daniel probably saw in the vision. In 509 BC, the city of Romulus threw off its Etruscan yoke, abolished monarchy, and created a republic instead. Absolute authority was replaced with two elected consuls who held the imperium for one year. In emergencies, this power could be extended. Each consul could veto the other. The senate was a body of conscripted aristocrats of the patrician class who belonged to one of the four principal colleges. The pontifical college was over all religious concerns and was headed by the Pontifex Maximus, Rome's high priest.

The Roman people were divided into two assemblies called the *comitia curiata*, a tribal membership, and the *comitia centuriata*, a military one. These bodies could draft legislation. After some years, the plebian aristocracy won a voice in governance with the creation of a tribunate having the power of the veto. The common man in the street, or plebeian, had the power to stand outside and shout. They could make their feelings known in the arena by booing or catcalls and in the forum by breaking the arms and legs of statues or in other creative ways. Since the tribunes had the power to veto, they often spearheaded legislation accepted or rejected by the two comitias. If passed into law, the legislation went to the Senate, which voted money.

Octavian avoided the fate of his uncle Julius Caesar by not threatening the republic. When Lepidus died, Augustus became Pontifex Maximus. The treasury was divided into a civil one and military one, which guaranteed the army would always be paid. The senate controlled the civil treasury and those jurisdictions not part of the emperor's patrimony.

Augustus eventually stepped down as consul, becoming proconsul for life and holding the power of a tribune. Basically, this was the Augustan settlement and the beginning of the Roman emperors. Under Tiberius, the "law of majestas" allowed the emperors to confiscate the property of those living within the jurisdiction of the senate. Over the decades, this power gradually undermined the authority of that august body. The emperor was the ultimate magistrate, and in time those with legal problems looked to the imperium for their decisions rather than the senatorial magistrates. Appealing to the senate could be ruinous. The cost became prohibitive. Appealing to the emperor was every citizen's right and considerably less expensive.

Like Persia and Macedonia in their day, Rome was now the great prince of the Mediterranean world. Its influence was extremely powerful then and has reached down to our day.

Festival Cycle One

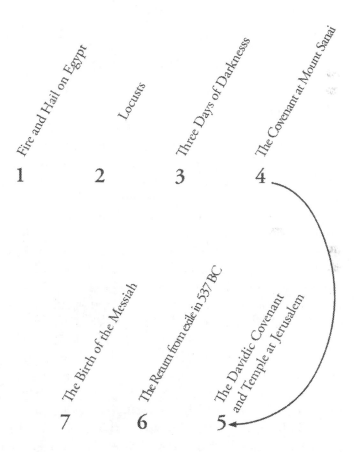

The three plagues in Egypt embody the entire scope of the material Theocracy. The first is the intervention of God in human affairs. The second is ongoing invasions of Israel until third the three days of darkness forecast the death and burial of the Christ.

10

THE GREAT PRINCE

By the Roman imperial age, the great ancient oracle centers of the Mediterranean world had faded from the glory they once had. Although the art of vaticination continued to be practiced worldwide, the oracle of Yahweh was setting a new and higher standard than any other deity in the antemedieval world. The name Yahweh transitions from Yahweh of Hosts or Armies to the Most High, the Eternal, and finally to almighty God the Lifegiver. To the post-exilic Jews, the oracle had proven the very existence of an almighty God. This much they knew.

Under the Ptolemaic pharaohs, a legal milestone had been created to promote the Apollo of God even further in the world. Imperial permission and patronage had been granted to the Jewish immigrants in Alexandria to translate the Aramaic-Hebrew Bible into Greek. This new collection was known as the Septuagint. It began with the Pentateuch and gradually expanded to include the histories of Kings and Chronicles, the post-exilic histories, wisdom literature, and prophets. The Greek Septuagint was the first witness to the original Bible in the post-exilic age. It was also the standard Bible among early Christians. This Bible gave the Jews a new tool to engage in proselytizing work. A fixed date could be referenced, and the great Hellenistic libraries of the eastern Mediterranean held copies of the Septuagint Bible for any Greek speaker to consult. Judaism began to attract new converts outside of Palestine. For the first time in centuries, Jews and pagans had an impartial means to measure the Apollo of God for themselves.

Specific rules govern the correct interpretation of all genuine oracles. They are as follows:

1. All oracles are prediction and prophecy. Not all prediction and prophecy are oracles.

2. A genuine oracle predicts, publishes, promotes, preserves, and proves its veracity.

3. All genuine oracles can be measured by external and internal evidence. Anecdotal evidence is not conclusive.

4. All genuine oracles end their lives as recorded history and nothing more. They do not become a greater oracle with a greater fulfillment in a more distant future.

The violation of this rule has caused much disappointment. The past is littered with the sufferings of those who foolishly listened to the colorful imaginings of eschatologists that would not prove to be. The failure of William Miller's interpretations in the early nineteenth century caused profound disappointment in his community, which has translated to the present. Yet time and again, wild-eyed eschatologists surface and create a bigger and better mousetrap for those who've been to Disneyland more than once. History can, and at times does, recreate similarities to past events, but never an exact duplication. Similarities mix with distinct differences to make each historical event unique.

One of the contributing factors to the misunderstandings of eschatologists is the use of "metatype" in Scripture. The Messiah of Israel is a latter-day Moses, David, or Solomon. Jesus referred to John the Baptist as a latter-day Elijah, by association casting himself as a latter-day Elisha. He also regarded himself as greater than Solomon. Indeed, there are some striking similarities. The reference is helpful to our understanding, but *caveat lector*! Let the reader beware!

In the mind-set of many eschatologists, interpretation of prophecy and oracles combines with metatypes to produce a grandiose hybrid thinking that invariably misses the mark. Some eschatologists use metatypes to an extreme, creating spiritual and symbolic interpretations at every turn. Today, the presence of "spiritual" and "symbolic" in any given interpretation has become code for caution. One eschatological society has offered the ultimate extreme by offering "antitypical" along with prophetic interpretation. The idea appears to be that the opposite meaning can typify. Can good be typified by evil? Can black typify white? Can Satan typify Christ? These eschatologists pride themselves on their flamboyant imaginations, perversely thinking that imagination is synonymous with the Holy Spirit. But the record of failure and disappointment follows them to their inevitable demise.

5. The only exception to this general rule occurs when a future oracle calls an historical event forward in history to become a greater oracle through a future oracle. It appears the prophecy in Daniel 4 is called forward into the future by the book of Revelation's reference to "Babylon the Great." Revelation also calls forward "Gog of Magog" from Ezekial's oracle. It is only these exceptional cases authorized by the oracle of Jesus Christ that set the general rule aside.

6. Interpretations of oracles must always be reduced to their smallest size until all the elements fit perfectly. No element must be omitted.

7. Oracles are not an extension of the prophet's subconscious. They are never given in dreams. Dreams are subjective in nature and is not a proper conduit for divine interpretation or inspiration.

8. A genuine oracle is given through cherubic representation. This representation delivers the oracle to the prophet. The prophet functions as secretary by recording verbatim what is said and seen.

9. Most genuine oracles use ambiguous language as an internal security device. Ambiguous language protects the meaning and words from alteration by copyists. It can serve to expose abuse and false interpretations. The ambiguity is designed to disappear after the fulfillment is achieved. A unique historical event often emerges.

There are examples when an oracle's ambiguous language cannot be interpreted with any competent certainty. Eventually, most historians who rigorously pursue knowledge of our past must concede there are some things they will never know. There may be a wealth of archeological remnants and artifacts concealed below earth's surface that will never come to light. The same can also be true of oracular etymology. There may be words or expressions impossible to render into modern usage. The cryptic meaning has been lost. Healthy conjecture can raise reasonable possibilities and sometimes completes the picture, but often conjecture fails. Interpreters may have to accept these gaps as inexplicable in the same way historians do. Indeed, any oracular interpretation that appears to be perfect should be instantly viewed as suspect.

10. Overly ambiguous language is often a good indicator of a bogus oracle. Multiple interpretation is not the function of a genuine oracle. Any interpreter can extract his own meaning from an overly ambiguous oracle. Numerous interpretations never resolve a useful meaning.

11. Because all genuine oracles end their lives as recorded history, zealots can fraudulently write history in oracular style to give the impression it is "God speak" when, in fact, it is not. Consequently, the student of oracles must be cautious and forensic in his thinking.

12. The oracle will always interpret forward and never into the past.

The above are some of the rules I discovered to be operative in my search for the Apollo of God. They set a high standard, as one would reasonably expect from a genuine, existent deity.

In the summer of 43 BC, Antipater the Idumean died. His oldest son Phasael had been made governor of Jerusalem and Judea, and Julius Caesar had appointed his younger brother Herod ben Antipater governor of Galilee. Each of the Idumean brothers had to contend with two factions attempting to seize their power. Antigonus, descended from Aristobulus, wanted the throne at Jerusalem, while Hyrcanus wanted the high priesthood. In former times, Queen Salome Alexandra (76-67 BC) had created this division by making her oldest son, Hyrcanus II, high priest and her youngest son, Aristobulus II, commander of the army in Judea.

This local rule had worked for Rome since 63 BC, when Pompey had marched south from Antioch, making southern Palestine a Roman possession. In the previous year, Pompey had simply abolished the old Seleucid empire, adding Syria to the Roman domain and sending its last king into retirement. The next twenty-four years saw Egypt go from weakness to weakness while the new empire of the king of the north was consolidated into Roman hands.

Palestine was briefly conquered when the Parthian king Barzaphranes invaded and overran Syria in 40 BC. Antigonus hurried north to Antioch and made his bid for the rule of Jerusalem, which the Parthian king granted. Both marched south into Galilee, forcing Herod out and south to refuge with his older brother in Judea. Making his campaign in Galilee, Barzaphranes sent his general Pacorus to invest Jerusalem. Herod realized the city would fall to Parthian forces after a siege and fled to Petra of the Nabateans. The city did fall to Pacorus's army, and Antigonus became the new ruler of the Judean capital. Barzaphranes sent Phasael and the high priest Hyrcanus into permanent exile, where both died.

At Petra, Herod did not receive the support he had hoped for. The Nabateans sent him away, and Herod took his family to Masada. From there he journeyed alone to Alexandria and took passage on a ship to Rome, where Octavian and Marc Antony received him as a loyal friend. Both triumvirs detested Antigonus and were determined to replace him with Herod, driving the Parthian invader out. The triumvirs assembled the senate, which granted their wish, making Herod king of Judea and voting him money and troops.

The new king of Rome's province "beyond sea" landed at Ptolemais in 39 BC at the head of an expeditionary force. Moving south along the coast, he took Joppa and marched from there to Masada to rescue his family. Turning northward, he invested Jerusalem. While the siege progressed, Herod used the time to secure Idumea to the south and then recapture his former territory of Galilee, isolating the Judean capital circa 39-38 BC. From Galilee he marched north to assist Marc Antony's siege of Samosata on the Euphrates. When Samosata finally fell to Antony's troops, Herod returned south with Roman troops to end the siege at Jerusalem.

However, Herod's march was met by Antigonus's troops in Samaria, where the forces engaged and Herod inflicted a heavy defeat on the usurper's hopes of relief. Returning to the city of David, Antigonus prepared for Herod's rapid advance. Sometime in 37 BC, Jerusalem fell and its population was slaughtered. Antigonus was captured and sent to Antony in chains. What a terrible death he must have suffered.

The year 37 BC saw the end of Hasmonean rule in Judea. From then on, legitimacy would be determined by Rome. They had decided an Idumean would be master of Judea, establishing Herodian rule. As the prophet Zechariah said, the spirit of Yahweh would come to rest in the north country. Indeed, it had come to pass. Rome was the new king of the north and it would tolerate no opposition to its rule. Herod the Great (37-4 BC) would firmly root Judea in the Roman east, where it would remain for the next six hundred years.

> He shall march and pass through other lands like a flood.
> He shall enter the land of the holy covenant and a thousand
> times ten shall fall victim
> However, Moab, Edom and the essential part of Ammon
> shall escape his purpose.
> His hand will reach out to other lands and Egypt will not
> escape.

In 40 BC, the triumvirs divided the Mediterranean world among themselves. The Pontifex Maximus Lepidus held North Africa, while Octavian received the western region from Italy to Spain and Marc Antony ruled from Greece to the border of Egypt. Since Antony's wife Fulvia had died, he took Octavian's half sister Octavia for wife to complete his alliance with the nephew of Julius Caesar.

Antony's alliance with Cleopatra, the queen of Egypt, linked him with the "Pharaoh of the South." The fact that the king of Egypt was a woman is one of the reasons eschatologists have not applied Daniel 11:40-45 to the right place. Indeed, the fate of Egypt was actually an intense struggle between two women in competition for the soul of one man, a love story that became legendary in Rome. Octavian waited on a favorable outcome of one of history's famous amours. Octavia was Antony's dutiful wife while Cleopatra was the infamous mistress. In a contest launched into the public arena, both women were determined to have Antony as their prize, alive or dead. Two sets of feminine wiles engaged in the deadly competition, one as admired as the other.

While Antony made preparations for a return expedition against Parthia, he received an offer of alliance from the king of Media against Phraates in Parthia.[189] This was exactly what the great Roman commander needed for a successful campaign in the east. The mounted archers would be crucial to his military strategy. Though his previous expedition could claim some eighteen victories against the Parthian host, Antony was unable to capitalize on them because he lacked an effective cavalry that knew the terrain and the enemy. The horse archers could also effectively escape a bad engagement to fight another day.

When the Romans returned to Palestine, Antony lost one third of his force. At Alexandria, he received word from Octavia of her arrival at Athens with clothing, baggage, and money for his soldiers, along with two thousand hand-picked troops for his coming expedition. Yet foolish Antony chose to remain in Egypt with Cleopatra and postponed his campaign to Parthia. This was clearly a mistake, since the kingdom was suffering internal turmoil. Yet he did form a marriage alliance with the Median king, whose daughter wedded one of Antony's sons by Cleopatra.

In Athens, Octavia continued to assist her husband's business by taking care of his children by Fulvia, and her faithfulness served to damage Antony's reputation among the Romans. At Alexandria, he added insult to injury by making Cleopatra queen of Egypt, Cyprus, Libya, and Coele-Syria, and by making Caesarion, her son by Julius Caesar, co-regent with

---

189. See "Antony" in Plutarch's Lives.

his mother. His son Alexander by Cleopatra was styled "King of Kings of Armenia and Media." To Ptolemy he granted Phoenicia, Syria, and Cilicia. When Parthia was overcome, it would be given to Alexander.

Antony's younger son Ptolemy was presented to the Egyptian populace in the attire of a Macedonian successor, while Alexander wore the costume of a Median ruler. Ptolemy received a Macedonian bodyguard and Armenian soldiers attended Alexander. Cleopatra appeared in the guise of the goddess Isis. The separation from Rome was completed when Antony leveled an accusation against Octavian for not sharing his gains with him. After deposing Lepidus, Octavian had kept all of North Africa. He had also taken all of Sicily from Sextus Pompey and kept the ships Antony had loaned him for the war.

> He shall raise up his might and set his mind against Egypt of the south.
> And Ptolemy of the south shall raise a greater army to wage war against the north.
> But those who recline at his table will plot against him and succeed
> They will break him,
> His plan shall be swept away and his army will suffer many killed.
> Because their minds devise evil the two Kings shall lie to each other at the same table.

As stated earlier, Daniel 11 has two endings. The first ending (above) concludes at verse 28, and the second ending begins at verse 29. What the prefix to the second ending was we do not know, but the redactor included it in the text as a postfix to the main oracle. The prefix and infix to the second ending is lost. It is also possible verses 40 to 45 were a continuation from verse 28, but the redactor may have inserted verses 29 through 39 as part of the infix to the original oracle.

As a result, eschatologists have been deceived into thinking the King of the North is exclusively Antiochus IV Epiphanes. Verse 22 can only apply to Rome, however. Antiochus had had some success against Egypt and inside his own kingdom, but not to the extent Rome did. Once again the antipathy of Jews toward Epiphanes has clouded their judgment, causing an adulterated text. Yet with proper insight the reader can correct the minor corruption. The original text may have been constructed as follows before the redactor went to work: Daniel 11:1-20; 29-39; 21-28; 40-45. This reconstruction makes more sense than the current rendering.

Antony's preparations for the war had positioned him well ahead of Octavian. The collection of taxes for Caesar's preparations brought the western kingdom to the brink of revolt, but Antony delayed the war's prosecution, making a major error in his timing. At this time two of his friends of consular dignity, Titius and Plancus, deserted him for Octavian. Cleopatra, they insisted, should not have come with the army. Antony's force was larger than Octavian's two hundred and fifty ships and ninety-two thousand troops. The king of the south had mustered five hundred warships and one hundred twelve thousand soldiers.

Cleopatra wanted a decisive engagement at sea, while Antony and his best officers knew his real strength was in his land force. Canidius and other of his commanders advised that Cleopatra be sent back to Egypt and Antony retire to Macedonia or Thrace, where Dicomes, the king of the Getae, agreed to join him with a large army. But Antony's allies and friends were deserting him. Two kings, Amynatas of Lycaonia and Galatia along with Deiotarus, went over to Octavian. Domitius his long-time friend also deserted to Caesar.

Cleopatra insisted on a battle at sea and Antony relented. Although twice the size, the fleet was poorly manned. Of the two hundred ships brought by Cleopatra, only sixty were serviceable. While the battle was engaged, Cleopatra in her flagship, the admiral-galley *Antonias*, led her remaining fleet south to the Peloponnesus and then to Alexandria. Here Plutarch gives his verdict of the star-crossed lover: "Now it was that Antony showed to all the world that he was no longer actuated as a commander or a man, but as the saying, 'the soul of a lover lives in the body of another', proved to be true in him. It was as if he could not bear her absence. Seeing her ship sailing away he abandoned the battle and all those dying for him and sailed after the woman who had begun his ruin and would now accomplish it."

At Taenarus, the fleet of Cleopatra put in. News arrived of the naval victory won by Octavian and the destruction of her fleet. The land forces under Canidius were intact and Antony ordered them withdrawn to Asia. However, Canidius and his officers deserted to Caesar and the army under their command made their submission to Octavian. The king of the north then included Greece in his domain. At Paraetonium in Africa, Antony and Cleopatra parted company, and during his stay there Antony sank into despair and solitude of the kind that was witness to betrayal. When his forces in Africa and their commander declared for Caesar, he wanted to die, but his two companions prevented him. While Cleopatra, now in Egypt, was making preparations to escape into the Arabian Gulf with her treasure, Antony only wanted to be left alone and live the life of Timon, the famous Athenian misanthrope.

Antony ultimately did kill himself, but he could not do so on the field of battle after his remaining naval forces at Alexandria and his cavalry deserted to Octavian. The doors to this honorable escape now closed to him, he retired to his private chamber and ended his misery by his own hand.

When Octavian entered Alexandria, he managed to keep Cleopatra alive until he had discovered the whereabouts of her treasure, gaining control of Egypt's wealth. Of all Antony's children, only Antyllus, his eldest son by Fulvia, was put to death. The remaining six were raised by Octavia, a truly remarkable woman. It was from Antony's two daughters by Octavia that Rome produced two emperors, Claudius Caesar and Lucius Domitius. The latter was adopted by Claudius when he was the great prince of Rome and is known to history as Nero.

Octavian was now master of the Roman world in the dying days of the great democratic republic. Unlike his uncle Julius Caesar, the great prince of Rome was careful to preserve its fiction. Yet all the essential powers were in his hands. He was at once commander-in-chief of Rome's legions and head of the Roman empire as its Pontifex Maximus and high priest in the pontifical college. After ten years as one of the consuls, he relinquished that office for the office of proconsul, and he held the power of the veto as Rome's foremost tribune. He was representative of the patrician and plebeian aristocracies, and lifelong magistrate with the highest honor embodied in the name of Augustus, Rome's first citizen and prince of her domains. His private patrimonies were Spain, conquered by Scipio Africanus; Gaul, conquered by Julius Caesar; Syria and Palestine, subjugated by Pompey; and Egypt.

The emperor Tiberius added the law of *majestas* to the Roman code, permitting the emperor to prosecute anyone in the empire and confiscate their estates if convicted. Over time, this later provision in the law was to gradually increase the landholdings of the princeps. As the foremost magistrate, citizens found the emperor was more approachable than the senate and less ruinous financially. These powers and conditions served to elevate the princeps higher than intended, leading eventually to an absolute monarchy after some two hundred years.

It was early in this process, when Tiberius was Rome's great imperator, that an event in Palestine was to signal a change in the Mediterranean world. Herod the Great (37-4 BC) was dead and Judea had been given to his son, the ethnarch Archelaus (4 BC-6 CE). Galilee and Perea were given to Herod Antipas (4 BC-39 CE), while Judea and Jerusalem were ruled by procurators from 6 CE onward. These territories were governed by the emperor's patrimony of Syria. Herod Antipas was a client-king, whereas the procurators were Roman officials and direct representatives of Augustus through Antioch.

During the middle years of his procuratorship, Pontius Pilate was asked by the Jewish religious leaders at Jerusalem to execute a Jew named Joshua ben Joseph. In the normal course of events, the Sanhedrin court would have exterminated Joshua without any recourse to Roman authority, but Joshua was no ordinary man.[190]

The trial of Jesus Christ is an interesting study of how local and Roman jurisprudence interacted with each other in the imperial age. The gospel accounts are useful in giving the historian all the essential elements, but the chronology is deplorable. We must remind ourselves the biblical record is idealized and often is not actual history. The actual history can be discovered from the essential elements embedded in the text. Add to this other historical references along with commonsense interpretation in order to realize a reasonable perspective of what most likely occurred.

To properly understand how events unfolded, we require a basic knowledge of Roman law, an understanding of Herod Antipas's political situation, and Roman policy for the region. The first trial was a preliminary hearing before the high priest, Annas, who did not acquit Jesus but determined to submit him to the Sanhedrin court presided over by the other high priest, Caiaphas.

Jesus ben Joseph went on trial for his life. He faced two counts of blasphemy. First, he had claimed to be the Son of God. Second, he had also claimed to be king of the Jews. Although Jesus defended himself during the preliminary hearing, he remained silent during the second trial until the very end, when he made reference to Daniel 7:13-14. As we know, he was convicted on both counts and sentenced to die.

However, Passover was very close and the priests wished to remain ritually pure. They also knew how popular Jesus had become among the people. They would have to adhere scrupulously to the law on this occasion. Jesus would die by Roman hands. Pontius Pilate didn't wish to be troubled with their request. "Do it yourselves!" he retorted. But the Jews dug in their heels and insisted.

When Rome's procurator learned that Joshua had been sentenced to die for claiming to be the Son of God, he ordered his soldiers to take Jesus into custody without delay. As the emperor's legate and tribune, he could not permit the judgment of the Sanhedrin court to stand. The Romans were as scrupulous about their law as the Jews were about theirs. He would not

---

190. Acts 7:58.

execute any man for claiming to be God's son. All men were sons of God. It was not a crime under Roman law.

The Romans used two legal codes to govern their empire. The *Jus Civile* or civil code was the less liberal of the two and used to settle disputes among all Roman citizens. It carefully guarded and enforced the Roman state's authority and the privileges of its aristocrats and institutions.

The *Jus Gentium*, or common law, was used to settle disputes between Roman and non-Roman and also could be applied between non-Romans. In the latter situation, local courts would usually hear the case. The *Jus Gentium* tended to be more liberal in its outlook. It was developed from common practice and application around the Mediterranean, initially to settle trade disputes. The Romans wanted a code recognized by other nations that could settle disputes without war. It was a successful effort and gradually expanded to include other legal issues. As Caesar's tribune in Judea, Pontius Pilate applied the provisions of the *Jus Gentium* to Jesus.

The third trial in the governor's palace examined the question of Jesus's claim to be king of the Jews. "My kingdom is no part of this world. If my kingdom were part of this world my attendants would have fought in order that I should not be delivered up but, as it stands, my kingdom is not from this source." To Pilate this was an adequate defense. This Joshua could not be a threat to Roman authority in the region. He therefore aquitted Jesus and took his verdict out to the waiting Jews. 'I find no fault with this man. He's a nice Jewish boy.'

In the confrontation that followed, Pilate learned Jesus was a Galilean and a resident of Capernaum. The ruler of that particular tetrarchy was Herod Antipas, who was in Jerusalem for the Passover feast. To break the impasse, Pilate sent Jesus under guard to Herod for a fourth trial.

The injunction of Moses at Deuteronomy 23:7-8 allowed that any Idumean/Edomite or Egyptian resident among the Israelites could be legally admitted to the assembly of Israel from the third generation. Antipas was second generation. This entitled Herod's successor to become a legal Jew and ultimately legal king of the Jews. This also entitled Herod's successor to claim rulership in Judea at Jerusalem. This was the potential that lay ahead for Herod the Great's grandchildren.

However, Antipas's first wife was the daughter of the Arab king Aretas. In Rome's eyes, this marriage alliance was a good thing for business. But Herod had alienated the Arabs when he divorced the daughter of Aretas, and then alienated the Jews by marrying the wife of his brother Herod Philip while Philip was still alive. The stability of Herod's rulership was under a cloud.

Now standing in front of him was the disciple and successor of John ben Zechariah, also known as "the baptist." Antipas's wife Herodias had been responsible for John's death. Herod's investigation of Jesus had uncovered an impressive lineage.[191] Jesus could trace his family back to King David ben Jesse, not only from his mother but from his adoptive father as well. Jesus was a Judean royal with exceptional credentials. What if Pilate decided to make him king?

Antipas would see to it that never happened. But he had to be as cunning as a fox. To obscure the legal issue, Herod clothed Jesus in a royal robe, essentially admitting that Jesus was Israel's rightful king. If things turned bad, that would provide enough ambiguity to protect his family. Herod then concluded his examination and sent Jesus back to Pilate with a letter of explanation.

Jesus, the letter said, was a Judean, and Herod's letter was accompanied by a genealogical record that traced ben Joseph's family back to the Maccabean revolt at least. By implication, Jesus was a descendant of Jewish rebels. Perhaps Herod thought this would raise suspicion about him. According to the treaty of 161 BC, signed by envoys of Judas Maccabeus and the senate of Rome, Jesus, as a Judean royal, had automatically been granted Roman citizenship at birth. Roman records registered his birth at Bethlehem, where his father and mother were also registered. Therefore Jesus should have been tried under the provisions of the *Jus Civile*. The claim of being the "Son of God" was still not a crime under the Roman civil code, but the claim to be a king was another matter. The claim to be king of anything without Caesar's permission was a direct violation of the law of majestas enacted by Augustus. Tiberius rigorously pursued and punished any violation of this law, no matter how small.

The notion that Pilate "cut a deal" to save his butt is not a plausible one in my opinion. It is not difficult to imagine that the Jews would have worked hard to have every procurator investigated by Antioch or Rome on one charge or another. Investigating each procurator on the basis of Jewish accusations would have been business as usual for the Romans and part of their appeasement policy. In fact, any procurator in Judea not under investigation at Jewish instigation would have probably been suspicious. Yet in spite of it all, Pilate served ten years in Judea when the average term was some three years. Only Valerius Gratus, his predecessor, served longer.

In light of the above facts and Herod's approach, Jesus went on trial for the fifth time. He was convicted of treason and sentenced to die a usurper's death. But as tribune, Pilate had one more option left, and he decided to use

---

191. Luke 3:23-38; Matthew 1:1-17.

it. This reinforces John's contention in his gospel that Pilate exerted himself to save Jesus's life. In a sixth trial, the procurator appealed to the court of public opinion and asked the people of Jerusalem to choose between Barabbas, a convicted and known criminal, or Jesus. To his dismay and the dismay of those who attended his court, the public chose to exonerate Barabbas and execute Jesus. In disgust, Pilate washed his hands of the whole sorry mess and handed Jesus over to his soldiers.

Jesus's execution began immediately. The soldiers began by breaking his resistance. They flogged and humiliated him, slapped and spit on him, and degraded his person in every way they could. At the same time they were doing all this, however, they were also making Joshua ben Joseph the last legitimate king of Israel by legal means. They placed a purple, royal robe on him and crowned him with a diadem made of thorns. Then Rome's soldiers hailed him as king of the Jews and did obeisance to him.

History has proved there were four ways one could be made a king by the Romans. The emperor could make someone king in his patrimony if he wished. As procurator and legate at Jerusalem, Pontius Pilate was the emperor's direct representative, holding and exercising the emperor's powers. Secondly, the senate could vote someone all the powers necessary to rule. Third, the praetorian guard could pave the way to the throne if they liked the candidate and the donative was lucrative enough, Fourth, the soldiers could hail someone as king. All these were recognized, constitutional means to the throne. Although ignominiously done, Joshua ben Joseph ben David became the last legal king of Israel. The emperor's representative even assented by placing a sign above his head that said, "King of the Jews." The Jewish religious leaders were disturbed by this exercise in legal minimalism and objected. After all, a dead martyr was more dangerous than a live rebel.

The issue of establishing material legitimacy as set out and practiced by human institutions needs to be highlighted here. Faith and legitimacy in this case go hand in hand. Both must be part of the same equation. Faith is not meant to be a road unto itself nor isolated from material reality. Almighty God has always respected human institutions and the governments we choose or allow. The planet is our home, after all, and almighty God respects that. We get to pick our political poison. Abraham ben Terah was a man of faith, but he also had to be a Shemite to inherit the promise. In the arena of rulership, legitimacy played a conclusive part. Jacob was a descendant of Abraham through Isaac. David ben Jesse was a legal descendant of Jacob's son Judah. Similarly the prophet Elisha had to be commissioned by Elijah, who had been sent out to do this by the authority of the grand council at Horeb. Jehu ben Nimshi had to be duly anointed by Elisha's servant. In the natural course of events, Jesus also had to travel the road of legitimacy as a companion to his faith.[192] All too often faith is overemphasized. Jesus had to become the last legal and legitimate king of Israel by human institutional law. He also had to be the only fitting sacrifice that almighty God would actually accept from human hands.[193]

> The scepter shall not be dismissed from Judah,
> Nor the rulers staff from between his feet,
> Until the one appears who owns the right, to claim the peoples' obedience.

By this time, Judah was losing its legitimacy and right to independent rulership in Judea. It's highest court had to go cap in hand to get permission from the Roman authority to execute a fellow Israelite. Jesus was last legitimate king was made by Roman constitutional means. Yet the legal scepter did not depart from Judah until 70 CE, when the Roman legions under Vespasian's son Titus destroyed any hope of future Davidic legitimacy in the material world. If there was any doubt, the emperor Hadrian put an end to any real speculation. Judea's capital city was rebuilt as a Greco-Roman example and the temple has never been rebuilt to the present day.

Finally, like David his forefather, Jesus was also a member of Israel's community of prophets. This was how John ben Zechariah, "the baptist," presented him to the Jews. John was the son of a Levite priest and a member of the wilderness prophetic community. But John was more interested in the messianic prophecies that had forecast the advent than a career as a temple priest. In his day, that advent was expected by many. Even the priests came out to inquire of him. When a dispute arose between Johns' disciples and those of Jesus over the issue of baptizing, the Baptist openly designated Jesus to be his successor. Jesus patterned his ministry after the prophet Jeremiah of old, and his itinerant teaching was based on themes linking his message to the spiritual meaning of the great Jewish festivals the people saw enacted every year at their temple in Jerusalem. He was also a spiritual descendant of Zechariah ben Barachiah, who lived during the reign of the Davidic king Joash.[194] A religious renaissance took place during Joash's reign, when Judah had fallen under the control of Ahab ben Omri's daughter Athalia. Judah was recovered by the priests in Jerusalem,

---

192. Tacitus, The Annals Bk. 15:44; John 19:13-19.
193. John 16:2; Jeremiah 19:4, 5.

194. 2 Chronicles 24:20-22.

no doubt with the help of the prophets, beginning a type of messianic age. Jesus was also a new age prophet.

> He was hated and thrown out by men, one made to suffer and hurt. We viewed him as someone rejected who hides their countenance from us as someone with no use.

These words of the prophet Isaiah describe the suffering servant the Jews had developed in their own eschatological outlook. The book of Esther creates this same image of a despised deliverer. The king's official Haman ben Hammedatha was given the second place after the Persian king. He is described by the king's edict as a man "who excels among us in sound judgment, and is distinguished for his constant goodwill and unchanging fidelity, and has attained the second place in the kingdom—." Ahasuerus then described the Jews as an obstinate people who defied the laws of kings and promoted disunity in the kingdom. They were a people, he contended, who opposed every nation. The king gave Haman the authority to destroy them. This law was never rescinded, and we are told the Jews were given the natural right to defend themselves, as all humanity has.

Haman was executed by the Persian monarch for the sake of his Jewish queen. Haman was sacrificed for her deliverance and that of her people. The execution stake meant for Mordecai became Haman's. The end result was the deliverance of the Jews. To this day, Haman is despised by the Israelis and the Judaizers who support them. They make a pastry for the festival of Purim called Haman's ears. They do this to mock the man who was honored, yet executed, by the highest authority.

The similarity between Jesus ben Joseph and Haman ben Hammedatha is too striking and comprehensive to be coincidental. Jesus was in fact the greater Haman who was executed for the deliverance of Israel. Not only is the book of Esther an important historical book, but it is also part of the oracle. To this day, Judaizers acknowledge the death of Haman was part of the Most High's divine plan of deliverance for Jews, but their lack of understanding and absence of Holy Spirit is evident when they celebrate Purim near the Easter holiday and mock the memory of Haman, whose death delivered them. Now we can understand the words of the resurrected Haman to the angel.[195]

The Christian church of the later second century CE appears to have missed the close similarity of the Esther story as well. If there was a distinction needed to repel the Jews in the post-Hadrianic world, this was

---

195. Revelation 2:8-9 of Smyrna.

surely one of them. One can understand the Judeo-Christian church of the first century CE would have avoided the comparison to the Amelekite Haman because the character had become deeply odious to the Jews. The comparison would not have persuaded them to become converts to the new Judaism. It was not used because it did not suit their purpose at the time, and/or they had lost the spirit given to the apostles and were unable to recognize the deeper spiritual connection.

This dark image of the messiah, though disturbing to Israelis, is not out of context with the times. Speaking of the material Jewish age, the prophet Daniel saw its end: "Like a flood its end shall come in the midst of war. Desolations are decreed."

Although the greater Haman was then in a position to prevent the Roman and Islamic desolations, he did not. This was because the Jewish age ended after six hundred years (537 BC-63 CE), even if modern Israelis won't admit it. What was decreed was carried out.

As one would rightly expect, an act of God would irrevocably change the course of human history. The first advent surely did. All of western and eastern Europe became Christian. The expansion continues around the world to this day.

Jesus ben Joseph ben David was registered circa 7 CE during the Augustan census. Caesar's legate at Antioch in Syria, P. Sulpicius, and his new procurator of Judea named Coponius administered the census locally. As provided by the Treaty of 161 BC, Jesus became a Roman citizen at birth because both his parents were members of the Judean royal family. This was common practice in Roman treaties with allied nations. Consequently they were required to register their names at Bethlehem ben Jesse's birthplace. It was not necessary that Jesus be born there. The prophecy in Micah 5:2 only stipulates their messiah would "come out" of Bethlehem. Jesus was likely born somewhere else. The entire nativity story in Matthew is bogus. How old Jesus was at the time of his registration is not known.

When his adoptive father Joseph died, Jesus became the head of the household, and he decided to move the family and their business to Capernaum on the Sea of Tiberius. His mother at Cana treats him as such.[196] Since a Jewish man became independent of his father from age thirty, people outside of Nazareth probably assumed he was at least thirty. How old he actually was is not known.

Was Jesus a married man? We should not be surprised if he was. Jewish custom and practice at that time would have essentially mandated it. If

---

196. John 2:3-5.

Joseph and Mary decided he would take a wife before age thirty, then that would have been that. However, I'm inclined to think Jesus was probably only betrothed, at least to the lady from Magdala, at the time of his death. The intimacy reflected in their brief conversation contained in John's gospel, and the fact that Jesus manifested himself to her first, indicate a genuine concern for Mary's well-being. She, of course, would have been relieved to know he was alive. A huge burden would have lifted from her shoulders. This was necessary business. At this point it becomes difficult to believe Jesus wasn't married. If he was single, why did he not appear to his mother first? After all, she was still the family matriarch.[197] Whatever the facts, marriage was not central to his ministry and message to the world. If he was actually married, it would have served him well. His understanding of the human race would have been fully completed. If Jesus had any children, Herod Antipas would have seen to it they perished as well. Knowing this, I seriously doubt Jesus fathered any children. It is also possible the lady from Magdala was infertile and unable to bear children.

When Jesus came to the Jordan for baptism, John ben Zechariah knew who he was. After receiving baptism from his cousin, Jesus journeyed into the eastern desert where the prophets were. They had their own communities with scriptoriums and published scrolls of the law and prophets. They were also expecting and looking for the Messiah. Among them, he presented himself as the "greater Moses" the prophets spoke about. Here Jesus made his first disciples. New Israel had been created.

He then retraced Moses's steps, symbolically entering allegorical Canaan as a sign to an Israel alienated from God. Upon reaching the Jordan, these new disciples would have been baptized with some additional members of New Israel such as Peter and Andrew among others. With all the meaningful symbolism intact, Jesus now led his little flock into future history.

Political Judaism had failed to bring about the prophesied restoration spoken of by the prophet and priest Ezekiel. Consequently a division came about between mainstream Jews in Judea and Jerusalem and the community of prophets in the wilderness. The Jews in Judea were a very exclusive religious community who despised all outsiders, and for the first eighteen months Jesus conducted his ministry in Galilee, going to Jerusalem only for the festivals held at Herod's temple. He traveled to neighboring villages and

---

197. However, as is typical of a younger man who is unmarried when he knows he's about to die, John the apostle records that Jesus thought of his mother and not the Magdalene. This is the only evidence we can point to that Jesus was single.

towns, including his own, and taught in the synagogues on the Sabbath day. Then he would return to his home in order to continue the family business. The gospels give us a glimpse of what he taught on these occasions, and much is preserved in Matthew's Sermon on the Mount which, along with the gospel of John, is worth preserving.

The gospel of John is the only reliable history of Jesus Christ. Of all the disciples and apostles chosen by Jesus, it is clear he completely trusted only John. Indeed, he gave the care of his own mother into John's hands. Jesus had four brothers and an unknown number of sisters, yet he never gave the care of his mother to them. This speaks volumes about Jesus's confidence in John and why he told Peter that John would outlive him and all the other apostles.

The greatest oracle ever written was also entrusted only to John while he was witnessing on Patmos Island. To wait until all the other apostles had died and then give ben Zebedee the book of Revelation expressed a deep-seated trust in John. This means that should Peter, James, Paul, or others have failed in their assignments, John would be available to see the Christian mission continue. This in fact was the case when the Neronic persecution savaged many of the disciples who were called to Rome in chains. When the Flavian dynasty ended the persecution, John remained to deliver the oracle of Jesus Christ to the seven congregations and fulfill the oracle's trust. By then his spiritual growth, as evidenced in his letters, defined him as an apostle worthy of the confidence given him.

John's gospel was written to set the record straight and was pre-Revelation. It is clearly at odds with the synoptic gospels. By writing his gospel, John confronts the Christian believer with a dilemma of sorts. To the democratic mind, the synoptics seem to act as three witnesses against his history. As a result, John's gospel tends to get placed in the back and is often neglected. Indeed, because of the difficulty it creates with the synoptics, the bishop of Rome at one time advocated it be excluded from the Christian canon, together with all of John's letters and Revelation. Some who work at being fair-minded have attempted to blend all four gospels into a scholarly whole, which essentially is impossible.

Here is where the mind of Christ proves invaluable to the student. Implicit in the history of Jesus and the oracles he spoke is an abiding trust in John ben Zebedee. As a second witness, Jesus gives the testimony needed to break the difficulty. Consider: did not Jesus say, "My load is kindly and my load is light"? In another place he says, "A slave is not greater than his master." And again, "And the father who sent me has himself testified on my behalf." When we line up the three witnesses on one side and the three witnesses on the other, which ones will you believe?

Yet, sad to say, many have opted to enjoin an impossible struggle on themselves, adding doubt to their faith and increasing their burdens. The solution is simple and reliable. Make John's gospel the standard by which all other histories are measured. Otherwise Christians invariably develop corrupted notions of Jesus's ministry. I t is also time to move on and leave the first century as a reference, not to fall into the error of making it a way of life. Historians and scholars are logically persuaded that the synoptic gospels should prevail, but such a belief proves to be misleading. Much confusion can be eliminated by recognizing the veracity and trustworthiness of the account in John's history. We can complete John's narrative by including the twelve parabolic oracles and Jesus's great prophecy from the book of Matthew. The reasons for this redaction will become apparent.

After eighteen months on the stump in Galilee and Perea, Jesus went to Jerusalem for the Passover. [198] While there, he spread his fame and brought his work into the open. The disputatious Jews helped make him famous when he made a whip of ropes and violently drove the moneychangers and other vendors out of the temple area. This created outrage but drew attention to the son of Joseph and his message. This "sign" drew more disciples into his fold.

After the festival, Jesus traveled about the Judean countryside for a time among the Jews.[199] It appears Jesus devoted his full time to prophetic ministry in the remaining two years of his life. During this time, a dispute arose between the disciples of John the Baptist and Jesus's disciples, instigated by the orthodox Jews. But John himself headed off the division by passing the mantle of succession to Jesus, just as Elijah did for Elisha, so all would know the anointed of God's holy mountain.

Herod Antipas feared John for the same reasons that previous rulers had feared distinguished members of the prophetic community in the past. Herod had no intention of killing John and may have actually liked him. The prophet would have been reasonably well treated in prison. After all, ben Zechariah could have been a useful propaganda tool for the ruler of the Jews. After feeding him and cleaning up his appearance, Herod could have given him a tongue-lashing and put him back out into the streets. The people would have seen their prophet had not been mistreated and, most importantly, that Herod was not persuaded by John's words of criticism.

But it was not to be. Herod's clever propaganda device misfired, turning into a public relations disaster. His wife Herodia and her daughter conspired

---

198. John 2:13-3:21.
199. John 4:45.

to have John killed. Herod could not persuade them otherwise, and he reluctantly gave them the head of the Baptist.

Six months after the Passover incident, Jesus created another stir when he helped a lame man walk again during the Feast of Tabernacles in Jerusalem. This was his second miracle. The orthodox Jews accused the man of carrying his mat on the Sabbath, and when they discovered that Jesus was responsible, they persecuted him also. Jesus defended himself and at the same time directly attacked the Jewish notion of the Sabbath by telling them that God continued working on their Sabbath as well. Jesus called on the prophets and God as his witnesses.

But his defense falls on deaf ears, and the son of Joseph fled to the other side of the Galilee on the east side of the Sea of Tiberius, where he took refuge in the mountains inside Philip's tetrarchy. During his temporary exile, he continued to engage in teaching. The crowds sought him out because he had apparently cured the son of a Roman official and had definitely cured a lame man at Jerusalem. This is where I believe Jesus gave his great Sermon on the Mount.

The notion that ben Joseph was a beggar is debunked when John and Mark tell us Jesus had two hundred denarii in his purse at the time. John tells us Jesus performed his third miracle on this occasion by feeding a crowd of five thousand with two fish and five barley loaves. At this point, people believed Jesus was the messianic prophet foretold by Moses. They then decided to replace Herod Antipas with Jesus, but David's son withdrew from the crowd and returned to Capernaum over the Sea of Galilee, where John reports they witnessed his fourth miracle.

At Capernaum, Jesus's theme was appropriately "the Bread of Life," since the Passover was near. At that time he also selected this twelve apostles and put them to the test when he expanded his teaching on the Bread of Life by defining his flesh as the bread and his blood as drink. "Very truly, I tell you, unless you eat the flesh of the Son of Man and drink his blood, you have no life in you." This teaching disturbed many, and like Gideon of old, he reduced his disciples to those who actually believed him, getting rid of those attracted only to his celebrity. When the Passover festival ended, Jesus entered his last year. He wanted only those who would assist in his task ahead around him.

John records nothing about the Passover feast in the spring. Jesus may have gone secretly or perhaps attended the one on the following month. The orthodox Jews were seeking to kill him. Perhaps Jesus celebrated the Passover privately, away from Judea. However, John skips directly to the Festival of Booths, and Jesus appeared in Jerusalem during the middle of the festival. He boldly entered the temple and began teaching. He continued to defend his actions from the previous year over the healing of the lame man. Circumcision was performed on the Sabbath, he declared, and helping an invalid on the Sabbath was not unlawful. He developed his teaching in such a way that the crowd at Jerusalem became volatile, and the orthodox Jews feared a riot. But Jesus now had a huge audience in one place, and their attention and focus were fixed on what he was saying to them.

At this point, Jesus's ministry reached a great crescendo. He spoke on all the themes he had used in the previous three years of his itinerant prophetic work. On the great day of the Tabernacles feast, he used the occasion of the water offering to proclaim his "Living Waters Sermon" that he had spoken of to the Samaritan woman and people of Sychar. "Let anyone who is thirsty come to me." Although the Temple police were ordered to arrest him, his charisma was such that they could not lay their hands on him. His huge audience was divided. Some regarded him as their long-awaited Messiah, while others denigrated him for being a Galilean.[200]

While at Jerusalem for the Festival of Booths, Jesus raised another controversy by curing a man blind from birth. Again he performed this healing based on applied medicine during the Sabbath.[201] This is not actually a bona fide miracle, although those who witnessed it, including his disciples, took it for one. Jesus was practicing medicine.[202] The city broke out in an uproar and the religious leaders refused to accept it as genuine. They confronted Jesus and moved to arrest him, but the son of ben Joseph managed to escape to the eastern side of the Jordan, where he remained until the Feast of Dedication a few months later. During that feast, Jesus was confronted directly by the religious leaders at the temple. Before he left Jerusalem at the end of the Feast of Tabernacles, Jesus had used the oracle of Ezekiel in chapter 34 as his theme. Now at the festival commemorating the restoration of Yahweh's temple by Judas Maccabeus, Jesus bluntly told them they were not among his sheep. By inference, he compares them to the exploitative shepherds in the oracle. The religious leaders decided they'd had enough of this prophet and attempted to arrest him, but Jesus narrowly escaped and spent his remaining time east of the Jordan.

Prior to Passover, Jesus heard his friend Lazarus was ill, and he journeyed to Bethany to see him. Jesus arrived to find Lazarus had been entombed for four days. Here Jesus performed the last and greatest miracle of his short life. He raised Lazarus from the dead. Those who witnessed it were electrified. This was his fifth miracle, unreported in the synoptic gospels.

---

200. John 7.
201. John 9.
202. John 10.

The first time we encounter a period of "seven times" is in Ezekiel. The priest turned prophet began his new career exactly seven years before Jerusalem was destroyed by the Babylonians in 586 BC. Exactly halfway into the seven years, Nebuchadnezzar laid siege to the city a second time. Exactly three and a half years later, Jerusalem fell. Some forty-nine years after that, the prophet Daniel used this same "seven time" model in his prophecy of the seventy weeks given in the first year of the satrap Darius the Mede.[203]. The seventy years of Jeremiah were nearing completion, as Daniel tells us in the introduction. Also the seven times spoken of in Daniel 4 had been completed when Nebuchadnezzar II suffered a collapse from illness for some seven years in 572 BC.

The destruction of the temple and city by the Romans in 70 CE ended the conditional covenant between the Israelites and Moses, bringing the old material theocracy to an end. Israel as a cherubic entity became fully dissolved by divine intervention. Membership in New Israel was based on other criteria and was no longer dependent on biological inheritance. This was the genuine restoration of New Israel and the post-exilic world. It was now dependent on a unification of spirit between Yahweh and the believer.

The mediator of the new covenant with "spiritual Israel" was the high priest Joshua, a spiritual descendant of Zechariah ben Barachiah. This was why the mother of Jesus Christ was instructed to name her firstborn son Joshua by the messenger of Yahweh. It made the linear connection to Zechariah 2:3-11 and 3:6-9, where he and the presence of Michael the Great Prince a subordinate creature spoke from Yahweh to the high priest Joshua while the prophet Zechariah ben Iddo listened. When the new nation of spiritual Israel was created on Pentecost in the same year that Jesus ben Joseph died, the resurrected high priest Joshua had already become the priest-king of the new nation. The priest Joshua in Zechariah was only an "omen or sign of things to come" and not the end result.

Clearly the Messiah bringing about restored Israel between 63 BC and 70 CE is none other than a legitimate descendant of King David ben Jesse through his mother Mary and his adoptive father Joseph. We know this man as Jesus Christ or Joshua ben Joseph ben David. It can be none other once we examine the evidence from the past.[204]

---

203. Daniel 9:24-27.
204. John 12:14-15. The oracle in Zechariah 9-14 set the tone of Jesus's ministry. Although the prophet who wrote this oracle may have had a more traditional viewpoint, Jesus inserts himself into it, perfectly taking ownership. Clearly some of it did not apply to the future, such as 9:13, but the overall theme fits reasonably well with Jesus's ministry. Indeed, Jesus may have deliberately

Jesus's great prophecy in Matthew 24 and 25 is largely based on Daniel's prophecy about the seventy weeks, and is meant to bridge the distance from Jesus's death to his second advent. We know from the historical gospels and independent sources that Jesus ben Joseph was put to death during the procuratorship of Pontius Pilate, who was a genuine historical person under the rule of Tiberius, the great prince of Rome. Consequently we can fix Jesus's death at or before 36 CE. This creates a measuring line to compare his prophecy in Matthew 24 and 25, along with the other ten parabolic oracles contained in Matthew's gospel, with the history that followed his ignominious death. As we will discover, this roots Jesus Christ firmly in the wilderness community of prophets spoken of by Isaiah. "A voice cries out in the wilderness. Prepare the way of Yahweh, make straight in the desert a highway for our God."

The second advent of Jesus Christ is one of the most misunderstood features of Christian eschatology. To the present day, Christendom has never understood the concept of the second advent. History is littered with the bodies of Second Adventist charlatans and those who believed them. Invariably one of the first concepts they stumble over is the "sign."

> Then the sign of the Son of Man will appear in heaven, and then all the tribes of the earth will mourn, and they will see the Son of Man coming on the clouds of heaven with power and great glory.

Jesus quotes from Daniel 7:13, and he knew he was standing in the period of time spoken of in Daniel 7:7. Verse 13 may have appeared to be a considerable distance away causing the early church to postulate the second advent was a long way into the future and that none of them in the first century would live to see it. However, Jesus's prophecy in Matthew 24 and 25 must be calibrated with Jesus's words recorded in the last chapter of John's history.[205]

Here is where latter-day eschatologists make another major error. Jesus had told his disciples on the Mount of Olives prior to his death, "But about that day and hour no one knows." The resurrected Jesus at the Sea of Tiberius

---

used it as a guide. Zechariah 9-14 appears to be, in style, one of the last prophecies before Jesus's advent, and exhibits a resemblance to writings about the Sons of Light versus the Sons of Darkness in messianic theology. This leads into the gospel age perfectly. We also see the Jews indulge in an act of human sacrifice the Almighty did accept from them.

205. John 21:20-23.

told John and James ben Zebedee, Simon Peter, and others that the apostle John would live to see the second advent. However, Simon Peter would not. Jesus specifically told Peter that Peter would suffer a martyr's death, and that would be the signal that Jesus's second advent was imminent. It would occur between Simon Peter's martyrdom and ben Zebedee's death.

However, verse 23 in John's gospel indicates the early church had fixed its focus on the "long into the future" fulfillment. When they heard of this modification in their viewpoint, they assumed John ben Zebedee would not actually die. This, of course, was nonsense. Not only did John die, but Matthew's gospel tells us ben Zebedee and his brother James would also die martyrs' deaths.[206] Therefore the notion that John lived to 96 CE is delivered a critical mortal blow. Clearly, many eschatologists have impaled themselves and others on their own neglect. The truth about the Christ is in the details. In fact, apart from the oracles, the truth in Scripture is very often located in the details of both canons.

The Christian writer James makes reference to this important conversation, and inspired by Jesus's words, he told the "twelve tribes" of mostly Christian Jews that the "sign of the Son of Man" or second advent was imminent.[207] We can therefore locate James's letter to a time shortly after Simon Peter was martyred. John ben Zebedee was still alive. Obviously the Neronic persecution was underway in Rome. Yet it has become abundantly clear our history reveals that many in Christendom have resisted Jesus's words and explanation in John's gospel and insist on their own views. Amazingly, many today still think the second advent is in the future! But Jesus had forewarned his disciples:

> Then if anyone says to you, "Look! Here is the Messiah!" or, "There he is!"—do not believe it. For false christs and false prophets will appear and produce great signs and omens, to lead astray, if possible, even the elect.

Anyone who postulates the second advent beyond the first century belongs in the above description. However, his elect or anointed disciples would not be fooled by latter-day charlatans, "Where ever the corpse is, there the vultures will gather." Interestingly, Jesus indicated his true disciples would be viewed as vultures and treated as such by outsiders.[208]

---

206. Matthew 20:22-23.
207. James 5:8-9.
208. Matthew 10:16-25.

Jesus's prophecy in Matthew 24:1-25:13 was a link between his own demise and his second advent or coming, which would decidedly occur in the first century CE. In fact, nation did rise against nation inside the collection of national groups known to us as the Roman empire. In the year 68 CE, the emperor Nero died. A civil war broke out in the year 69 CE, which is often called the Year of the Four Emperors. This civil war shook the empire to its roots and nearly engulfed it in massive chaos. To the rebellious Jews at Jerusalem, it must have appeared the war between the Sons of Light and Darkness was commencing. Roman historians reported the regular occurrence of celestial phenomena and earthquakes.[209]

However, Jesus told his disciples the forthcoming apocalyptic cataclysm would be cut short before the Mediterranean world collapsed in disaster. Indeed, that is exactly what happened when Vespasian ascended the throne, becoming the first of the Flavian emperors. Within a short period of time, he and his sons Titus and Domitian restored the *pax romana*.

Immediately after the suffering of those days the sun will be darkened, and the moon will not give its light; the stars will fall from heaven, and the powers of heaven will be shaken.

The Julio-Claudian heavens disappeared when Nero died without issue. The Flavian emperors were a new dynasty in Rome's governmental "heaven." Many of the Christian disciples and all the apostles still alive except for ben Zebedee died during the Neronic persecution. The heavenly aspirations of the old material theocracy in Jerusalem fell to the ground when David's city was destroyed by the Romans in 70 CE. The last stronghold at Masada fell in 73 CE. Besides the heavens above, the earthly heavens had also been decisively shaken and had received a new high priest and Great Prince Michael at almighty God's throne. The influence of earth's Great Prince was accepted by humankind's Creator as future King of our planet's population. On his way to becoming King, the Great Prince would make his influence felt within his true church first and the rest of the world second. The second advent took place in 63 CE, some thirty years after the death of Jesus Christ.

That this is so was previewed by Jesus in his parable of the ten virgins. The Jewish day ends and begins at sundown. Since Jesus gave this parable in the spring, the length of time from sundown to midnight was about four to five hours—enough for a literal wedding feast but a short period of time. Both groups from the bridal party brought enough oil for that time period. However, the discreet or wise took enough oil to last should the feast go

---

209. Tacitus 2:47; Pliny the Younger in Natural History; Seneca.

beyond midnight to early morning. They did not put their faith in human timetables as the foolish or insensible virgins did.

This is why second adventist eschatologists have consistently failed over the centuries. Like the foolish virgins, they constructed schedules and timetables based on their own imaginations. When those timetables ran their course, the "oil supply" was depleted and the eschatologists missed out.

In fact, it was the Christian writer James who raised the shout, "Look! Here is the bridegroom! Come out to meet him." When James wrote his letter, the year 63 CE had passed and the Christians, including Peter, had been hauled in chains to Rome and killed at Nero's pleasure. The death of the apostle Peter was the signal the five discreet virgins were waiting for, and it came at the right time—see Revelation 3:20.

In another place, Jesus had specifically said to his disciples before his death, "When they persecute you in one town, flee to the next; for truly I tell you, you will not have gone through all the towns of Israel before the Son of Man comes." Clearly, this again indicates a short period of time and not hundreds of years. Some eschatologists postulate this occurred when Jesus was transfigured. This is not the case. They did not see Jesus coming to Kingdom power but simply conversing with Moses and Elijah. This is looking backward, not forward. The second advent would not occur as his disciples expected, which is why they were cautioned to be alert. But some would miss out on the wedding feast and not share in the marriage of the Lamb. As Jesus indicated, a major split would take place in the early church. As it turned out, many to the present day have been unable to recognize or accept the second advent as it actually happened.

"Then two will be in the field; one will be taken and one will be left." This passage does not refer to any kind of rapture. The term "rapture" does not appear in Scripture and is a human invention. What Jesus meant was that one would be "taken" into the wedding feast because that one had prepared to meet the bridegroom when he appeared, whereas the foolish virgin would be left. In the same way, "Two women will be grinding meal together; one will be taken and one will be left." When Jesus told his disciples they would not know the "day or hour," he was not speaking in figurative terms but meant it exactly as he stated: a literal day and hour. When he also stated, at the end of the first part of his prophecy, that "this generation will not pass away until all these things have taken place," he was speaking about his own, contemporary generation and not something figurative as some suppose. Again, when he said, "Therefore you also must be ready, for the Son of Man is coming at an unexpected hour," he meant a literal hour of a literal day.

"Look! He is coming with the clouds; every eye will see
him, even those who pierced him; and on his account all
the tribes of the earth will wail."

Here is another passage Christendom has stumbled over for centuries,
and they still have failed to understand its true meaning. The meaning
is quite clear. Indeed, many have witnessed this but have been unable to
recognize what they were seeing. The second advent has been under their
noses for centuries, but Christendom has consistently proven themselves
to be "blind guides" to the present day.

The apostle John ben Zebedee was the first to witness the second
advent while he was on Patmos Island exactly seven years before Jerusalem
fell to the Romans in the summer month of Ab on the tenth day in the year
70 CE. The Revelation to John is the second advent! Anyone who reads
Revelation becomes an eyewitness, whether one realizes it or not. Over
time, "every eye" will see him.

A description of Jesus Christ resurrected is given us in chapter one. It
bears a close resemblance to the one given in Daniel.[210] The fact we can see
an image of the resurrected Great Prince Jesus Christ/Michael tells us he is
not almighty God. No one can see the Almighty and survive the experience.
We can only have his oracle and see his Son.

The description given in Revelation 4:3 is completely surreal and not
one we can really understand. The same is true of the picture given in Daniel
7. John would have immediately made copies of the "oracle of Jesus Christ"
and sent them to his fellow apostles who were still alive around the empire.
Paul's second letter to the Thessalonians indicates he had seen a copy of
the new oracle.

Revelation begins the third through seventh cycles, completing the
forty-ninth and fiftieth years of the larger festival cycle. With the death
and resurrection of Jesus Christ, the pattern continues in its numbered
arrangement, but events of necessity change. The third cycle deals with the
final location of the church in Asia Minor. Chapter two of Revelation gives
us the first four locations of Ephesus, Smyrna, Pergamum, and Thyatira.
In the summer of 63 CE, the church of Asia Minor is strong and faithful,
although it is being persecuted "by those who claimed they are Jews but are
not." These are things the church must overcome, but on the whole there is
more good than bad till at least 110 CE.

However, when we get to the last three, the church of Sardis and
Laodicea come under some serious criticism that overreaches the good

---

210. Daniel 10:5-6. See also Zechariah 2:3-4:14.

they can claim. Of Laodicea, no good thing is mentioned at all. On the other hand, the church at Philadelphia receives all praise and no criticism, in marked contrast to the other six. In this later period, those who are weak are very close to extinction, whereas those who are strong are much more so than at the beginning.

In chapters four and five, the apostles saw a detailed description of the way the "powers of the heavens been shaken." The great high priest, in the manner of Joshua ben Jehozadak, also named Joshua, with the legitimate claim to the Kingship of the "Jerusalem above," had arrived at almighty God's throne. This Greater than Solomon would now spend the future centuries building the new Temple of God, made up of living pillars taken from humankind. Earthly Jerusalem would no longer be the capital of the new kingdom but would be located in Asia Minor, among seven literal cities inhabited by the anointed of God. They are the new age prophets and angels of God.

We should understand the reappearance of the Christ was never described by Jesus as a second advent, but more correctly as the "Sign of the Son of Man." Again, the term second advent is a human invention. A sign, omen, or portent prefigures something future. Many in the early church may have stumbled over what at first appears to be a subtle difference. Just as the post-exilic high priest Joshua ben Jehozadak and his fellow priests were an omen of future events that would have a larger and more important impact on the human race, so also the Revelation. It was a sign or list of events with a direct impact on humanity for the years ahead. However, in the interval, many Christians began cultivating Jewish eschatological notions of a fantastical, apocalyptic event in their thinking. This led them away from the expectation of a mere sign. They wanted more than what had been promised.

When the Sign of the Son of Man finally appeared to the apostle John on Patmos Island in the summer of 63 CE, it fell short of Christians' apocalyptic designs.[211] Like the foolish virgins, they were away buying oil at the marketplaces or elsewhere when the sign of the Bridegroom appeared. Today, the five foolish virgins of Christendom continue to buy into any and all fantastical eschatologies the marketplace has to offer. They want more than what Jesus promised them. The end result is they are shut out of the wedding feast and do not share the good things enjoyed by the five wise and discreet virgins belonging to the Bridegroom.

In 66 CE, the Jews were in revolt against the Romans, whom they expelled from Jerusalem. The Syrian legate Gallus marched south with a

---

211. See Matthew 24:17, 32. Jesus indicated it would occur in the summertime.

punitive force but was badly routed at the Beth-horan pass by the Jewish rebels in the autumn months of that year. Finally Nero dispatched Vespasian to destroy the revolt. Early in February 67 CE, exactly three and a half years before Ab 10, 70 CE, Vespasian marched his punitive expedition south into Palestine.

In Rome, Jews and Christians were actively persecuted by Nero and his court, but he was unable to appease the Romans. His crimes against the aristocracy were tolerated by the people of Rome, who often viewed it as entertainment. But when he tried to divorce Octavia, they made such an outcry the emperor had to take her back. The fire and its destruction of their city had motivated Nero to offer lavish sacrifices on the altars of the gods to appease them. This was Nero's usual practice in the aftermath of his criminal behavior. This convinced the people it was the emperor himself who had ordered the flames. Rightly or wrongly, they perceived it as a crime against them. Their seething resentment could be felt by Nero and his Jewish mistress.

To deflect their anger, the emperor launched the first Christian persecution in an attempt to appease his mistress Poppea Sabina and the people of Rome. However, the attempt misfired. Although the Romans hated the Jews, the imperial heavy hand was perceived to be raised even higher against them. This was all part of the Sign of the Son of Man foretold by Jesus in his great prophecy. Christians empire-wide were alerted that the second advent was at hand. When Vespasian became emperor, "those days were cut short." The *pax romana* had been restored.

> They left our association because they belonged to someone else. That is why they did not remain in our company. By leaving they advertised the fact they actually never did belong to us.

With the death of Peter and James, John emerged as the faithful and discreet slave Jesus had predicted he would be.[212] The Great Prince Michael had returned, and to his faithful slave John he entrusted his belongings: the authority of the church, and the Apocalypse located among the seven congregations in Asia Minor. From that time forward, they were the apostolic church. Yet many in early Christendom did not recognize the Apocalypse as the sign of the Son of Man. Many withdrew their support from the seven congregations in Asia Minor. The writings of John the apostle were rejected by many, and in particular the Revelation.

---

212. Galatians 2:9.

However, by the end of the second century, the Muratori canon did contain all the writings of John, including the Revelation. The Muratorium set down the Bible and Christian canon in its most widespread form. It is also an early milestone to prove Revelation was known in the second century. The monk Jerome translated the Muratorium from the Hebrew-Aramaic and Greek into Latin near the end of the fourth century, providing another legal milestone.

In his canon, Jerome favored the revised Hebrew Bible produced by the Jamnia school of rabbinic Jews founded by Johanan ben Zakkai. When Johanan saw the fall of Jerusalem was inevitable, he petitioned the emperor's son Titus to allow him and his fellow rabbinic scholars to leave the city and set up a school directly west of Jerusalem, near coastal Philistia. Titus agreed and gave them safe conduct there. However, in the eastern church, the Christian Greek canon was the Septuagint until the Old Testament portion became so corrupted that it was ultimately replaced by the revised Hebrew canon.

Under the Flavian dynasty, the Roman empire settled down to enjoy a long period of peace for the next one hundred years. Vespasian ruled with an even hand, passing the imperium to his able son Titus, who ruled for two years before he died. Titus had been well respected most of his life and proved to be his father's strongest official. Indeed, one could reasonably conclude Titus was actually a co-emperor with his father. His younger brother Domitian succeeded him, and unlike his father and older brother, he ruled in the manner and tradition set down by Julius Caesar, Caligula, and Nero. They gravitated to the oriental, despotic style of rulership, with the end result they all died prematurely.

Although the Flavian rulers, including Domitian, never engaged in an open persecution of the early church, the law enacting the Neronic persecution against Jews and Christians was never repealed. It was used only by local rulers away from the imperial gaze. The Christian church had survived its first major crisis. John ben Zebedee had received the last will and testament of Jesus Christ, sealed with seven seals in the Roman style.

Jesus Christ the Great Testator left behind one of the greatest oracles ever written. Almighty God had bequeathed to his resurrected Son, Michael the Great Prince, the Holy Roman empire. He gave his "belongings" to the church on earth, beginning with the apostle John and the seven congregations. They are the faithful and discreet slave Jesus spoke of in his prophecy.

Festival Cycle Two

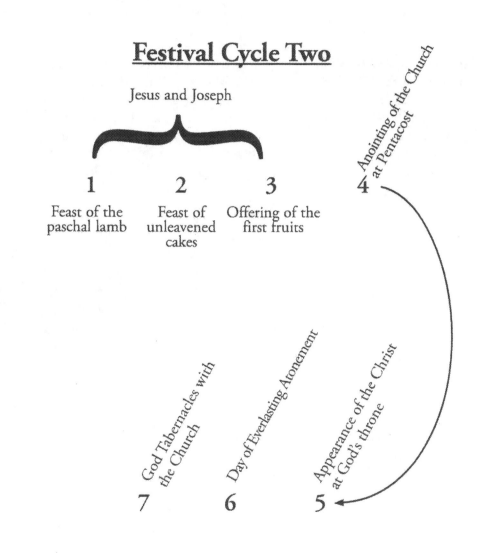

Jesus and Joseph

1
Feast of the
paschal lamb

2
Feast of
unleavened
cakes

3
Offering of the
first fruits

4 Anointing of the Church
at Pentacost

5 Appearance of the Christ
at God's throne

6 Day of Everlasting Atonement

7 God Tabernacles with
the Church

11

THE FALL OF ROME (98-193 CE)

> Considering the fourth beast there shall be a mighty empire
> on the earth that will differ from all the others—
> It shall devour the whole earth breaking its kingdom into
> pieces.
> The ten horns mean ten kings who will arise
> And an eleventh horn will rise among them
> He will rule differently than the others and he will trample
> three of the horns.

These ten kings represented as a crown on the Roman she-wolf are the ten emperors during Rome's zenith. Historians refer to them as the Antonine or adoptive emperors of the second century. If we count Lucius Verus as co-emperor with Marcus Aurelius, then we count from Trajan. If we exclude Verus, then we simply count from Nerva.

"But troubling news from the north and east shall distress him and he will send his armies to war and destroy many." It is this prophetic flourish at the end of Daniel eleven that elevates it to a genuine oracle. To a lesser extent, it is also present in Daniel 9:24-27, with the last line "and in their place shall be an abomination that desolates, until the decreed end is poured out on the desolator." Consequently, Daniel 9:24 through 12:3 takes a place in the Apollo of God as a bona fide divine prediction. Daniel 9:3-23, on the other hand, is more apocryphal in nature and can be left behind.

Just as the oracle predicted, the two areas of greatest concern to the Antonine rulers were the empire's northern and eastern frontiers. The greatest concentration of its military strength was based along the Rhine and Danube rivers and near Antioch in Syria. Trajan added to the northern defense system with the Dacian salient in the Carpathian bowl. Armenia south of the Caucasus mountains provided Rome with a forward listening post and a check on the Parthians in the east. Hadrian continued this process of defense with his famous wall in northern Britain.

On Hadrian's assumption of the government on August 11, 117 CE, the Jews in Cyrene and Egypt were in rebellion again causing considerable desolation there. To counter the opposition to his principate, Hadrian became a traveling emperor who regularly visited the extent of his empire. This had the effect of reducing the importance of Italy and its capital city. The emperor's court was wherever he happened to be.

In 132 CE, this "spiritual Greek" ordered the devastated city of Jerusalem to be rebuilt in the Greco-Roman style. This gave rise to the so-called Bar-Kochba revolt, when Rabbi Akiba proclaimed him "son of the star" and the long-expected Messiah. It became a bitter and ruthless war that ended Jewish eschatological expectations for centuries to come. The Romans slaughtered the rebels in their thousands, leaving Palestine depopulated for many years. The persecution of Jews became widespread to the extent that Christians began to distance themselves from them. Many Jews sought refuge in the Parthian empire. It is reasonable to say that from 135 CE onward, Rome was no longer a tolerant and welcoming place for Jews.

However, the early church experienced rapid growth in the empire. From Jerusalem it spread to Antioch, Damascus, and on into Asia Minor. From there it crossed the Hellespont into Macedonia and Greece. Egyptian Alexandria hosted the evangelical movement south and then westward into north Africa.[213] Even Rome itself became a launching point, spreading the Christian gospel further west and north into Gaul.

The center of the church continued to be among the seven congregations in Asia Minor, particularly the city of Ephesus. From Edessa in Syria, the church spread the gospel eastward into Mesopotamia and Persia. Roman roads and the longing in the empire for a personal salvation drew many into the growing number of congregations in the Mediterranean world. Regardless of the personal or ethnic background of converts, all were welcomed into the association of Christ.

However, all was not bliss and blessing in the early church. Gnosticism was a formidable force inside the church. The secret knowledge or *gnosis* was a direct counterclaim to those gifted by the Holy Spirit. Those who

---

213. Since the Hadrianic persecution, Alexandria had become the theological center for developing neo-Christian doctrine to repel the Jews. Alexandria still boasted a Jewish diaspora from Ptolemaic times. It was the best place to draw a difference between the Christians and the Jews. From 230 CE to 630 CE, Alexandria led the way in wielding the sword of separation.

lived by faith and not perfect belief had a very difficult time separating the two. Consequently, the church began the process of setting down Christian dogma and authorized Scripture, keeping control of the church in apostolic hands. The rise of Montanus in the mid-second century clearly demonstrates the emphasis on prophecy among the apostolic churches in Asia. In particular, the book of Revelation received strong focus.

The Roman state also had its problems with the growing movement. Like the Jewish community, Christian society was a literate one. Individuals who could read and write were employed by business and the civil administration. For this reason, the emperor Trajan advised Roman officials to adopt a "don't ask" policy toward Christians. Yet Christians in the empire were not members of a legal Roman collegiate, nor were their leaders represented in the pontifical college. Because they stood outside of the legal norms they were viewed as renegades and lawbreakers.

Christians viewed Rome as "Babylon the Great." Between the reigns of Trajan and Marcus Aurelius, the great apologists began to emerge, a trend that continued into the third century. Both sides became entrenched in a war of words. The writings of Justin, Tertullian, and Origen were on one hand, and the *Meditations* of Marcus Aurelius on the other.

The pagan empire and its philosophers were, in fact, not defending themselves very well. During the princeps of Marcus Aurelius, things began going wrong in the empire. The military campaign in Mesopotamia brought a contagion among the ranks into the empire that devastated Rome's well-trained legions. The panic to reinforce her frontiers with new legions cost the loss of the fine espirt de corps and discipline among her soldiers. Persecution of the Christians followed when it was believed Rome's deities were angered by their existence.

The adoptive principle was dropped from imperial succession when Commodus replaced Aurelius on the throne. Historians have pondered why Marcus allowed this succession. Perhaps he had no choice. Commodus, a practicing gladiator, may have been a big help to his father in restoring Rome's defenses on her frontiers. Perhaps gratitude to his son compelled Marcus to raise Commodus to the throne. However, the resources of the empire begin to diminish. The silver denarius was becoming devalued, and Rome's silver supply showed signs of exhaustion. By 193 CE, Rome had had its fill of emperors. Commodus was strangled in his bath by an athlete and succeeded by the elder Pertinax, who was the seventh of the Antonine emperors.

When Pertinax was installed as Rome's great prince, he soon discovered the treasury was bankrupt. He could not pay the promised donative to the Praetorian guard. Like Galba, he advocated austere economy in order to restore the government's finances. The Praetorians were not willing to wait, nor did they condone his stringent measures. Their solution was simple and direct. They murdered him during a riot. They then put the office of emperor up for auction. The unfortunate candidate with the best bid was one Didius Julianus. The senate was so outraged by this event that they convened and elected Clodius Albinus in Britain to be their emperor instead. Albinus was voted all the powers. In Syria, the legions proclaimed Pescennius Niger the new emperor by acclamation. In Upper Pannonia, the Danubian legions and Rhenish soldiers hailed Septimius Severus their new emperor. Like the year 69 CE, Rome had four emperors. History appeared to be repeating itself.

All four candidates had come to the princeps by legal means. Clodius Albinus, the governor of Britain, probably had the strongest claim, but was the farthest away from the empire's capital. Didius Julianus, a senator, lacked the support of the senate and although he was at Rome, he could not use his influence or wealth to appease his colleagues. Of the two raised by the soldiers, Septimius Severus was the closest to Rome. Niger could sail with a small entourage from Antioch, but his armies would take longer to follow in his train. The advantage fell to Severus.

At Ravenna, the fleet and town proclaimed their support for Severus. From there he marched to Rome. The Praetorian guard began to desert Julianus. Sensing his own difficulty, Julianus offered Severus a joint rule. Severus refused. The consul Silius Messalla summoned the senate, which passed a resolution deposing Julianus. The unfortunate senator was conducted into one of the palace lavatories and decapitated. Nine days later, Severus marched into Rome with his own Illyrian guard, and the senate convened, making him the new emperor and voting him all the powers. In deference to the conscript fathers, Severus offered the succession and office of Caesar to Clodius Albinus, who accepted. However, Albinus was no fool. He left the task of Niger to Severus. Meanwhile, he made preparations to battle the victor for recognition as Rome's imperator.

Severus wasted no time consolidating his grip on power. He summoned the Praetorian guard and banished them. His Illyrians replaced them. On July 9, 193 CE, Septimius Severus marched his armies to the east, where he engaged Pescennius Niger at Perinthus. Defeated, Niger fell back on Byzantium. The governor of Asia, Asellius Aemilianus, met Severus's supreme commander Claudius Candidus outside the town of Cyzicus. The battle went to Severus's forces.

While Severus's troops occupied Nicomedia, Niger moved into Bithynia. On the plain between Nicaea and Cius, a decisive engagement went against Niger. He fled to Antioch to rebuild his army. While he was there, Egypt revolted against him and went over to Severus. Leaving Antioch, Niger marched his new army to Issus but was routed by Severus's armies once more. His flight was intercepted at the Euphrates, and his pursuers killed Niger there. After a siege of two and a half years, Byzantium fell to Severus over the winter of 195/6 CE. The east was now firmly in his hands. Possibly one of the contributing factors in the eastern success was Septimius's marriage to Julia Domna, a member of the Syrian aristocracy and the network of alliances in the Near East.

With Niger out of the way, Severus marched his troops westward to confront Clodius Albinus. At Viminacium, Severus openly supplanted Albinus by appointing his eight-year-old son Bassianus to become Caesar on June 30, 196 CE. Julia Domna was made *Mater Augusti*. She and young Bassianus Antoninus were worshipped as the holy mother and child. Of course, this made Septimius a living god-king.

The Severan dynasty and its connections to the Near East and North Africa began the process of introducing oriental religion into the Roman west. In the first century, the emperor was a noble Roman in every sense of the word. Everything about him was Roman. In the second century, the emperor became a Greekling. Marcus Aurelius represented the ultimate Greek ideal of a philosopher-king.

In the third century, Rome's emperors became spiritual Orientals. This trend had been referenced by such early princeps as Caligula, Nero, Domitian, and Commodus, but the noble Greeks and Romans had a low tolerance level for such despotism. But the Severan dynasty was to root absolute monarchy in the imperial system according to the Greco-Oriental style. The defeat of Clodius Albinus and his death on the battlefield near Lugdunum on February 19, 197 CE, truly ended an era and began a new system.

> Then I saw the Lamb
> Open the first of the seven
> seals and one of the living
> creatures commanded with
> a voice of thunder, 'Go!'
> There came a white steed!
> It's rider was an archer;
> and he wore a crown.

He set out conquering and to complete his conquests.
Rev. 6:1 & 2

> As I watched I heard
> the arrogant words made
> by this horn
> As I continued watching
> Its beast was slaughtered
> It's body was given over
> to the fire to be consumed.
> As for the other beasts their
> domains were removed but
> there existence continue for five seasons.
>
> He shall boast words
> against the Most High.
> And shall attempt to
> change the sacred
> seasons and the law;
> They shall be handed
> over to his control
> for fourteen seasons.
> Daniel 7:12-25

Thus did the "little horn" defeat the three kings Didus Julianus, Pescennius Niger, and Clodius Albinus, who were the last of the ten kings from Trajan.

In 193 CE, Septimius Severus ended the Imperial Republic of Rome. The return of absolute monarchy, much feared by republicans, was an inescapable reality. The dominion or hegemony of Italy was taken away, and it became just another province in the empire. Italian Romans were prohibited from military service, and the senate included more provincials. The government of the new empire would become more cosmopolitan as time went on. With Severus, the focus of governance changed from "What is best for Rome and Italy?" to "What is best for the empire?"

The Near Eastern half of the empire was in the ascendancy, being the wealthiest half, while the western half began to decline. The old classical Roman empire, dominated by the west, had gone, its lofty ideals replaced. The season of change (193-283 CE) had come.

Septimius Severus created a new elite corps of his own called the royal archers, mounted on horseback. They were mostly from the eastern provinces of Syria and Osrohene. Severus had taken a page from the military handbook of the ancient pharaohs of the New Kingdom dynasts and their successors. The idea was to dispatch the royal archers as a rapid response unit to any trouble spot in the empire. In some cases the problem could be solved by them. If not, they would attempt to contain it until the legions arrived. To the troublemakers, the arrival of the royal archers was a signal their activities had been noticed and were going to be dealt with. Their very arrival was sufficient in some cases to cause the offenders to withdraw. Sometimes the emperor went with the archers.

The four horsemen of Revelation came fully into play during this first season from 193 to 283 CE. It is then followed by a time of 360 years (284-643 CE) when the lives of the other national groups prior to Rome are extended as part of the empire. By 643 CE, Armenia, Roman Mesopotamia, the entire Near East, Egypt, and North Africa to Tripoli were swallowed up by the hordes of Islam.

At first the Severan dynasty opposed the Christian church, and in 200 CE Septimius Severus banned evangelism and the act of becoming a Christian convert. However, by the time of Alexander Severus, Jesus Christ had become one of the emperor's personal deities. Not only had the new empire become a harsher place for Christians, but Septimius's son and successor Caracalla made it a harsher place for many of his pagan subjects. When Caracalla issued the double denarius, the fiction of the denarii came to an end. Inflation was the result. Caracalla also granted Roman citizenship to all freed persons in the new empire. The end result was higher taxes for most, who also came under the *Jus Civile* law code instead of the more liberal *Jus Gentium*.

Caracalla was murdered by Opellius Macrinus on April 8, 217 CE, who in turn was defeated and killed by the forces brought together by Julia Domna's sister Julia Maesa around the son of Julia Soaemias named Elagabalus. This boy-priest, whose name was Bassianus became the new emperor by June 218 CE. Styled Marcus Aurelius Antoninus, he introduced oriental religion into Rome in a big way. The worship of Sol Invictus, the unconquered sun, was his contribution to the pagan empire. The introduction of monotheism to pagans was the end result. Elagabalus was a latter-day Ikhnaton. In Egypt during the fifteenth century BC, there were four religious tribes who opposed Ikhnaton's religious reforms. Similarly, the old Roman religion was represented by four colleges. Elagabalus was the Pontifex Maximus of all of them. As the early Byzantine empire unfolded its developing character, we see more and more why the oracle of Jesus Christ described it as "Sodom and Egypt in a spiritual sense."

The Severan dynasty was divided into two periods. The death of Caracalla ended the first period. The last half was governed by the "Syrian Princesses": Julia Maesa, the sister of Julia Domna; Julia Soaemias, the mother of Elagabalus; and Julia Mammaea, the mother of Alexander Severus (222-235 CE). The four Julias had a very powerful presence in the new empire and did much to give the Byzantine state its Greco-Oriental flavor. Their sons sat on the throne, but the kingdom was ruled by the women. Julia Maesa was a member of the now cosmopolitan senate. However, her prestige in the government was seriously threatened when Elagabalus exhausted the imperial treasury in his four short years in power. Although he was married a number of times, the emperor produced no heirs. Maesa persuaded her grandson to adopt her other grandson by Mammaea named Alexianus. Once Alexianus had established himself as the new Caesar, the emperor was duly murdered.

Styled Marcus Aurelius Severus Alexander, his rule was a reactionary one in much the dame way that Claudius's rule was a reaction to Caligula's. However, the glory of the Augustan rulers and Antoinine emperors were gone. The army was in the ascendancy and the road to ultimate power. Severus protected them from the coming inflation by doubling their wages. "Protect the army," Septimius is reported to have told his sons, "and forget the rest."

For a short time, it appeared the empire would recover from the excesses of Elagabalus, but the peace was shattered by wars along the northern and eastern frontiers.[214] In the spring of 232 CE, Alexander Severus marched his troops from Antioch into Mesopotamia to confront Parthian incursions there. His army suffered horrific casualties, but the Parthian king Artaxerxes withdrew suddenly, making Severus imperator by default. He stopped long enough in Rome for a magnificent triumph in 233 CE before leaving for Mainz in Gaul in 234 CE to defend Illyricum and Italy from the Germans.

The emperor's pacific gestures to the barbarians annoyed his Illyrian legions, who decided they wanted one of their own for the princeps. In March 235 CE, they proclaimed a Thracian officer named Julius Verus Maximus emperor, after which they murdered Alexander Severus and his mother in their palatial tents. The era of the Syrian Princesses and the Severan dynasty came to an end. Yet the Greco-Oriental character they ingrained into the empire was to remain.

Indeed, the eastern influences gave rise to the feudal system in western Europe during the medieval period. The era of chivalry and fully armored

---

214. Daniel 11:44.

knights is a throwback to the Persians of the third century. They were known as "cataphracts." Supported by a peasant infantry, they were no match for the well-trained Roman legions. But campaigns to the east were often difficult due to the depradations of contagion, famine, desert terrain, and other causes. The armies of Rome could conduct a successful expedition into the Middle East, winning battle after battle, yet return as if they had been badly defeated.

In the sphere of religion, Christianity and Judaism were influenced from the east. Artaxerxes, the first of the Sassanides, hosted a great synod of the Magi to create a uniform Zoroastrian religion in the Persian kingdom. Persecution fell on all schismatics and other non-Zoroastrian groups.

The members of the early church were the disciples of Jesus Christ. As time passed, they became disciples of other religious influences they incorporated into Christian doctrine, such as Zoroaster, Plato, Socrates, and Aristotle. Plato and Aristotle lived at a time when the Greek world much admired the Persian east. Orientalism found a ready channel to the west through Asia Minor and the Levant. The seven congregations of the early church found themselves on a battlefield of theological influences, east and west. The casualties were to prove heavy indeed.

The remaining forty-eight years in the "season" see the emergence of the era of soldier-emperors. During this period the other three make their appearance. From emperor Maximus to the death of Claudius II Gothicus (235-269 CE), the new empire went through one of its darkest periods. The military and its leaders were all-powerful. They were largely indifferent to the senate and civil population. Its enemies within and without had forced the military to fall back on itself. Their needs and aspirations came first.

The military segregated into three main branches. The emperor and his elite corps and bodyguard were over all the land forces. The legions were by now a barbarian rabble. The cavalry and navy operated separately.

While the Romans desperately sought for the right commander-in-chief from within, the barbarians from the north broke through the frontier defences along the Rhine and Danube rivers, sweeping into Gaul, Italy, and Spain. In the east, the Parthians took Mesopotamia and Syria, capturing the emperor Valerian (253-260 CE). The reign of Gallienus saw the empire reach its lowest point. It also saw the reforms of Septimius Severus brought fully to the fore. A rise to power no longer came from the patrician or plebeian aristocracies but through the military ranks. The path to power was vertical.

Prior to the later barbarian invasions, the Christian missionaries had been active among the Gothic tribes. Some tribesmen were becoming converts. In the mid-third century, the bishop Ulfilas constructed a Gothic alphabet. The Muratori Bible was translated into the new written language. As Christian doctrine and theology spread among the Goths, so also literacy expanded. As a result the Gothic tribes became persuaded the pagan gods were powerless among the Neo-Romans and should be destroyed. The God of Jesus Christ would give them victory. This was not what Christian aspirations looked for among them, but once the consensus was created from within, their leaders were able to organize the Gothic community for the great task ahead.

Claudius II Gothicus (268-269 CE) undertook the defense of Italy from the Alamanni and of the Balkans from the Goths. When his advance cavalry met with disaster, he made Aurelian the commander-in-chief of all his horse soldiers.

> When the second seal was opened the second living creature cried out, "Go!" A red horse came into view and its soldier was granted to make war on the earth to take away peace so that the earth should slaughter one another; and he was given a long sword. [215]

Near Lake Benacus, Claudius won a major victory over the Goths, killing half their number. The survivors then linked up with the Heruli and Peucini tribes to build some two thousand ships for some 320 thousand warriors. Launching their fleet from the Danube into the Black Sea, their lack of sailing skills and experience soon got them into trouble. Unable to carry their large number, most of the soldiers disembarked, leaving the Gothic fleet to a smaller force. The landed barbarians eventually were confronted by Aurelian's cavalry and Claudius's infantry at Naissus, suffering another heavy defeat from imperial forces. The imperial navy commanded by Probus sailed from Egypt to engage the remaining Gothic fleet, forcing the barbarians to retreat northward.

While Aurelian's cavalry pursued the fleeing Gothic remnants, Claudius Gothicus marched his infantry to confront the Vandals in Pannonia and the Juthungi in Raetia. However, at Sirmium, Gothicus and his infantry were wiped out by the plague. Only Probus at sea and Aurelian's cavalry on land remained. In 270 CE, Aurelian was invested with the crown and all its powers, becoming the first horseman of the Apocalypse.

By this time, the Neo-Roman kingdom was reduced in size. All that remained under imperial control was Italy, Greece, Carthage, and Cyrenaica. The west had fallen to some two dozen warlords while Asia Minor and the

---

215. Gibbon, Decline and Fall, Vol. 1, Chap 1:17.

Levant became the domain of the Palmyrene kingdom. Egypt was ruled by a renegade governor.

Aurelian's cavalry force proved to be an improved asset for the emperor and his elite royal archers. The cavalry could move more rapidly than an infantry. This enabled a rapid reconquest of the east, including Egypt, and by 274 CE he was in the west to recover Spain, Gaul, and Britain. As he went, troops deserted to him, making it a quick victory. A magnificent triumph was given him in Rome. While there he undertook to reform the currency.

> When the third seal was opened the third living creature said, Go! I saw a black horse. The rider upon it held a pair of scales above his head and a voice from among the four living creatures said, "a quart of wheat and three quarts of barley for a silver denarius. But do not harm the olive oil and the wine."

Wheat, barley, olive oil, and wine were the staple diet of the Roman empire. In the second century CE, an army modius of wheat cost half a denarius. Consequently, a full denarius at that time would buy 15.36 quarts of wheat and 46 quarts of barley. The period of time this horseman refers to was an inflationary one.

The Roman monetary system was a trimetallic one spread out over four official coins. At the top was the old aureus, standardized by Octavian Augustus at 1/40th of a libra. A libra was equivalent to 327.45 grams in todays measure. Below the aureus was the silver denarius. One aureus was the same as 25 denarii. Below the denarius were two copper coins: the sesterce, which was used to measure personal worth, and the smallest coin called the as. Ten as and four sesterces would purchase one denarius in the first and second century CE. In the second century, one quart of wheat cost less than two as. Wheat made the bread of choice for the army. Barley was for the bread of punishment.

Under the Roman emperors from the second century, the silver denarius was the coin they debased. They had the good sense to leave the aureus alone and the copper coins were not worth the trouble. By the time of Septimius Severus, the denarius had been devalued by half its face value. The army's pay was doubled to two denarii per diem.

Inside the empire, the denarius continued to trade at face value. However, traders outside the empire to the east noticed the devaluation, and what used to cost one denarius now cost two. Astute merchants then took their devalued denarii coins inside the empire and traded them at face value for the gold aureus. In this way, they enhanced their profit by receiving an additional 50% discount on their gold purchases. This had the effect of draining gold out of the empire's coffers.

When Aurelian reformed the monetary system, this practice was stopped and the silver denarius became defunct. The gold aureus became smaller and was revalued at $1/50^{th}$ of a libra. The sesterce became the sestevtii revalued at 1/2500 of a libra, while the as became the sestertius valued at 1/5000 of a libra. It wasn't until the fourth century that the silver coinage was replaced by the seliqua. Consequently the first three horsemen must have completed their ride by 275 CE. Death had always been with the earth, and death by plague seriously entered the empire from the princeps of Marcus Aurelius onward.

From his temples dedicated to Sol Invictus, the unconquered sun Aurelian was vice-gerant of his monotheistic deity. As such he was a man-god and anyone touching him without his permission was put to death on the spot. At Rome, his senators became *pontifices dei Solis*, meant to cultivate the personality cult of the emperor. Although Aurelian was probably unaware of it, in the overall scheme of history and the oracle, he had become a surogate for the unconquered Christ, who had described himself as the "root of David and the bright morning star." Our resurrected Lord had become the Apollo of God.

The elevation of Aurelian to a god on earth made it more difficult for his enemies to assault his person. It also enabled him to be a strict disciplinarian. From his troopers he demanded sobriety, chastity, and frugality, and prohibited the arts of divination. His soldiers were trained for optimum readiness. A new esprit de corps emerged. Though Aurelian's punishments were cruel, they were effective. "The public allowance is sufficient for the soldiers' support" he said of his military. "Their wealth should be collected from the enemy spoils and not the tears of the provincials." His monotheism and rigorous adherence to strict moral living and service attracted Christians and their offspring into the military. In the summer of 275 CE, Aurelian fell to an assassination plot.

Modern eschatologists who attempt to fit the four horsemen into a grandiose symbolic function make a fundamental error in their interpretation. The four horsemen of Zechariah were down to earth and specific, appearing once and only once in events that occurred in real time. It's the same old technique of bombastic charlatans who like to throw symbolic or spiritual explanations at what they actually do not understand. Yet these religious imposters have their uses. They serve to attract an element of the public like themselves. Those who have an astute insight into how an oracle lives and breathes know who and what to avoid.

> When he broke the fifth seal open I heard the cry of those faithful to the good news under the altar who had been killed for the witness they had given: They plead, "Sovereign King, holy and faithful, when will you avenge the righteous blood of your servants on those who slaughtered us?" A white robe was given to each and they were calmed. "Wait a little longer until your number has been fulfilled for your fellow slaves and their associates are also about to be killed."

The persecution of Christ's disciples began in Jerusalem and gradually spread through the empire. It was a constant threat to the New Israel of God. But the power of Pentecost could not be overturned. The hundred and twenty apostles and disciples spread out over the empire, making a significant impact on local populations. In the east, the power of prophecy and its probability as the word of God was a powerful tool for making converts among Jews and Gentiles. In the west, these eastern, swarthy-looking people appeared among them, able to speak their language, which in many cases was not written down. Among the barbarians, this was a miracle in itself. What is more, the easterners spoke about some Messiah named Jesus Christ who could give them a better life.

However, the early church was actively opposed by the Jews in most cases. They, in fact, were the first to create Christian martyrs, beginning with Joshua himself. In the initial stages most early Christians, being Jews themselves, were willing to forgive their brethren, but as time passed resentment turned to animosity. In the last half of the first century, the apostle John began labeling Jews the anti-Christ. He would be joined by Gentiles in the years to come, among whom would appear many Christians. This collective anti-Christ showed its face during the persecution launched by the emperor Nero in Rome. He was assisted in this effort by Jews and Gentiles alike. The Jewess Poppea Sabina, his mistress turned wife, was one of them. How many Christians turned traitor is not known, but Roman money would have discovered them. The Apocalypse of John admonishes Christians at Smyrna not to fear the collective anti-Christ, who are a synagogue of Satan. In the Christian mind-set, anyone who opposed Joshua ben Joseph ben David as the Messiah of God was the anti-Christ.

The edict enacted by Nero was never repealed by the Flavian or Antonine emperors. Trajan advocated a "don't ask" policy, but Christians continued to suffer persecution and martyrdom in the second and third century. Much of it was prosecuted by the locals for local reasons. During the princeps of Marcus Aurelius, events began to turn against the Romans on a larger scale. The currency was in the process of being devalued, the well-oiled legions had been devastated by a plague from the east, and the early invasions of barbarians from the north beset Rome's frontiers. The gradual absence of Jews from the empire after Hadrian crushed the last Jewish rebellion exposed Christians to the frustrations of the Roman governing class. They needed a scapegoat, and Christians were local and few enough in numbers.

Septimius Severus extended the edict of Nero to include a prohibition on converts. This struck a direct blow against the evangelical mission of all Christians everywhere. The followers of Christ went deeper underground as a result, and the church continued to grow. Instead of defeating the church, its oppressors merely added an increasing mystique to the community of disciples.

Roman intellectual life continued to advance its boundaries, but its pagan system of belief and institutions began more and more to feel like a dead weight around its neck. In times of crisis, cherished notions come under scrutiny, and their worth is measured in the light of day. Expediency ultimately determines what is useful and what is not. Survival ingrains the new perspective into common practice. When the emergency gradually abates, the survivors build monuments to the institutions that contributed to their salvation. Generally those institutions are a mixture of old and new. Each crisis that follows serves to test the new institutions and their relationships to the old ones, as well as the growing or declining commitment made by individuals or the collective. This was the process visited on the first one hundred and fifty years of the new Byzantine state and the early church alike.

The governor of Egypt at the time of Aurelian's death succeeded the choice of Claudius Tacitus by the senate's *inter regnum* and Florianus, the prefect of the guard, who may have murdered Tacitus after a six months' rule. Probus effectively continued the conquest begun by Aurelian until the enemies from without and within had been subdued. Before his death in 282 CE, the emperor was turning his attention to domestic works inside the empire. Building projects and agricultural endeavors were launched by his armies to restore confidence in the new empire.

Goths were settled in Thrace to correct the loss of population there, and many were employed in the infantry. The continued decline of discipline in the infantry resulted in horrific casualties among them. Some historians, including Gibbon, point to this policy as one of the main reasons the empire fell, the policy may have actually been a deliberate design to reduce the numbers of warlike barbarians who resisted discipline. As previously stated, the premise of Gibbon's excellent history is in error. The fact is the empire of classical Rome ended in one year. The year 193 CE.

The so-called "dark ages" are said to be such because of a lack of correspondence about the period. Yet periods of zenith in some histories are just as dark. For instance, we know very little about Antoninus Pius. who preceded Marcus Aurelius. Human nature is easily fooled by outward appearance. To say an absence of correspondence means a period of decline is not necessarily true.

Festival Cycle Three
The Seven Congregations

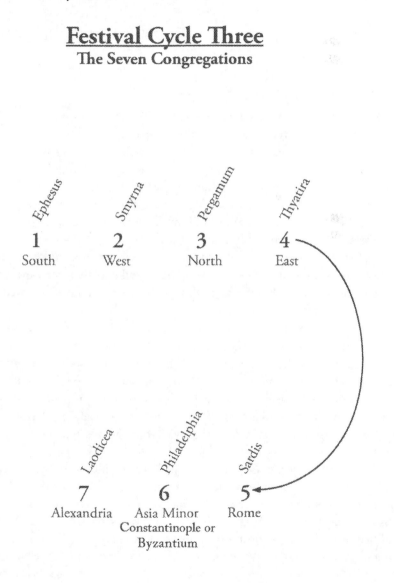

Ephesus	Smyrna	Pergamum	Thyatira
1	**2**	**3**	**4**
South	West	North	East

Laodicea	Philadelphia	Sardis
7	**6**	**5**
Alexandria	Asia Minor Constantinople or Byzantium	Rome

12

THE CHRISTIAN ORTHODOX STATE

It was the emperor Aurelius Carus (282-283 CE) who recognized that Rome was not the true capital of the new empire. Nor was one ruler adequate to govern so vast an area. The legal, imperial language in the west was Latin, while Greek was spoken in the east. He appointed his son Aurelius Carinus as western Caesar and raised his younger son Aurelius Numerianus to be co-Caesar. The emperor took Aurelius Numerianus with him into Mesopotamia, restoring that province when he captured Seleucia and Ctesiphon. He probably had in mind making Numerianus eastern Caesar, but died before he could do so. His son was proclaimed Augustus, but both he and his older brother were murdered shortly afterward. It was left to Diocletian (284-305 CE), who made his capital at Nicomedia in Asia Minor, to effect the intentions of Carus.

In the summer of 285 CE, Diocletian raised one of his colleagues, Maximian, to be Caesar. The following year, when Maximian's troops made him emperor, Diocletian accepted his elevation, making him western Augustus with his capital at Milan. Diocletian was senior Augustii of the east and Maximian was junior Augustii of the west. All edicts were published in their joint names, while each retained initiation of all legislation in his respective jurisdiction. It was in this way that the western empire came about.

C. Aurelius Valerius Diocletianus, an Illyrian soldier of humble birth, was a perfect example of how the military was the road to imperial power. His vertical rise from the son of a slave through the ranks made him consul in the government for one term. In years past, that would have qualified as a senatorial promotion. His talent clearly lay in organization and administration, which the old republican system would not have used for the simple reason that he was not an illustrious member of the patrician or plebeian aristocracies. In the new Byzantine system, however, merit and service went hand in hand to yield the new empire its rulers.

As senior Augustus, Diocletian also followed Aurelian, styling his princeps as an oriental god-king. The only part of Aurelian's person the petitioner could touch was the emperor's big toe, showing homage by kissing it. Under Diocletian, the entire residence of the emperor was a holy sanctum. He would condescend to hear his subjects' petitions in specially created environments designed to present himself as a god. He wore a purple robe over a splendid white tunic that matched the white cosmetic on his countenance. On his feet were scarlet boots. He reposed on his throne, the sun casting a kind of spotlight on his serene demeanor. His guard dressed in red tunics and gold armor, which must have been very intimidating to the average petitioner.

Religiously, Diocletian was somewhat regressive and out of step with the changing times. Designating himself as the "House of Jove" and Maximian as the "House of Hercules," Diocletian invoked the old Greco-Roman, pagan forms of anthropomorphism. The worship of Sol Invictus was far more spiritual in nature and had as its fundamental premise the launching of human spiritual capability beyond symbols and ancestor worship. It was a new religious awareness for a new age. As a god-king in the Greco-Oriental fashion, Diocletian enhanced the outward form of the monarch but fell short of the spiritual expectations envisaged by the symbols.

In the western empire, Maximian had to contend with renewed barbarian invasions into Gaul. Paradoxically, their own depradations served as a weapon against their incursions by decimating their ranks with famine and plague. In turn, civil war would erupt among them with obvious results. To assist his governance, each of the Augustii secured the help of a successor made Caesar. Galerius Valerius became eastern Caesar stationed at Thessalonica in Greece, while Maximian adopted Constantius Chlorus, locating his Caesar's capital at Trier in Gaul. A northern road gradually developed between the Danube and the Mediterranean, linking the four capitals.

The western Caesar Constantius elevated an officer named Carasius to be commander-in-chief of the navy in 287 CE and gave him charge of the fleet to clear pirates from the rivers, the Channel, and North Sea. Carasius achieved the desired results but was accused of misappropriating pirate booty to his personal coffers. Carasius sailed the entire fleet to Britain making himself Caesar, then Augustus there. Perhaps the new tetrarchy would have let him be for a longer period of time, but Carasius began minting his own silver coins, styling himself as a member of the ruling fraternity. A supply of silver meant a new coin could restore the old monetary system. The result to Carasius was fatal.

The government of Diocletian became a bureaucracy of officials who received fixed wages for their service. The system of taxation was taken out of the hands of farmers and completely reorganized based on the ability of farmland to produce. During this time the feudal system was couched in law. The new Byzantine state was on the threshhold of the medieval age. The new taxation system yielded new revenues, enabling government to finance new endeavors. However, the age of conquest was over, and the empire built a defensive military system designed to intercept invaders. The new age invented a new utilitarian architecture designed to last. Roman forts became stone castles. More and more, Europe was adopting the outward appearance of the Middle Ages.

The religious policy of Diocletian brought him into conflict with the syncretizing of his era. In 296 CE, he took action against the Persian religious sect of the Manichaeans, who combined Zoroastrianism, Neo-Platonism, and Christianity in their religious outlook. He published an edict against them, and to avoid persecution, many Manichaeans sought refuge among the Christians.

About 298 CE, according to Lactantius, certain pagan priests were unable to obtain omens from their sacrifices and blamed it on the Christians present, who made the sign of the cross. In response, Diocletian ordered all Christians to be discharged from government service. Finally, after consulting the oracles, he published a general edict against the disciples of Christ on February 23, 303 CE. Their rights as citizens were abolished until such time as they returned to the "old time religion." All Bibles and related literature were to be surrendered and burned. Church buildings were closed and religious assembly prohibited. Two fires in the palace at Nicomedia led to the arrest and detention of the clergy. Most were forced to make official sacrifice to the pagan deities and then released. Those who did not were imprisoned or martyred. In the spring of 304 CE, this practice was extended to all Christians in the empire.

The breaking of the fifth seal signaled the last great persecution to fall on Christendom by imperial direction. While the imperial persecution progressed among rank and file members of the church, Diocletian and his colleague Maximian abdicated the princeps on May 1, 305 CE. Gallerius, who was considered the prime instigator of the Christian persecution, replaced Diocletian as Augustus in the east and Constantius Chlorus replaced Maximian in the west. As soon as Constantius was confirmed in power, he effectively halted the persecution and honored the edicts by demolishing a Christian church or building every now and then. In the east, however, the seven congregations were savagely devastated. Galerius and Caesar Maximin Daia created havoc in the eastern church and raised schismatic quarreling for years into the future. The *lapsi* were everywhere. Finally, the persecution was halted by edict in 313 CE, and the eastern church was left to recover what it could. Like the pagan Romans in Nero's day, many non-Christians were appalled at the persecution they had witnessed. Christians were, after all, fellow citizens. It was probably a good thing Diocletian retired during that time. His credibility as an oriental god-king was in all likelihood seriously damaged.

The tetrarchy of Diocletian began to unravel in the west. Galerius held a very strong hand at court by confining Maximian's son Maxentius inside the city of Rome and holding Chlorus's son Constantine as hostage in Nicomedia. He had bypassed the heredity principle by having Flavius Valerius Severus installed as western Caesar. However, in 305 CE, Britain was invaded by the Picts and Constantius demanded his son join his campaign there. Reluctantly, Galerius complied, and Constantine joined his father at Boulogne in early 306 CE to accompany the expedition. The Picts were crushed, and while in York, Constantius died on July 25 of that year. The legions in Britain proclaimed Constantine the new western Augustus. He wrote to Galerius explaining the situation and suggesting his recognition as Augustus would prevent civil war. Instead, Galerius compromised, making Severus western Augustus and Constantine western Caesar. Constantine accepted. However, in Rome the praetorian tribunes and the tribune of the *forum suavii* who commanded the urban cohorts, openly complained about their loss of prestige in the new empire. Inflamed and provoked to further action by the senate and city population, they proclaimed Maxentius emperor on October 28, 306 CE. Maxentius then sent the purple insignia to his father Maximian, who accepted the title of Augustus with the senate's approval. The western empire was now at civil war.

Galerius ordered Flavius Valerius Severus to crush the revolt. The rebels held the loyalty of central and southern Italy only and Severus marched south from Milan to end the insurrection in 307 CE. In a surprise move, Severus's troops mutinied and went over to the rebels. Severus hastily retreated, pursued by Maximian to Ravenna. There he surrendered to Maxentius's father and abdicated. At Rome, Maxentius was raised to co-Augustus with his father, and this time he accepted.

What of Constantine? Maximian wasted no time and marched into Gaul, confronting him at Trier. Constantine relented and married Fausta, the daughter of Maximian, to confirm their alliance. Constantine retained the office of western Caesar.

Galerius took the field against the western usurpers but was forced to abort the expedition at Interamna. Spain declared for Maxentius. When Maximian attempted to denounce the growing support of his son to the legions, his efforts misfired and the aged emperor was forced to flee. Constantine gave him succor. By the spring of 308 CE, Maxentius was recognized as sole Augustus in the west.

In November of that year, Galerius, supported by Diocletian as fellow consul for that year, concluded a conference at Carnuntum to attempt a resolution in the west. Galerius proposed that Maximian resign as Augustus in exchange for a full pardon. Maxentius would be declared a public enemy with all the attending consequences. Constantine would remain western Caesar but Galerius nominated Licinianus Licinius to be western Augustus.

All parties refused to accept Galerius's proposal. To make matters worse, Maximin Daia, the eastern Caesar, was hailed as eastern Augustus by his troops. In Africa, a revolt elevated the *vicarius* of a praetorian named Domitius Alexander as another candidate for the purple. In 310 CE, Maximian reappeared at Arles, having himself proclaimed as Augustus by the troops there. Two Augustii in the east, three in the west, and one Caesar. The Byzantine state and the tetrarchy of Diocletian were becoming basket cases.

One can only wonder why Galerius so staunchly resisted Constantine's elevation to be western Augustus. Twice he passed him over. What was it about the son of Chlorus that the House of Jove rejected? Was it because Constantine fundamentally rejected the idea of the tetrarchy, or was it his religious views? Constantine, like Aurelian, worshipped Sol Invictus and was receptive to the ongoing developments within and outside the empire. Unlike Galerius, he probably appreciated change was inevitable and those unwilling to change, especially in the imperium, deserved to be pushed aside. The military instrument, on which the emperors' power rested, was changing, and the imperium had to change with it. In fact, in an ideal world the emperor should have been the one leading those changes.

In 311 CE, the emperor of Rome, Maxentius, sent his praetorian prefect to put down the rebel Domitius Alexander in Africa. When his task was accomplished, the food supply from Carthage was restored to the old capital, thus revealing its outside dependence. By May, Galerius's efforts to recover the eastern empire ended when he died of a wasting disease.[216] In the far west, Constantine brought the Franks to heel and Spain was

---

216. Jews and Christians of that time liked to imagine their enemies dying of disease, causing exquisite torture to their tormentors such as Galerius,

recovered to his support. In the east, Maximin Daia marched from Syria into Asia Minor and Pontus. Licinianus Licinius laid claim to the eastern empire and made an alliance with Constantine. In response, Daia proposed an alliance with Rome, which Maxentius accepted.

While Licinius moved to engage Maximin Daia, Constantine assembled an army of forty thousand troops and moved on Italy to unseat Maxentius. The conquest of northern Italy proved expensive, and Constantine marched on Rome with a reduced force of some 25,000. Fortunately he was able to capitalize on an awkward position Maxentius was in near the Milvian bridge, which led to the destruction of Maxentius and the end of any rivalry in the west. By force of arms, Constantine had become western Augustus. In the east Licinius had triumphed against Daia becoming Augustus there. In 313 CE, Constantine and Licinius met in Milan, concluding an edict that ended the persecution of Christians in both east and west. Constantine's sister Constantia married Licinius as a symbol of their alliance.

> When the sixth seal was opened I saw a great earthquake;
> The sun turned black as coal,
> The full moon became red like blood;
> And the stars of heaven fell to the ground
> Just like a fruit tree lets go its winter fruit in a strong wind.
> The sky disappeared like a finished scroll
> And all the mountains and every island was shaken from its place.
> Then the kings who rule among those of influence, the military leaders, the wealthy and poor, slave and free hid in the network of caves, calling to the rock and mountains above them;
> "Cover us over and conceal us from the ones seated on the throne in its place save us from the Lamb's anger and fury for the great day of wrath has come and who can bear it?"

These words are reminiscent of Jesus's words in his portrayal of the "Portent of the Son of Man" in his great prophecy reported in Matthew. Just as the political empire changed then, so it was to occur again during the life of Constantine. The western emperor's victory at the Milvian bridge reminded

---

Herod Agrippa (Acts 12: 21-23), Antiochus IV (2 Maccabees 9:5), Jehoram (2 Chron 21:15, 18-19), and Judas Iscariot (Acts 1:18).

Constantine of his oath regarding the Christian faith. That victory made him sole Augustus of the western empire and the first Christian emperor. The ten years of peace between himself and Licinius enabled Constantine to renovate the worship of Sol Invictus into the worship of Jesus Christ, the root of David and the bright morning star. Perhaps this tendency in Chlorus's son had been foreseen by Galerius, which may have been why he opposed Constantine's elevation in the Tetrarchy.

In the east, Licinius was to continue this Galerian opposition to the Christian church. But the lines had been drawn between Christian and pagan. Licinius may have been the eastern Augustus of Jove's house, but Constantine had abandoned Hercules for Jesus Christ. As western Augustus, he ruled by divine right. He would tolerate no opposition from anyone. Constantine had a stake in the eastern empire as Licinius also did in the west. Constantine would concern himself with the safety of the church in Licinius's domain equally as his own. In the same way, the pagan emperor would be watchful toward the west.

During the ten years of peace, each emperor occupied his time consolidating his grip on power within his respective domain. Once that was accomplished, each would begin overtly interfering in the other's jurisdiction. There were old scores to settle, and the new material theocracy rising in the west had a long scorecard.

Constantine appointed his brother-in-law Bassianus to be Caesar at Trier in Gaul while his children were still young. Licinius was able to instigate a conspiracy with Senecio, the brother of Bassianus. He in turn persuaded the western Caesar to revolt against his brother-in-law. Constantine discovered the plot before it became serious, and Bassianus was tried, convicted, and executed. Senecio was at court in, or around, Nicomedia, and Constantine demanded Senecio be extradited to his custody to answer for his part in the plot. Licinius revealed his complicity by refusing. East and west were once again at war.

The emperors engaged their respective armies at Cibalae in Pannonia on October 8, 314 CE, but Licinius withdrew. Though Licinius appeared defeated, it was not a clear outcome, and both forces met in Thrace at Campus Mardiensis. Again the battle was inconclusive. There followed a conference wherein both emperors concluded a treaty ending the tetrarchy. From 315 CE onward, the old Roman domain and its boundaries were no more. Two empires were legally recognized, separate and distinct: the pagan empire of the east and the Christian Holy Roman Empire of the west. To give credence to the notion of unity, each emperor became consul for the year 315 CE in a republic that no longer existed.

And he shall wear out the holy ones of the Most High, and shall attempt to change the sacred seasons and the law, and they shall be given into his power.

In 318 CE, Constantine recognized the authority of the episcopal courts on equal terms with the civil jurisdiction. If all parties to a litigation agreed, their case could be heard and adjudicated in either a civil or an episcopal court. Any dissent would compel the case to be heard exclusively in a civil court. This option was bound to create problems in the east, where the central authority and strength of the church rested.

In 321 CE, a rescript in the west allowed any citizen to bequeath his property to the church. The church at Rome also became a civic corporation and a legal religious college. The bishop of Rome became a member of the pontifical college, second only to the Pontifex Maximus Constantine himself. The patriarchs would have been offended at this elevation of one of their subordinates. The bishop of Rome, of course, would have seen his role in the church from a much different perspective. From the emperor's point of view, his church was now a legal entity, an objective that Christians and the old Roman state had clashed over.

In times of crisis, emperors like Decius and Galerius were vigilant to ensure all citizens were law-abiding. Because Christians were not a legal college involved in various day-to-day transactions, they were viewed as lawbreakers. Under the Roman system they, in fact, were. Constantine removed this impediment by rooting the church in law.

These reforms in the west prompted the eastern church to seek reciprocal comforts from their emperor. Instead, Licinius banned all Christian synods and restricted all philanthropic activities in his dominion. These measures smacked of another Christian persecution on the horizon. It appears Licinius had signaled it was time for Christians to migrate westward. However, in 320 CE, Constantine turned back a Sarmatian invasion in Pannonia and then marched his troops into Thrace to confront an incursion by the Goths. Clearly this latter move was a provocative act, and Licinius decided to view it as such. In 324 CE, the empires again went to war.

On July 3 of that year, Licinius was badly defeated at Adrianople, and his land forces fell back on Byzantium. While Constantine besieged the old Greek city, his son Crispus, who was now Caesar, attacked Abantus's fleet in the Dardanelles. Licinius's fleet was destroyed. Unable to be reinforced and supplied by sea, Licinius withdrew across the straits to Chalcedon in Asia Minor. Occupying the straits with his fleet, Constantine landed in Asia, giving battle to Licinius's forces at Chrysopolis on September

18, 324 CE. Fleeing to Nicomedia, Licinius and his court sued for an honorable surrender. Constantine arbitrated an agreement, sending the defeated emperor into exile at Thessalonica. Licinius was caught in an intrigue against Constantine's life, and the emperor asked the senate in Rome to decide Licinius's fate. They sentenced him to death. The whole Byzantine empire was now in the hands of a Christian emperor, and the world had changed forever.

> As I watched,
> A succession of thrones were put in place
> And an Ancient of Days set among them
> His garments were pure white and his hair like fine wool;
> His throne burned with fire
> And his carriage was fiery flames
> Fire like a river poured out from his being.
> Millions attended him.
> Books were consulted as the court sat in judgment.

As we've learned from Ezekiel's book, the description of a throne in chapter one was occupied by the Neo-Babylonian king Nebuchadnezzar II at the time. The glory of God could be reflected by human kings. Christendom's eschatologists have consistently concluded, incorrectly, that the description in Ezekiel is of God himself. Yet the Scriptures make it quite clear that no human can see God and live.[217] Thus, the Creator communicates by oracles. The notion that Jesus Christ was God on earth is nonsense. The description of the personage in Daniel 7:9 matches that of Revelation 1:12-16 and is indeed the same. The passage in Daniel 7:13 gives no description just as Revelation 4:2-3 gives no material description, only an aura that fits the person of God. It is a distinctive atmosphere surrounding a given source; a luminous radiation; an energy field that is held to emanate from a living being.[218] Yet Christendom's eschatologists assume the Ancient of Days is one and the same when, in fact, it is not. Just as Jesus said to the Jews through John's gospel, the Father judges no one at all but has given all judgment to the Son.[219]

Consequently, more than a superficial reading is required to understand the oracle. All too often, Christendom's eschatologists miss the mark by making assumptions that never did exist. The ongoing failure rate is

217. John 1:18.
218. Merriam-Webster's Collegiate Dictionary, Tenth Edition 1996.
219. 5:22.

a sure testimony that this is true. Even today, with the growing amount of impressive materials available to the student, the tragedy of failed expectations continues. In some cases, lives have been needlessly lost. Eschatologists become rooted in their oppressive, authoritarian structures, unwilling to change.

The synthesis of a Greco-Oriental culture, observing the Christian religion, held together by Roman law, within an imperial framework created the Byzantine material theocracy. The pagan sky was being rolled up like a scroll, opening heaven;s gate to all who lived in the Christian *oikoumene*. The new thrones were those of the emperors at Constantinople and Rome and the bishops of Christ. All the emperors' subjects would be welcomed inside Christendom's mountain-like "caves" made of stone, where worshippers would plead, "Fall on us and hide us from the face of the one seated on the throne and from the wrath of the Lamb."

One can fully appreciate the oracle's meaning by reviewing the massive church structures with their cavernous interiors. Those outside the boundaries of the Orthodox Holy Roman Empire would also have heard of her fame and journeyed to the "mountains of Rome." However, to experience the fullest impact, one need only journey through old Capadocia in Central Turkey and see some of the oldest Christian churches carved out inside mountains to hide congregants from the persecutions. Some are quite awe-inspiring. Monasticism was also becoming a feature of Christendom in this period. Christian monks literally lived and worshipped in caves.

In 325 CE, the first ecumenical synod was brought together at Nicaea to bring about a unified confession in doctrine and canonical law. In that same year, the solar legend disappeared from imperial coinage, replaced by Christian motifs.

On May 11, 330 CE, Byzantium on the Bosphorus was inaugurated as New Rome and became the new imperial capital. Later it was renamed Constantinople, the city of Christ and his church and the center of the Middle Ages. Gradually, Rome became a provincial capital only, and eventually just a provincial city when Ravenna became the provincial imperial capital. On the other hand, Constantinople went from glory to glory, rising to become the great capital city of the medieval period. Hagia Sophia, still standing in Istanbul, became the first great Christian edifice and temple of Christ in the material theocracy. New Jerusalem on earth became the gateway and bridge to heaven. Constantinople's ideal location controlled the major trade routes east, west, north, and south, making its wealth legendary. In time, Constantine's city became an impregnable fortress. It could easily defend its wealth and power. Its highly professional cavalry was the best fighting force in the Mediterranean world. Its navy became the forerunner of twentieth century battleships, able to destroy the enemy fleet from a distance. For centuries, no one dared to confront it. Even the empire of Islam learned to keep its distance.

The old material theocracy of ancient Israel paled by comparison, but its experience was similar in many ways. Just as Old Israel had become like Sodom and Egypt in a spiritual sense, so would Christendom. As the Christian material theocracy developed, one can see the similarities between old and new. "The Kingdom of the heavens," said Jesus in one of his parables, "is like the master of a household who brings out of his treasure what is new and what is old."

Here we can introduce the parabolic oracle used by Jesus in his ministry. In our redaction of the Bible and reconstruction of the oracle of God, the parabolic oracles contained in Matthew 13, 18, and 20 should be preserved as part of Jesus's great prophecy in chapters 24 and 25 of Matthew's gospel. These ten parabolic oracles can be listed between verses thirty and thirty-one of chapter 25, for a total of twelve parabolic oracles.

> After this there were four angels at earth's four corners restraining the four winds so that no wind could harm the earth, sea, or any tree.
> Another angel having the living seal of the Almighty
> And ascending from the east shouted to the four angels who had authority to harm the earth and sea
> "Cause no harm until we have sealed the slaves of the Almighty on their foreheads."
> There were sealed out of every tribe of Israel's people one hundred forty-four thousand in number.

The picture we see here is the orderly construction of the Christian material theocracy.[220] This is the heavenly church, which is still bound to the earth. Like his ancestor ben Jesse, the greater David groups them in an orderly fashion to serve at the altar before God, where the people can see these holy priests perform their sacrifices and atonements. They occupy the holy compartment in the sacred place. It is lit by the golden, seven-candled menorah representing the seven churches of the Christ. They eat the sacrificial bread and drink the sacred wine, offering prayers of atonement and well-being on the altar before the allegorical curtain separating heaven from earth.

---

220. 1 Chronicles 24:7-19.

The great high priest, in the manner of Joshua ben Jehozadak, passed through the curtain into the Most Holy of heaven itself, where he offered the value of his perfect blood at the mercy seat of almighty God's throne. His perfect life, represented by his shed blood, was the purchase price accepted by God for the human race, past, present, and future. The deal is done. The Great Prince Michael owns humankind. We are his slaves. How we are treated by the Master will depend on each of us individually.

No one can say to our Master, "You don't understand." It would be an empty accusation. Those who are anointed by God to the first resurrection belong exclusively to the Great Prince and are the priesthood. They pass from the first and second death into everlasting life to serve at God's throne. These are the twenty-four elders. Those of faith who follow with the second resurrection from the first death will occupy the earth during the millennium to come. This is the group described at 7:9-17 in the oracle. At the end of the millennium, they will have an opportunity to pass through the second death into everlasting life, provided they have been perfected to God's approval.[221] Again, it will depend on how they live their lives. Because God has promised a resurrection to humankind does not obligate a resurrection of everyone at the beginning of the millennium. Only those whom God favors will begin the second resurrection. Each will then follow in order depending on what God thought of them.[222] Most will receive their resurrection in the middle years of the millennium. However, those who narrowly qualified will receive theirs at the end. You will receive your resurrection as promised, but that may be all you get.[223] It will depend on each individual and how he comports himself. Some will not negotiate their way past the first death. They will simultaneously suffer the second one as well. For them, there will be no resurrection.[224]

The resurrection of Lazarus as recorded in John 11 was, in my view, a genuine miracle performed by Jesus himself in his own power. It was done that way to show that although Jesus is the Lord of the resurrection, his power is limited because Lazarus died again. Christ can give life for a thousand years, but only almighty God can give immortality with everlasting life. Again, it is up to the individual during the millennium. (See 1 Corinthians 15:20-28)

The silence in heaven is a half hour. The time does not relate to earth time as humans would understand a half hour. In the eyes of heaven, it

---

221. Revelation 20:7-15; 1 Corinthians 15:20-28.
222. John 5:14-29.
223. Revelation 20:15.
224. John 3:17-21.

is a much longer time span. By comparison, the average human life span would amount to six minutes.[225] Consequently, as the oracle establishes when correctly interpreted, an "hour" describes a period of six hundred years from the fourth century onward. From the time Constantine established the Christian material theocracy at Constantinople in 330 CE, the "half hour" began to count forward to the seventh century. When Jesus said, "The hour is coming and indeed it is now," we can conclude he said that in 30 CE.

During this three hundred year period, the Byzantine state moved to entrench orthodox Christianity as the state religion. Constantine had already patronized the western church. Now he extended that to the Greco-Oriental east. Indeed, the preference for the east among Byzantine rulers can be demonstrated when Byzantium became the new capital of the Christian oikoumene. We should understand at this juncture the Mediterranean world never knew themselves as Byzantine. They saw themselves as "Romanian" or East Romans. "Byzantine" was a period between 270 CE and 1453 CE that we use to distinguish the later Romanians from the early Romans of the republic (509 BC-270 CE). Roman governance was a universalist concept that brought diverse national groups under one state. The traditional view is the Byzantine period began with Constantine, but the Apollo of God marks the beginning during the rule of Aurelian. I support the latter view. Historians don't mark the beginning of the Persian empire with Darius Hystapes, even though he changed the state religion and relocated the capital eastward to Persepolis.

Byzantium was that part of the Roman empire that survived the depredations of the third century and left it in a hegemonic position relative to the west and east. Inside the new Byzantine state, the universal church was a match for the Roman concept of universalism. Survival determined them as allies. Over the centuries, these two powerful entities were joined at the hip. One disciplined the other. They were like the pharaoh and the four priestly tribes. Byzantium was in a spiritual sense like ancient Egypt. The Byzantine emperor ruled by divine right and not official democratic consensus. He answered only to God. The church had its authority from Christ.

At the first ecumenical council of Nicaea in 325 CE, the church realized this imbalance of power would dog them for years into the future. Christian doctrine had clearly made Christ subordinate to God.[226] Arrius had postulated a Platonic and Philonic version of that fundamental apostolic

---

225. Based on one minute equals ten years.
226. Revelation 3:2, 12.

tenet. But Athanasius and his supporters determined by sophistry what would evolve into the Trinity doctrine, unknown to the apostolic church. The emperor's claim to be vice-gerant of God could not be overturned, but the bishops of Nicaea collaborated with Athanasius to doctrinally elevate Christ to be equal with his Father in a dual Godhead. In this way, the church could at least claim equal status with the emperor.

Unfortunately, Constantine was an unbaptized Christian because of the occupation of arms. Only when he set them aside could he be baptized. The church had not reconciled that one could be a soldier and a Christian in good standing. The proof that Constantine was a faithful Christian is in his children. All his sons and daughters were raised in the faith and remained devout all their days.

Sincerity and devotion to the Christ cannot really be measured by humans. This, in my opinion, is true of any religious calling. The human conscience belongs to God and no one else. In that secret chamber, two cannot hide the truth and the lie will never prosper. There is no collaboration. The truth will always be the measuring line of God on our lives.

The church cannot escape that fact either, but its function is one of a servant to the average Christian of faith. True, the church has filled its stalls with theological vanities like a huge bazaar. Yet over the centuries it has provided a fundamental service to Christians everywhere, often in difficult circumstances. On the one hand like a huge modern-day shopping mall that caters to every religious whim one could imagine, the church on the other hand has also provided an essential government service, like a postal outlet that everyone uses on a regular basis. From the church, the Christian associate has been provided the sacraments of baptism, the eucharist, marriage, and the preservation of the Hebrew and Greek scriptures.

In Christendom, churches sprang up everywhere for assembly and learning. All her walls and ceilings illuminated picture-book stories for those unable to read, while bound copies of holy writ were available to those who could. The Jewish synagogue was the forerunner of the modern church. Scripture was read aloud from the pulpit for most to hear on a regular and repetitive basis, year in year out. Like Israel of old, many sins can be laid at Christendom's door, but like it or not, the church has rendered a useful service to God.

Each Christian convert must work out his own salvation. This is true of any religion. Infrastructure is there to be of assistance. However, it will not do everything for the individual. Some essential needs it will provide; others it will not.

In Matthew's gospel, Jesus related twelve parabolic oracles to help Christians understand what Christendom's journey would become. In his great prophecy in Matthew 24 and 25, Jesus follows up the parable of the ten virgins with a second parable of a man who commits his property to three slaves.[227] He distributes eight talents of gold or silver money to each of three slaves based on their individual abilities. Each of the slaves was expected to do business and increase his Master's holdings. Then he departed on a long journey.[228] Earlier on in his short ministry, Jesus had related ten other parables in a similar vein.

> The kingdom of heaven is like yeast that a woman took
> and hid in three measures of floor until all of it was
> fermented.

Christendom did ultimately collect into three main groups around the Mediterranean which still exist today. In Constantine's day, the eastern church was centered on Ephesus and then Constantinople. Asia Minor, Thrace, and Greece were its heartland for centuries. Alexandria and Antioch formed the axis of Egypt and Palestine and were a strong theological influence in the development of early ecumenical doctrine. In the west, Rome and Carthage serviced the Latin church. Inside these three main spheres, each Christian could work out his own salvation or lack thereof over the centuries to come.

Jesus explained the length of this journey in chapter thirteen in the second parable of the wheat and the weeds.

> The son of man sows the good seed,
> The wheat producing seed are the kingdom heirs
> And the world is the field.
> The enemy who sowed the weeds is the devil
> And his children are the weeds.
> The reapers are God's servants
> And the harvest is the end of an era.

When the Master was informed that weeds were growing among the wheat, his slaves assumed they would be instructed to remove those weeds. However, the Son of Man cares for all the sheep and would not risk harm to any of them. He decided the good and bad would grow together. When the era of harvest arrived, they would all be uprooted from the soil and separated into two piles. The wheat would be saved and the weeds collected

---

227. Matthew 25:14-30.
228. See also Matthew 18:23-35.

into bundles for burning. At the end of this great work, the weeds would be dried and burned.

See 13:47-50.

> The kingdom of heaven is like someone who planted mustard seed in his field.
> Although it is one of the smallest seeds it becomes a great shrub and eventually a tree.
> Birds make nests in its branches.

Jesus assured his disciples they would have success in their work of evangelism. It would not come in a perfect form, as some might have expected, but it would cover the globe. Today we see it taking place. Christendom is all over the world in one form or another. However, each individual must determine his own disposition. Beginning with the first parable at chapter thirteen, the balance of the parables concern the individual's response to this great work.

> The kingdom of heaven is like a field with buried treasure
> Someone finds it and purchases that field with all their belongings.

Jesus Christ as the smallest of mustard seeds was planted through the gospel in the world, and rooted in the Mediterranean world at Pentecost. Now under Constantine and his successors, the church would be protected and nourished by the Byzantine state, creating a springboard to the rest of the world. The "half hour" of silence was the patience of heaven as the empire rooted and spread Christendom within and outside its borders.

Christian influence ended Roman expansion by force of arms and placed the Orthodox Byzantine state on a defensive footing. In a violent world, the exercise of arms would still be necessary. The sons of Constantine were already baptized Christians and the Church could not unbaptize them. Constantius II inherited the reforms of Diocletian that were completed by his father.

Surprisingly, the tetrarchy had survived in the new imperial administration. The four great praetorian prefectures encompassed a close approximation of the four imperial domains. Italy and the Orient were governed by the two most powerful prefectures, while Illyricum and the Gauls were formerly the territories of the Caesars. The military function and civil function had been separated within the diocesan jurisdiction and down into the provinces. The provincial governor handled the civil administration while the *dux* or duke commanded the military in each of the hundred and twenty provinces. In turn, these provincial jurisdictions were collected in fourteen dioceses under a diocesan governor and a vicar. Above them were the four great prefectures, inside which the civil and military functions came together under the praetorian prefect. The military function was later removed, making the prefecture a civil body only. Second only to the praetorian prefect was the city prefect. Constantinople, Rome and all the great cities of the empire became separate jurisdictions under a city prefect. He was a foremost member of the senate, and in him survived all the traditions of the republican age of Rome. He was responsible for law and order, the courts, and the entire economic life within a municipality's boundaries.

At the center of this huge bureaucracy was the imperial court. The person of the emperor was protected by the *scholae palatinae* or imperial guard, who were usually eunuchs like the *praepositus sacri cubiculi* or grand chamberlain who cared for the emperor's household. At times the chamberlain's office became the most powerful at court.

The *quaestor sacrii palatii* oversaw all judicial matters affecting the empire. He drafted laws and countersigned all imperial decrees. The finances of the kingdom were handled by the Fiscus and *res privatae*. The treasury would calculate its projected expenses for the coming year and then tax the empire for that amount. Its financial projections were always accepted.

Over all this huge bureaucracy, the emperor appointed a watchdog in the *magister officiorum*, who employed *agentes in rebus* as carriers and spies to inspect, overtly or clandestinely, the workings of the emperor's officials to ensure compliance with the court's expectations. This court was crowned with a magnificent visual and sensual splendor that was at least intimidating to the visitor. The court's orthodox splendor reached such a height that many came to believe Constantinople was the gate of heaven.

Outside of the court and its growing hubris lived the farmers, merchants, and vast numbers of peasants called *coloni*. Diocletian's reforms and taxes gradually collected them into hereditary serfdom. Constantine reformed the currency to become one of the strongest and most stable in the medieval period. The gold *solidus* and silver *seliqua* were the coinage of choice for the next thousand years. Each solidus had 4.48 grams of gold content. The silver seliqua was $1/24^{th}$ of a gold solidus and weighed 2.24 grams. By that time, the denarius, outside the imperial coinage since 275 CE, was defunct. The emergency under Diocletian had entrenched a strong barter economy in the empire that survived a long time, particularly in the west.

The Council of Nicaea and its outcome caused religious division in the empire. In 337 CE, Constantius II became eastern emperor in command of the *pars orientalis,* where the military center had shifted. Constans became western emperor after the death of his brother Constantine in 340 CE. Constantius was a devout Arian whereas Constans was an orthodox Nicene Christian. Paganism continued to be more widespread in the west. The Council of Sardis in 343 CE could not reconcile both confessions, but Constans was in a position to force his older brother to reinstate the orthodox bishops of the creed to their former stations in the east. Arianism further undermined its own position by splitting into two camps.

The defeat and death of Constans at the hands of the pagan usurper Magnus Magnentius in 350 CE, and Magnus's crushing defeat the following year by the forces of Constantius II were viewed as a blow to Nicene orthodoxy. The bishop Ulfila, consecrated bishop by the Arian Eusebius of Nicomedia in 341 CE, translated the Bible into the Gothic language and was instrumental in spreading Arian Christianity among the barbarians. The tenets of Arius continued to hang on. Julian the Apostate (361-363 CE) attempted to return the empire to paganism but failed with his early death. From the reign of Julian, the old Roman empire's boundaries began to shrink. He signed a treaty with the Sassanid Persians, giving them control of Armenia and much of Mesopotamia. Byzantium was now embroiled in unending problems east, north, and west from the Persians and barbarian invasions.

In the west, Britain was invaded by the Saxons, Scots, and Picts. The Alemani on the Rhine and Neckar rivers began incursions southward, as did the Quadi and Sarmatae in the Danube basin. These encroachments became serious when the Visigoths, settled in Thrace, began plundering imperial lands along with the Huns and Ostrogoths. The eastern emperor Valens (364-378 CE) rushed from the Persian front to Constantinople and then, hearing of the enemy's whereabouts, marched his forces to Adrianople, engaging the Visigoths and their allies the Ostrogoths on August 9, 378 CE. Valens and his imperial forces were wiped out. This crushing defeat signaled the defeat of Arian Christianity in the east.

Both Valentinian the western emperor and his successor Gratian (375-383 CE) decided to settle the barbarians in the western empire by agreement. The Ostrogoths settled in Pannonia and the Visigoths in northern Thrace. They were tax-exempt and enlisted as *foederati* in the imperial army. On January 19, 379 CE, the western emperor Gratian raised Theodosius the Great to be eastern Augustus. In that same year, he abandoned the title Pontifex Maximus, which was then adopted by Pope Damasus (366-384 CE) in Rome.

The second ecumenical council at Constantinople in 381 CE ended Arianism in the east, and orthodoxy was decreed to be Nicene. Theodosius the Great (379-395 CE) rooted Christianity as the state religion by outlawing paganism in all its forms and any sect opposed to Nicene orthodoxy.[229] The successors of Theodosius Arcadius in the east and Honorius in the west saw further declines in the empire, more serious in the west than east.

In 395 CE, the monk Jerome completed his translation of the Hebrew-Aramaic and Greek Scriptures, Old Testament and New, into Latin. The translation formed the basis for the Latin Vulgate Bible in the west. This Latin translation became another milestone we can use to measure the book of Revelation and its contents against medieval history.

The reigns of Valentinian III (425-455 CE) in the west and Theodosius II (408-450 CE) in the east saw the halves of the empire go their separate ways. The west had been overwhelmed by the barbarian invasions. Britain was now outside and beyond their control. Alaric and his Visigoths had sacked Rome. Constantinople was powerless to help. The Greek language disappeared and the official Latin tongue was being replaced by the Germanic and Gothic languages. The *pars occidentalis* was a world away. In Byzantium, the government of Theodosius had reduced the population to permanent serfdom. The feudal system contrasted sharply with old notions of freedom. Theodosius recodified Roman law in the Codex Theodosianus and surrounded the capital with a system of walls and defenses that made Constantinople an impregnable fortress for a thousand years.

In the three spheres of the church, all had ultimately accepted the Nicene Creed as their confession, making Christ consubstantial with the Father in a dual Godhead. The next controversial debate centered on the nature of Christ. The theological school of Antioch taught two separate natures coexistent in Christ, but emphasized his human nature as predominant. This Nestorius upheld as true doctrine when he became patriarch of Constantinople. However, the leading school in Christendom was in Alexandria, and Cyril, its bishop, postulated that Christ was God made man in a single nature. He was backed by the influential Egyptian monks and by Rome. This issue was one of the major debates at the next ecumenical council at Ephesus in 431 CE. The Alexandrian theology won

---

229. Banning paganism by imperial decree essentially guaranteed its incorporation into Christian practice. Slowly at first, pagan motifs began to surface in various ways at various times. It would have been better to have kept paganism separate, although that would have offered no guarantee that pagan influence would have died in the Christian oikoumene. It would have offered a comparison, however.

the day and Nestorius was branded a heretic. The bishop of Alexandria was rising to prominence in Christendom.

However, the successor of Cyril in Alexander's city, Dioscorus, and his representative Eutyches at Constantinople developed their doctrine, maintaining the two natures of Christ became a single, divine nature at the incarnation. This was the monophysite controversy. A synod at Constantinople pronounced Eutyches a heretic, and Pope Leo in Rome published a tome and condemned the monophysite doctrine. Monophysitism did win a triumph at the second ecumenical council at Ephesus in 449 CE, but the high-handed domination of the council by the bishop of Alexandria and his supporters caused a violent reaction from the emperor Marcian and the empress Pulcheria. In 451 CE, Marcian replaced the "Robber Synod" of 449 CE with the official fourth ecumenical council at Chalcedon. The monophysite doctrine was rejected and orthodoxy decreed the dyophysite doctrine of two distinct natures in Christ.

Chalcedon recognized the bishop of Rome's primacy in honor among Christians, but clearly the patriarch of Constantinople and the *pars orientalis* emerged as the center of ecclesiastical policy. In Syria, Palestine, and Egypt, the monophysite view persisted. The reign of Anastasius (491-518 CE), a monophysite, demonstrated a Byzantine emperor had to be a dyophysite. A monophysite invited revolt from within. Vitalian's rebellion drew considerable support from the emperor's orthodox subjects.

The emperor Justin rose from the ranks of the military and brought forward one of the great Byzantine emperors of the early period. His nephew Justinian (527-565 CE) had a great hand in the affairs of the empire during his uncle's reign. At that time, Byzantium enjoyed a theoretical sovereignty in the old Roman Mediterranean world. Even though many of the western territories were controlled by Germanic and Gothic kings, they did acknowledge the emperor at Constantinople as the great Roman king. He was at the zenith of the *orbis romanus* and the Christian oikoumene of which they were a part. Theodoric the Great, Odoacer and others were styled *magister militum* in the west and acknowledged the Roman emperor as their suzerain.

This arrangement was limited in any practical application, but Justinian attempted to expand this theoretical orbis romanum. He established ecclesiastical restoration with the church of Rome and its bishop. He then began his campaign of reconquest in the areas that mattered most for Byzantine control. In 533 CE, his commander Belisarius sailed with a force of 18,000 to North Africa, establishing Byzantine power at Carthage and ending the control of Gaiseric and his Vandals. The islands of the

Mediterranean were also taken and the Great Sea was once again a Roman lake.

Italy was retaken from the Ostrogoths in a long and difficult campaign lasting twenty years. The Visigoths in Spain then saw Byzantine power occupy the southeastern corner of Spain. A long-term peace treaty with Chosroes Anushirvan, the great king of Persia, in 532 CE made the western conquests possible. From these positional strongholds, Constantinople held all the high cards from where it could expand its influence, gradually turning its theoretical sovereignty into a restoration of the orbis romanum.

The Nika riot[230] at Constantinople had far-reaching results for the cities in the empire. The last vestige of Rome's republican sentiment and tradition had survived in large urban centers. The Nika riot essentially ended the old civic freedoms there. Officials of the government exiled by the demes were now reinstated and their authority increased. In the wake of this almost fatal incident, Justinian built the great Hagia Sophia[231] in the capital, which dominated the Christian landscape for centuries and still stands in Istanbul to this day.[232]

Under the direction of a man named Tribonian, the emperor Justinian codified Roman law from the time of Hadrian. Based on the Codex Gregarianus, the Codex Hermogenianus from Diocletian's day, and the more recent Codex Theodosianus, the Codex Justinian was first published in 529 CE. In 533 CE the *pandects* or digest was published.

Justinian's reign was the zenith of imperial influence on the church, east and west. Yet his dream of recapturing the old Roman territorial boundaries was not to be. The unified church proved to be more divisive than paganism ever was. The monophysites of Syria and Egypt were implacable in their opposition to the orthodox center. Their sentiments had turned separatist. In the west, the bishop of Rome had backed the patriarch of Constantinople in the theological debate, but in his new role of Pontifex Maximus of the pontifical college, he began cultivating illusions of grandeur all his own. The church of Rome began to view itself as the true center of Christendom-the just inheritor of the orbis romanum. Later popes saw themselves as the direct descendants of Augustus through Constantine. After all, Constantine was western Augustus before he became sole emperor. They viewed the east as the "schismatic Greeks" who staunchly refused to acknowledge their ecclesiastical suzerain in Rome as the spiritual descendant of the apostle

---

230. 532 CE.
231. 532-537 CE.
232. The habit of burying monarchs in churches is another indicator of Egypt in a spiritual sense. Cathedrals became latter-day pyramids.

Simon Peter ben John. Christendom had split into three spheres of influence that Byzantium's emperor and patriarch could not reconcile.

During the reigns of Justin II (565-578 CE) Tiberius Constantine, and Maurice (582-602 CE), the dream of rebuilding the old Roman empire into a unified Christian oikoumene quickly unraveled and ultimately collapsed. In 568 CE, Italy was invaded by the Lombards, ending Byzantium's western base. Cordova in Spain was retaken by the Visigoths in 584 CE. Only Carthage in North Africa remained. The constant war with the Berber tribes made it a costly possession.

The dream of universal authority in the west had vanished. Byzantium consisted of Greece, Thrace, Asia Minor, Syria, Palestine, Egypt, and North Africa, including Carthage and its immediate territories. It was just as well that Constantinople's focus should return to the east. Under Justinian, Byzantium's prestige in the east had suffered at the hands of the Persian kings. The great emperor's nephew, Justin II, ended the tribute paid by his uncle to the Persian king of kings, thus breaking the treaty.

The war with Persia was fought around the possession of Armenia. The migration of Germanic peoples from the empire had left a vacuum in the pool of military recruits the army could draw from. The battle for Armenia was important for Byzantium to replenish the ranks of her military. Finally, Chosroes II Parviz concluded a peace treaty with the emperor Maurice's government in 591 CE. Much of Persian Armenia came under Byzantine control.

Maurice also took steps to strengthen the remnants of Byzantium in the west at Carthage and Ravenna. Each was placed under the authority of the new exarchs. This signaled the militarization of the coming Byzantine administration introduced by Heraclius, who came from the exarchate of Carthage. Ravenna maintained the presence of the fleet in the Adriatic while the balance of the navy was located off the southern coast of Asia Minor in the east Mediterranean.

From this period, the bane of Byzantium's existence was the gradual penetration of the Slavic peoples into the Balkans and the growth of independent kingdoms on Byzantine territory. It was during the war with the Avars and Slavs north of the Danube that disaffection broke out in the army. In 602 CE, the army resorted to an old Roman practice and raised a junior officer named Phocus to the imperium. At the head of his mutinous army, he descended on the capital.

Inside Constantinople, the collapse of Justinian's absolutism had brought in its wake a revival of republican forms in the main cities of the empire. People began to raise their voices. This widespread internal deterioration and growing dissension brought Byzantium to a new precipice. The reign of Phocus permanently ended any dreams of restoring the old Roman state. Byzantium became convulsed with a wave of indiscriminate killing and looting. The aristocracy was singled out for hostility by peasant and emperor alike. Phocus directed a persecution of monophysites and Jews inside the empire, while the demes raised the hostility among themselves. The Greens backed Phocus in the early years of his reign but then turned against him, the Blues then stepping up to support his rule. The empire was engulfed in civil strife and war.

The Avars and Slavs took advantage of internal discord among the Christians and permanently occupied the Balkans with little opposition. In the east, the Persians swept into Asia Minor, taking Caesarea. An advance Persian column reached Chalcedon before withdrawing. It appeared Byzantium of the east was about to yield to disintegration when the exarch of Carthage, Heraclius, sailed to Constantinople to overthrow Phocus. With Egypt's support he arrived at the capital with his flotilla on October 3, 610 CE. He entered the city and ended the bloody rule of Phocus. On October 5 he was crowned emperor by the patriarch of Constantinople.

The reign of Heraclius (610-614 CE) ended the early Byzantine period and began the middle period. (610-1081 CE) Heraclius received a kingdom in turmoil and exhausted. The system in place no longer worked. Early attempts to expel the Persians in the east met with failure. The religious morale of the Byzantines was wounded when the city of Jerusalem fell to the Persian invaders. The Church of the Holy Cross was carried off to Ctesiphon. By 615 CE, the capital was being attacked by the Persians from the east and the Avars and Slavs from the north. By 619 CE, the Persians had reached Egypt, threatening the important corn and wheat supply to Constantinople. To western Christendom, it must have looked like the eastern empire was about to be swallowed up by the judgment of God.

To cope with the emergency, Heraclius reorganized the military and administration on the model of the western exarchates at Carthage and Ravenna. In Asia Minor, land was exchanged for military service, much like the old Roman system of *limes* on the frontier defenses. The system of limes had collapsed on the frontiers, and the soldiers had withdrawn into central Asia Minor. From there they were organized into inalienable land holdings inside a unit called a *theme* controlled by a military *strategus*. Next to the strategus was the proconsul of the theme, who ran the civil administration. In Asia Minor, four themes were created: the land forces of Opsikion, Armeniakon, and Anatolikon, and the maritime force of Carabisiani on the south coast. Mercenaries were expensive and notoriously unreliable, and the system of themes drew its recruits from among those who had a stake in the country. Each soldier was required to provide and maintain his own armaments and horse. While on campaign, each was provided with modest pay from the government's treasury. It proved to be a better system at significantly lower cost. The old praetorian prefectures had been replaced. The finances of the central government were managed by *logothetes* in independant departments connected to the provincial theme administration.

This reorganized military then turned its focus on the war with Persia. Heraclius mustered out his new military and placed himself at its head, leading them on the very first medieval crusade. In the new land army, the cavalryman was all-important, along with the emperor's elite mounted archers. Heraclius marched first to Armenia, forcing Persian units to abandon Asia Minor altogether. In Armenia, the forces engaged in a decisive battle, with the Byzantines defeating the army of the Persian general Sahbaraz.

Heraclius was forced to return to Constantinople over the winter of 622/3 CE, but returned in the spring to resume the crusade. The fight for Armenia proved difficult, and by 626 CE Constantinople had to face another dual invasion. The Persians took Chalcedon and camped their forces on the Bosphorus. From the northwest, the Avars, Bulgars, Gepids, and Slavs laid siege to the capital with land and sea forces. On August 10 a massive attack to take the city was first defeated at sea, causing the Slav fleet to withdraw. The Avar khan's land army was routed next with terrible losses. Sahbaraz had no choice but to withdrawal and pull back to Syria. His second-in-command Sahin remained behind, but was badly defeated by Theodore, the emperor's brother. Heraclius made an alliance with the Khazars who warred with the Persians from the Caucasus. Near old Nineveh, the Byzantines closed with the Persians and almost wiped them out. The war was over.

Chosroes was assassinated, and his son Kavadh-Siroe negotiated a new settlement with Byzantium. Armenia, Mesopotamia, Syria, Palestine, and Egypt were once again in Byzantine hands. On March 21, 630 CE, Heradius restored the holy cross to Jerusalem, bringing Christendom's first religious crusade to its end.

> Then the angel filled his censer with fire from upon the altar and scattered it upon the earth; and there were the sounds of thunder, rumblings, lightning flashes followed by an earthquake.

After three hundred years of struggle, the half hour of silence saw the church triumphant in the world. Religious, pagan Rome had been converted to Christianity. Almighty God had granted deliverance to the nation of spiritual Israel. Only its citizens are genuine Jews.

Yet in spite of this great victory for the Great Prince Michael and his church, the transition toward renewal and reconciliation does not go well during the half hour of silence. Just as material Israel fell into apostasy after its deliverance, so also does the earthly church. Just as almighty God set his face to punish Israel of old for its unfaithfulness, so also happens to spiritual Israel during the Middle Ages. The second intervention differed from the first in that it began with the reconciliation phase of the fifth cycle. The "Orthodox Holy Roman Empire" became "Sodom and Egypt" in an allegorical sense. Although Christendom in the east continued to expand, its relationship with almighty God and his crown prince became estranged.

The power of Persia and the Avar khan was broken permanently by the might of Byzantium. The Slavs revolted against Avar rule and created their own domain. The Bulgars above the Black and Caspian seas concluded an alliance with Heraclius that saw their ruler Kuvrat baptized a Christian. At Constantinople in 619 CE, he received the title of patrician. Later, the Bulgars settled in the Balkans. The Croats occupied the northwest while the Serbs moved into the southwest. In terms of realpolitik, the Bulgars allied themselves more closely to the Slavs than the Byzantines. Constantinople was viewed at a distance. However, the Avar problem had been solved, and a new Christian mission had been opened.

The reading of the last will and testament.

Festival Cycle Four

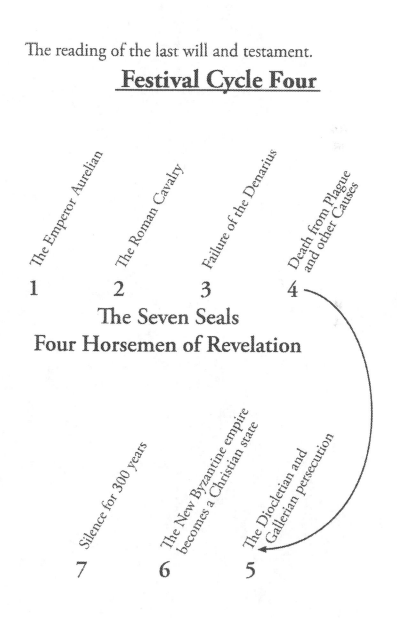

The Emperor Aurelian

The Roman Cavalry

Failure of the Denarius

Death from Plague and other Causes

1   2   3   4

The Seven Seals
Four Horsemen of Revelation

Silence for 300 years

The New Byzantine empire becomes a Christian state

The Diocletian and Gallerian persecution

7   6   5

EPILOGUE

From the founding of the world, humankind developed an interesting relationship with what they considered the four basic elements of life: earth, wind, fire, and water. Of these powerful elements, only the wind had an intangible and mysterious quality. In John's gospel, Jesus reflects this belief by comparing the Holy Spirit with wind. Though one cannot see the wind, its effects can be clearly discernible at times. The movement of earth's wind was viewed as the power of a god or the gods themselves. This was especially true among those living near or among dense woodlands, where frequent manifestations of this mysterious, god-like power were evidenced. Today, of course, we know and hopefully understand the scientific reasons for wind, but in the remote past it awakened in humankind a longstanding desire to believe in life and deity beyond themselves and outside of the material world we all live in.

In time, the power of death prevailed over the human species, and though some accepted it, many did not. On the bold, broad landscape there appeared nothing to prevent it, however. Gradually the idea of a messianic figure began to appear. He would be a man-god who would defend the people from all their enemies. He would be sacrificed and appear before the highest deity to appeal the human case to the giver of life and bring about a reconciliation between the parties. This common human desire and its proposed purpose to attain enternal life is found in various forms across the historical spectrum. The Egyptian king Osiris is one example of a beloved king resurrected to Orion's home to assist in the orderly governance of the planet Earth and its inhabitants.

The message of the Apollo of God is that although our several religious ideas and practices reflect our deep longing for eternal life, none of the mythologies fostered by our race ever produced the outcome we hoped for over the centuries and long millennia. Yet the proven, genuine oracle tells us that one individual did achieve that goal, and that he was exactly who he said he was.